From Filmmaker Warriors to Flash Drive Shamans

From Filmmaker Warriors to Flash Drive Shamans

Indigenous Media Production and Engagement in Latin America

RICHARD PACE, EDITOR

Vanderbilt University Press
Nashville

© 2018 by Vanderbilt University Press
Nashville, Tennessee 37235
All rights reserved
First printing 2018

This book is printed on acid-free paper.

Library of Congress Cataloging-in-Publication Data on file
LC control number 2017053890
LC classification number P94.65.L29 F76 2018
Dewey classification number 302.23089/98
LC record available at *lccn.loc.gov/2017053890*

ISBN 978-0-8265-2211-5 (hardcover)
ISBN 978-0-8265-2212-2 (paperback)
ISBN 978-0-8265-2213-9 (ebook)

Dedicated to the memory of Terence Turner

Contents

Tables   ix

Introduction

Embedding Aesthetics and Envisioning
Sovereignty: Some Definitions and Directions in
Latin American Indigenous Media Studies (Richard Pace)   1

Part One: Overview

1. Indigenous Media from U-Matic to YouTube:
   Media Sovereignty in the Digital Age
   (Faye Ginsburg)   31

Part Two: Indigenous Video and Videographers

2. Kiabieti Metuktire and Terence Turner: A Legacy
   of Kayapó Filmmaking (Richard Pace and
   Glenn H. Shepard Jr.)   49
3. Wallmapu Rising: Re-envisioning the Mapuche
   Nation through Media (Amalia Córdova)   59
4. Transformations of Indigenous Media: The Life and
   Work of David Hernández Palmar
   (Laura R. Graham)   75
5. Value and Ephemeral Materiality: Media Archiving
   in Tamazulapam, Oaxaca (Erica Cusi Wortham)   96
6. Making Media: Collaborative Ethnography and
   Kayapó Digital Worlds (Ingrid Carolina Ramón
   Parra, Laura Zanotti, and Diego Soares da Silveira)   106

Part Three: Sounds and Images

7. National Culture, Indigenous Voice: Creating a
   Counternarrative on Colombian Radio
   (Mario A. Murillo)   129
8. The Shaman and the Flash Drive
   (Guilherme Orlandini Heurich)   148
9. Kawaiwete Perspectives on the Role of Photography in
   State Projects to Colonize the Brazilian Interior
   (Suzanne Oakdale)   158

Part Four: Television

10. As Seen on TV? Visions of Civilization in Emerging
    Kichwa Media Markets (Jamie E. Shenton)   175
11. Reproducing Colonial Fantasies: The Indigenous
    Other in Brazilian Telenovelas (Antonio La Pastina)   197
12. Kayapó TV: An Audience Ethnography in Turedjam
    Village, Brazil (Richard Pace, Glenn H. Shepard Jr.,
    Eduardo Rafael Galvão, and Conrad P. Kottak)   212

Contributors   237
Index   243

Tables

10:1. Media Type, Ownership, and/or Access among the
Kichwa in Sacha Loma, Ecuador   180

10:2. Usage of Television and Other Media   181

10:3. First Impressions after Viewing Images   187

10:4. Responses to Magazine Image Prompts   189

12:1. Years of Televiewing among the Kayapó in
Turedjam, Brazil   219

12:2. Overall Opinions about Television in Turedjam   222

12:3. "What Is Good about Television?" in Turedjam   222

12:4. Daily Television Viewing in Turedjam   225

12:5. Enjoyment of Television Viewing in Turedjam   227

12:6. Number of DVDs Watched in Previous
Week in Turedjam   229

12:7. Genre of DVDs Watched in Turedjam   229

12:8. Favorite Genre of DVDs in Turedjam   229

Introduction

Embedding Aesthetics and Envisioning Sovereignty

Some Definitions and Directions in Latin American Indigenous Media Studies

By Richard Pace

The inspiration for this collection of Indigenous media research dates back to March of 2013 during field research in the Brazilian Amazon. On a hot day in the Kayapó-Mebêngôkre village of Turedjam, my co-researcher Glenn H. Shepard Jr. and I strolled through the circular village toward the river where we planned to take a dip to cool off. On the way, we were queried, as usual, as to our destination. *"Ba djua"* (to bathe), we responded multiple times. On this particular day I noticed between each inquiry and answer sequence there was an unbroken stream of sounds coming from different electronic and digital media devices in use. The sounds were easily audible through the palm thatching and makeshift plank walls of the dwellings, and people's activities were visible through open doorways.[1]

From a DVD playing on a television set, I heard Kayapó songs and speeches filmed during the *Bep* great name ceremony held in the village the previous month. On another TV in the following home, cartoons from a Brazilian commercial station entertained a young audience. Continuing along a couple of structures further, an elderly woman was using the community's two-way radio to speak in Mebêngôkre to a relative in another village. Three houses beyond that, a young man standing just inside the doorway was talking in Portuguese on a cell phone hooked up to an antenna mounted on a wooden pole extending several meters above the home. As we left the village for the path to the river I heard more Kayapó music. But this time the song was Brazilian *sertanejo* (country music) sung with Mebêngôkre lyrics, stored on a USB flash drive and played on a portable, battery-powered radio.

That I paid attention to these background sounds was not unusual. Shepard and I were in Turedjam as part of a larger research project to study media engagement in five small communities spread throughout Brazil.[2] What struck me at this moment, due in large part to the seemingly routine and quotidian nature of media engagement I observed, was that much of the media-linked sociocultural transformation well underway in Turedjam (as well as countless other Indigenous communities) could easily escape scrutiny by ethnographic researchers—and often does. This is particularly true for anthropologists who have more often than not received minimal training in media studies and potentially continue to harbor apprehensions, if not antipathy, toward media impacts (the old fears of cultural contamination, cultural imperialism, and Faustian contracts—see Ginsburg 1991; Faris 1992; Moore 1992; Weiner 1997; and Deger 2006, 43–44).

Notwithstanding some anthropologists' resistance, there is an important base of research on Indigenous media, albeit a literature that is uneven in scope and focus, with most scholarship centering on video production and far less exploring viewers' / listeners' / users' engagement with radio, television, cell phones, and social media.[3] When considering the tremendous potential for sociocultural change associated with media as indicated by countless studies among non-Indigenous peoples, it appears that the range and number of current studies pales in relation to the amount of change actually occurring (just for Indigenous video, for example, see Pearson and Knabe 2015, 37). Additionally, many of the studies that exist to date involve limited fieldwork, few take into account viewers' / listeners' / users' reception of media, and still fewer consider an overall media ecology (i.e., how multi-media engagement fits into the broader cultural milieu as understood in an ethnographic context—see Ginsburg, Chapter 1 in this volume). These types of studies, of course, are more difficult to conduct and tend to be time consuming endeavors (see La Pastina 2005). In sum, despite the potential for substantial sociocultural impact, particularly at this critical juncture of media phasing-in when rapid and fundamental changes can occur (see Kottak 2009 [1990]; Pace and Hinote 2013), it seemed to me not enough was being done to understand the process.

As Shepard and I pondered these changes, their consequences, and their relative neglect, we decided one way to help address the lacuna and encourage others to research the subject matter was to organize a conference as a forum to discuss the ever-widening range of media engagement occurring among Indigenous peoples.[4] After two years of planning and organizing, we held the first InDigital Latin American Conference in 2015, followed by a second one in 2017, on the campus of Vanderbilt University in Nashville. These events included significant interaction between media scholars from Latin America, North America, and Europe with Indigenous media makers from Brazil, Chile, and Guatemala. For many of the presenters this was the first time working through and writing up media-related observations. For others, the conference was a welcomed opportunity to discuss longer-term projects with a specialized and very attentive audience.

Among the many highlights of the first conference were Faye Ginsburg's keynote address summing up Indigenous media's past and exploring its current and future trajectories, and Terence Turner's commentaries on Kayapó filmmaking over the decades. Together, Ginsburg and Turner are considered by many to be the founders of Indigenous media studies (Ruby 2005, 164; Wortham 2013, 5). Turner's commentaries, alongside his long-time Kayapó colleague Kiebiete Metuktire, were particularly memorable as they were Turner's last major public presentation before his death only eight months later.[5] In recognition of his pioneering work and steadfast devotion to Kayapó media, we dedicate this volume to his memory.

This volume, then, is the next step in disseminating this group's diverse findings with respect to Indigenous media in Latin America. Many of the chapters are edited versions of papers presented at the first conference, although we have accepted a couple of submissions from people not in attendance and have incorporated a joint tribute to Kiabiete Metuktire and Terry Turner created from their presentations, interviews, and travel experiences in 2015. Altogether, the chapters in this volume explore the diverse ways Indigenous peoples have been creating and engaging media over the last few decades. Although we have limited the content geographically to Latin America, with studies examining groups in Brazil, Chile, Colombia, Ecuador, Mexico, and Venezuela, the subject matter remains broad. We build upon the mainstay scholarship of Indigenous video production and circulation by including studies of engagement with television, community radio, photography, cell phones, USB flash drives, and the internet.

Defining Indigenous Media

Indigenous media studies is a relatively new field; researchers have been combining innovative methodologies and theoretical perspectives from anthropology, geography, film studies, and media studies for about thirty years. Currently the subject matter of the field is evolving at such a "dizzying" rate of expansion (Ginsburg 2011, 238) that is nearly impossible to keep track of all the innovations, novel applications, and sociocultural impacts transpiring among Indigenous populations as they engage a range of media technology.[6] As might be expected, given the speed of technological innovation and the unpredictable nature of media production and engagement, defining what Indigenous media and Indigenous media studies mean can prove problematic (Magallanes Blanco and Ramos Rodríguez 2016, 11; Schiwy 2016, 39). Nonetheless, a review of the literature indicates scholars have been defining the topic by asking the following types of questions: Who does it? How is it done? And how is it unique? Less frequently asked, but equally critical, are questions on sociocultural impacts of Indigenous media (as well as non-Indigenous media) upon those engaging them. The answers to the first set of questions typically fall into a least three often-overlapping categories: ownership and authorship, technology and techniques, and goals. Answers to the latter question fall under the categories of reception and media ecology studies.

Foremost in the literature are definitions focusing on authorship or ownership of creations. Indigenous video and films, TV shows, music, music videos, digital archives, websites, and so forth are "loosely defined as forms of media expression conceptualized, produced, and/or created by Indigenous peoples across the globe . . ." (Wilson and Stewart 2008, 2; also see Córdova 2014, 123; Cardús i Font 2014, 2–3). The definition is broad and has led to some discussion about what threshold of Indigeneity needs to be incorporated into a production in order for it to count as Indigenous. This is especially true when dealing with productions that borrow substantially from non-Indigenous genres and representational/cinematic conventions as well as collaborative productions created with non-Indigenous media makers (Ginsburg 2011, 234; Schiwy 2009, 12, 41, 48; Wortham 2013, 12).

To hone the definition, Ginsburg (1994) coined the term "embedded aesthetics" to call attention to a system of assessment that does not separate textual production and circulation from the wider realms of social relations. Referring mainly to video and television, Ginsburg (2011, 1241) writes that "the quality of a work is assessed according to its capacity to embody, sustain and even revive or create certain social relations. Indigenous media, then, can be seen as a new kind of object operating in a number of domains as an extension of collective self-production in ways that enhance Indigenous regimes of value." To this Salazar (2015, 128) adds the need to consider "formal socio-technical assemblage of technologies, resources, social organizations, legal frameworks and bureaucracies, cultural principles, and imagery, into a representational and performative form embodied in processes that extend beyond the completed product."

Relatedly, Córdova and Salazar (2008, 40) describe Indigenous authorship as "socially embedded self-representation." The focus is on the media makers' social location vis-à-vis their subjects. Córdova and Salazar characterize this relationship as viewing culture "from the inside in." To this one might add direct accountability to a community or group for one's representations created (see Wortham 2013, 12; Salazar and Córdova 2008, 43).

There are problems with the concept of 'embeddedness,' however, ranging from the media makers' relationship to a community to the difficulty of defining what does or does not represent community values. For example, are the Indigenous media makers widely accepted members of the community or are they seen as outsiders? Are they culturally well integrated or are they somewhat marginal—as in not growing up in an Indigenous community and shar-ing certain beliefs or assumptions? (See for example Córdova, Chapter 3, and Graham, Chapter 4, in this volume.)

Likewise, to what extent are there internal disagreements within Indigenous groups over representations and values? If there are polysemic interpretations, how can they be contextualized in productions, or are they simply ignored? Each of these situations can lead to considerable friction if productions sim-plify the possibilities of representation. In "making culture visible" through producing videos, as Wortham (2013, 6) phrases it, how successful are media makers in capturing the plurality of ways of belonging and being that exist in a community? For example, in her research with Aymara and Quechua media makers in Bolivia, Villarreal (2017) details the intense debates and anxieties expressed over matters of "authenticity and the definition and performance of indigeneity in relation to their own undertaking of indigenous media imagery" (173; see also 182–88). She notes that media makers were "in permanent de-bate about how to produce images that speak about their realities" (193). In this volume, Wortham's study of Mexican Indigenous video also analyzes those types of frictions that occur not only during initial filming, but also a second time when the material is digitized and archived. By contrast, in our studies of Kayapó video, most of which documents communal ceremonies, community pressure to "get it right" (both the ceremony as well as the filming) in order to claim the status and prestige associated with the event constrains the ten-dencies for errors or alternative representations (see Shepard and Pace 2012). Agreement on representations—or cultural policing—therefore, is relatively speaking more ubiquitous.

There is also some variance in the use of the phrase *embedded aesthetics*. Does it mean the above-mentioned media makers' social position / insider point of view, or does it mean the unique cultural conventions embedded in the production (what Worth and Adair [1972] called "different visual languages" in their reference to film)? The latter discussion centers on whether or not "Indig-enous aesthetics" exist in an identifiable form. For example, can Indigeneity be found in the way images are filmed and songs recorded, how productions are edited, in the structural variations of the narrative, or in the way productions are received and used by Indigenous audiences?

Wortham (2013) addresses Indigenous aesthetics in her work in Mexico. Referring to video, she writes, "many formal conventions in video indígena are not embedded; they are for the most part taught by nonindigenous media professionals and the indigenous videomakers trained by them, or they are bor-rowed from mass media (television) formats" (9–10). She maintains, however, the media maker can still be physically and culturally embedded, even if the formal aesthetic is not (13). Citing the Zapotec filmmaker Juan José García,

Wortham notes that the videos are packed with distinctive symbols about communality unique to Indigenous communities, such as collectivity, language, facial features, and intimacy (10–12). Schiwy (2009) adds that Indigenous storytelling traditions and ways of knowing as in "myth, ritual, and dreams" (9) as well as the "complex forms of transmitting social values through textiles, dance, song, rituals, and the reading of an animated life world" (31) drive not only the narrative but also the aesthetics of videos even though media makers are usually trained in Western filmmaking traditions. Along similar lines, speaking about Canadian Aboriginal media aesthetics and filming conventions, Kristin Dowell (2013, 2) maintains that although there is no singular Aboriginal aesthetic, there is nonetheless a distinctive "tone, structure, editing, framing, and content on-screen" reflecting Indigeneity in films (also see Masayesva 1995).

On the other hand, Villarreal (2017) is not as optimistic, stating she is "less confident about the decolonizing possibilities of indigenous media . . . [which] cannot be dissociated from contradictions of colonial and state power" (4). She continues by questioning "the idea that intrinsically indigenous features make their way into film aesthetics" (209). She concludes that in Bolivia the aesthetic features "attributed to indigenous cultures in films and their production responds in a more contentious and dynamic way to a political need for expressing indigeneity rather than to inherent features of indigenousness that reveal themselves at the moment of filmmaking" (209).

At the opposite end of the Indigenous aesthetics continuum, Terence Turner (1992, 8) succinctly described the key features of a Kayapó film aesthetic (or "symbolic strategy," as he called it) based on shared ". . . cultural categories, notions of representation, principles of mimesis, and aesthetic values and notions of what is socially and politically important . . ." (also see Turner 1990, 1991a, 2002, and Chapter 2 this volume). As Shepard and Pace (2012) have observed, over the decades this film aesthetic has persisted in Kayapó film production despite the ever-increasing exposure to Brazilian television and the widespread viewing of Brazilian and foreign films on DVDs. In forthcoming research, Shepard and Pace further delineate the Kayapó film aesthetic in terms of features such as vantage point, focal length, gazes, smiling, disdain for time compression, inclusiveness, and particulars of filming body decoration and nudity (also see Chapter 2 this volume).

A second component to defining Indigenous media focuses on the technology and recording and editing techniques used. For example, Spitulnit (1993, 304) observes that Indigenous media encompasses a "wide spectrum of media phenomena, ranging from community owned and operated radio, television and video operations to locally produced programs that appear on national television." Ginsburg (1993, 558) emphasized in an early definition that Indigenous media represents local cultural specificities, rather than being overwhelmed by commercial interests requiring mass audiences. Sreberny-Mohammadi and Mohammadi (1994) and Wortham (2013, 11) use the term *small media*, meaning technologies that are relatively easy to obtain (tape recorders, camcorders) and do not require investments from large governmental or commercial organizations. García Espinosa's (1979) often cited term *imperfect cinema* likewise refers to cheap technologies and collaborative methodologies that challenge industrial quality and aesthetics standards.

Also important here are the directing techniques utilized. In addition to the discussion of embedded Indigenous aesthetics in the video mentioned earlier, Córdova (2014, 123–24) notes that Indigenous videographers often combine various techniques from experimental and activist filmmaking practices, particularly reflexive ethnographic documentary, with realism and cinema verité methods to produce hybrid documentary works that "give voice to multiple expressions of contemporary identities." Propios (2002, 581) in an earlier classification, grouped Indigenous video into three categories: maintenance of historical memory, educational videos, and reports or informative videos as witness and advocacy. Salazar (2015, 133) lists the typical themes as ranging from "journalistic reporting to traditional stories, told through short fictions, documentaries, news programmes for television, music videos and video letters." With the growth of collaborative films, production styles may be more expansive and incorporate docudramas, fiction, testimonial documentaries, melodramatic love stories, horror and suspense tales, alternating talking heads in documentaries, and expository and observational formats (see Corrêa 2004; Córdova 2014; Wortham 2013, 9; and Schiwy 2009, 6).

A third common component in the definition of Indigenous media is a reference to goals. For example, CLACPI (Coordinadora Latinoamericana de Cine y Comunicación de los Pueblos Indígenas [Latin American Coordinator of Indigenous Peoples' Film and Communication]) maintains that to be Indigenous media there must be "a strong compromise to give a dignified voice and vision of knowledge, culture, projects, claims, achievements and struggles of indigenous peoples" (CLACPI 2013). Salazar and Córdova (2008, 40) add that the cultural logic of Indigenous media is to create "effective strategies for Indigenous peoples to shape counter-discourses and engender alternative public spheres." Ginsburg (1999 and Chapter 1 in this volume) expresses it as the ability to "talk back" to or "shoot back" at structures of power.

Córdova (2014, 123) continues by noting that Indigenous media is meant to "promote advocacy, and ultimately, to foster self-determination among Indigenous groups." Or as Wortham (2013, 6) puts it, Indigenous media makes culture visible—"they make visible narratives and realities that have long and systematically been made invisible by dominant societies." Claudia Magallanes Blanco and José Manuel Ramos Rodríguez (2016, 11) specify the emphases on "capacity for self-representation and visibility of cultures, the usefulness as a form of resistance, the use in the negotiation of meanings with the dominant culture, the use as cultural, political, linguistic or environmental platforms, as well as practices of decolonization or as an expression of self-determination."[7] Pamela Wilson, Joanna Hearne, Amalia Córdova, and Sabra Thorner combine authorship with goals as they define Indigenous media "as forms of media expression conceptualized, produced, and circulated by indigenous peoples around the globe as vehicles for communication, including cultural preservation, cultural and artistic expression, political self-determination, and cultural sovereignty" (Oxford Bibliographies 2014).

Advocacy and sovereignty in terms of self-determination are two keys to these goals. For example, Wilson and Stewart (2008, 5) see Indigenous media as "the first line of negotiation of sovereignty issues as well as a discursive locus for issues of control over land and territory, subjugation and dispossession under colonization, cultural distinctiveness and the question of ethnicity and minority status, questions of local and traditional knowledge, self-identification and recognition by others, and notions of Indigeneity and Indigenism themselves." Specifically focusing on advocacy, Turner (1991b, 1992) described how in the 1980s and 1990s the Kayapó consciously used video to unify different villages by bearing witness (recording common threats like dam building or protests against the government), to hold politicians accountable for statements made, and to show or gain support from the outside world by communicating their struggles. For the latter, Turner described how the Kayapó employed video as a political action to consciously reproduce and defend their culture and autonomy through "objectification"—a process which both defines and champions their culture through self-representations as they negotiate with the broader Brazilian society. Turner (1991c, 304–5) stated, "By making their culture a political issue, and self-consciously making the dissemination of their cultural image in public demonstrations and news media a key aspect of their political struggle, the Kayapó not only transformed the meaning and content of their culture itself but also the political significance of documenting it and communicating about it to the non-Kayapo public."

In a similar vein, Jeff Himpele (2008, xvii) in his study of Indigenous media circulation in Bolivia writes, "Projects for self-determination that take up representational media use them as the means for political ends: moreover, these media are their own ends as well, since they demonstrate the human capacity of culture, agency, and self-representation at once." Likewise, Zapotec videomaker García emphasizes that the goal of Indigenous video is to record schemes of autonomy that Indigenous peoples already live in such a way that they become visible and self-conscious, at which point they can be overtly defended (Wortham 2013, 35). Wortham (2013, 10–11) suggests understanding these goals as a *postura* (a posture, stance, or position) from which to stimulate social change within Indigenous communities as well as the world beyond.

Although Indigenous media are widely employed as tools for empowerment, scholars are quick to point out substantial sociopolitical limitations. Wortham (2013, 26) acknowledges that making Indigenous video "does not lead directly to increased autonomy in ways that are easy to measure." But, she continues, "gaining access to the means of audiovisual communication is an accomplishment, a victory, in the process of securing control over lives long determined and represented by others." Ginsburg (2011, 253 and Chapter 1 in this volume) likewise surmises that Indigenous media singularly cannot overcome the power imbalances that exist in the world for Indigenous peoples, but she notes that they can certainly assist in calling attention to critical issues of self-determination, cultural rights, and political sovereignty, which are important components to the struggle.

A second key element of defining goals is the notion of visual sovereignty, a term used by Rickard (2011), Raheja (2010), and Dowell (2013), among others, that highlights an Indigenous community's or individual's right to visually create a space for self-definition and determination. It is "a way of reimagining Native-centered articulations of self-representation and autonomy that engage the powerful ideologies of mass media" (Raheja 2007, 1163). It is a formulation of cultural autonomy on-screen, addressing Indigenous audiences by reflecting their stories, and a desire to engage with non-Indigenous audiences, but on their own terms (Dowell 2013, 104). It is a way to "Indianize" video production, or "create continuities between complex indigenous systems of signifying and audiovisual aesthetics" through the cultural politics of decolonization which situates media technology as "a technology of knowledge" that challenges state hegemony, particularly the use of literacy to define Indigenous representations (Schiwy 2009, 14).

Valerie Alia (2010, 8) adds a focus on space, in the sense that Indigenous media has created a location or niche. She writes, "Indigenous people are developing their own news outlets and networks, simultaneously maintaining or restoring particular languages and cultures and promoting common interests." She labels this the "New Media Nation," which consists of the internationalization of Indigenous media audiencehood and media production (see, for example, Isuma TV). In a similar vein, Propios (2002) writes that Indigenous video helps create a new political ethnicity in the contemporary world with new meanings, practices, and discourses. "Citizen media" is another perspective interpreting Indigenous video as a material site to create citizenship through daily political practices (Rodríguez 2001, 158). Civil society is constructed by producing counter-public spheres that facilitate new kinds of collaboration based on unique cultural claims and representations. For Gabriela Villarreal (2017, 7–8), counter-public spheres are sites of politics that act as a motor to stimulate "collective political practices out of continuous disagreement and negotiation" to reshape common imaginaries or political landscapes. Her focus is on power relations, aesthetic tensions, and visual economies—or the impact of unequal social and economic relations on video distribution (8). Finally, building on the concept of visual sovereignty, Ginsburg in this volume introduces the term "media sovereignty," which includes Indigenous people's pursuit of their rights to control all the production and circulation of their own images and words.

Salazar (2015, 128) sums up the collective goals of Indigenous video—the best studied subset of Indigenous media studies—by highlighting the different approaches to decolonize or decenter the dominant Western view. He writes,

> After almost thirty years of development, growing within the fissures of commercial and state mediaspheres, indigenous video in Latin America—*video indigena*—continues to be framed today through a multiplicity of interrelated perspectives and voices: as a survival and fighting strategy in the creation and recreation of indigenous imaginaries (Sanjinés 2013; Córdova 2014); as a metaphor of indigenous resistance (Rodrígues 2013); as a means by which indigenous organizations and mobilizations articulate new claims on national politics (Zamorano 2009); as a life project, and ideology, a political attitude (García 2013); as an appropriated and self-consciously re-signified *postura* or political position, vital to indigenous struggles for self-determination (Wortham 2004:366); as a political practice for articulating an activist imaginary (Salazar 2004, [. . .]); as a proposal for cultural seduction (Carelli 2013); or as an integral practice of 'cosmoexperience' (Champutiz 2013).

The fourth component of defining Indigenous media emphasizes engagement. In other words, what does ownership, authorship, and achievement of all the various goals of producing media actually mean for Indigenous peoples in the broader sociocultural context? What impact, influence, or effect does self-produced media, as well as non-Indigenous (or even other-Indigenous) produced media, have? These questions add critical perspective to the existing scholarship on production and circulation, typically understood through historical and institutional analyses or studies of content/text. Study of media engagement also brings Indigenous media to the fore of the essential but contentious and often polemic debates over structure versus agency—from cultural industry to active audience approaches (Abercrombie and Longhurst 1998; Bird 2003; Corner 2000; Peterson 2003; Pace 2009; Pace and Hinote 2013). Here, debates rage over what kind of power media has to change behavior, to shape, mold, or even determine world view and social identity. Concomitantly discussed are the proficiencies of viewers/listeners/users to tease out social, political, and cultural constructions embedded in programming—if such messages are not overly polysemic or incoherent. Do viewers/listeners/users readily or reticently accept, reject, ignore, or subvert all or parts of media messages? Does this change behavior? Do the messages simply go unnoticed? Or is it the best we can do to describe what people do and say in "relation" to media—dropping pretenses for causal explanations? In this volume, Wortham (Chapter 5), Heurich (Chapter 8), Shenton (Chapter 10), and Pace et al. (Chapter 12) explore these complexities.

Why Indigenous Media Matters

However one chooses to define Indigenous media, as the research in this collection shows, when Indigenous peoples create or engage media they do so in manners that often diverge significantly from patterns seen among the better-studied non-Indigenous, and particularly Western, populations. The study of Indigenous media creation, distribution, and consumption, as well as analysis of Indigenous people's engagement with non-Indigenous media, therefore, can provide excellent examples of alternative cultural practices that both challenge and expand upon assumed norms of media engagement. Or as Faye Ginsburg (1995, 65), using an analogy to visual depth perception, phrases it, these studies can provide us with a parallax view of media in that they provide "different angles of vision" that provide a richer understanding of sociocultural complexity.

From a scholarly point of view, the study of Indigenous media adds much needed contrast that better informs media theory. In particular, it helps to de-center the West as the base, norm, or natural model for human-media interactions (see Peterson 2003). For example, an understanding of how different groups may watch, interpret, and sometimes create television messages; fashion and comprehend radio texts; construct and view their own cultural representations on video and upload them to the internet; build websites to archive culture materials; construct social networks in cyberspace among themselves and other groups; or even utilize cell phones to not only communicate but also film in culturally appropriate manners, collectively helps break down ethnocentric assumptions about the form, function, and focus of media use globally. Study of Indigenous media can provide a more nuanced understanding of media engagement beyond the previously mentioned traditional and sometimes parochial debates over passive versus active audience models (for example, see Himpele's comments [2008, 29, 32]).

From an activist point of view, Indigenous media provide crucial tools for subaltern populations to confront structures of power. As several authors in this volume argue, Indigenous media production can decolonize media by contesting national and colonial narratives that have erased or distorted Indigenous interests and realities. Whether it is preserving a disappearing language; encouraging intergenerational dialog and cultural transmission; establishing social networks within and beyond one's group; recording events for political leverage; exploring new marketing or consumption opportunities; or simply being expressive and creative in conceptualization of cultural identity; the use of cameras, laptops, DVDs, USB drives, the internet, cell phones, radios, audio-recording devices, and television open up new avenues for cultural survival.

On the point of activism, Salazar (2015) raises a caveat. He is wary of what he considers the failures of media scholars, especially media anthropologists, to fully engage with Latin American social movements incorporating novel uses of media. Salazar (2015, 123–24) writes that with a few exceptions, Latin American media anthropology "remains locked in the internal vicissitudes of critical anthropology and visual anthropology." By contrast, he maintains, Indigenous communities, organizations, and individual producers in Latin America are on the vanguard of decolonizing methodologies, shifting away from the traditional anthropological knowledge practices that emphasize analyses of texts and/or media acculturation toward the creation of cultural resistance and revitalization. In the long run, he posits, this divergence of focus can stimulate a rethinking and refashioning of engaged research. But for now, he maintains that the discipline has failed to take full advantage of the parallax effect unfolding before it and the promises it holds to achieve a richer and deeper understanding of the complexity of culture.

The Contents of This Book

From Filmmaker Warriors to Flash Drive Shamans is divided into four sections based broadly on media type. Because many of the essays topically address a number of issues concerning media engagement (i.e., not just production, circulation, or reception alone, but often a combination of approaches, sometimes set within a broader media ecology approach) we decided that organizing this way made the most sense because it does not imply to the reader that a chapter focuses on just one media engagement concern, but potentially on many. Following the introduction and overview is the section "Indigenous Video and Videographers," followed by an eclectic assemblage of chapters in "Sounds and Images" (radio, electronic recordings, and photography) and "Television." Although the Indigenous groups studied vary by geographic location, the Kayapó of Brazil appear most frequently in the volume's pages. In part the Kayapó prominence here is due to happenstance—relating to who attended the conference and presented research findings. But beyond this, the Kayapó are mentioned in many of the volume's chapters because they are one of the first Indigenous groups to engage media as activists when they took up camcorders in the 1980s and begin creating their own representations in politically explicit ways. They were also widely seen in two popular documentaries recording their struggles—The Kayapó: Out of the Forest (1989) and The Kayapó: Indians of the Brazilian Rain Forest (1987). And finally, their media engagement is extremely well documented through the strength of Terence Turner's scholarly and activist writings. As a result, most treatises of Indigenous media, especially those with historical content, typically have a section dedicated to the Kayapó experience.

Subsequent to this Introduction, Faye Ginsburg's Chapter 1, "Indigenous Media from U-Matic to YouTube," provides a historical summary as well as an update on the current issues in global Indigenous media research, circa 2015. Drawing upon her extensive background in media research, she looks for patterns of commonality, connection, and difference in Indigenous media engagement worldwide. She explores the prospects and complications, both geographically and generationally, that arise as groups engage digital technology. Building on the concept of visual sovereignty she introduces the term "media sovereignty" to describe Indigenous people's pursuit of their rights to control the production and circulation of their own images and words. Through cultural activism (political agency and cultural intervention), Indigenous groups use media to maintain or revive their ritual practices, local languages, and historical knowledge as they also shore-up intergenerational schisms and even provide new sources of revenue. Ginsburg discusses in detail concerns over the sustainability of Indigenous film projects and the archiving of film and video materials, which seems to have become a common theme globally (in this volume, Wortham explores the subject extensively, and it is mentioned by various other authors as well). Ginsburg ends her chapter with cautious optimism, noting the remarkable expansion of Indigenous media over the last two decades, despite logistical, political, and cultural obstacles.

In the second section, "Indigenous Video and Videographers," "Kiabieti Metuktire and Terence Turner: A Legacy of Kayapó Filmmaking" by Richard Pace and Glenn H. Shepard Jr. documents the last encounter between Kiabiete Metuktire, one of the very first Indigenous filmmakers, and his long-time collaborator and friend, anthropologist Terence Turner. The two were together for the first time in several decades during the days preceding and following the InDigital Latin America Conference. Chapter 2 transcribes their joint interviews and provides a review of their commentaries made during the conference. Turner, who was struggling with Parkinson's disease at the time, was particularly nostalgic as he expressed his pleasure at the continuance of the Kayapó Film project he had helped create nearly thirty years earlier. He was also impressed that a conference focused solely on Indigenous media of Latin American could attract such an audience and saw it as a promising sign for expanded research in the future. The chapter also documents Kiabiete's travels in the Southeast USA, including his visits to Cherokee, North Carolina, and Disney World, and his interesting cultural observations. Kiabiete describes himself as a "filmmaker warrior" (*guerreiro cineasta* in Portuguese) and is recorded in the National Geographic Society's short video *Amazon Tribe: "Video Is Our Bow"* (2015) as saying, "I always say video is our bow. It's our weapon."

Amalia Córdova's Chapter 3, "Wallmapu Rising: Re-envisioning the Mapuche Nation through Media," explores how the Mapuche of Chile and Argentina use media as a tool for advocacy, cultural affirmation, and creative expression. Córdova notes that by creating experimental and hybrid productions, which range from documentaries to music videos recorded in *Mapuzungún* (the language of the Mapuche), filmmakers give voice to alternate histories and contest contemporary misrepresentations and omissions created by mainstream media. She focuses on two important Mapuche directors, Jeannette Paillán and Jennifer Silva (who is also a hip-hop artist known as JAAS), and how they use media to rethink Indigeneity, revise history, and challenge assumptions about the practice of individual filmmaking. Córdova then expands her discussion to other media initiatives, such as bilingual radio programs and the use of new digital platforms (online news, blogs, YouTube, and Facebook). Although frequently harassed by the state, Mapuche media producers confront the vested interests of powerful industries (e.g., mining and hydroelectric complexes). She insists that Indigenous-controlled media serve as a critical tool in this struggle to save lives and seek justice.

In Chapter 4, "Transformations of Indigenous Media: The Life and Work of David Hernández Palmar," Laura Graham explores how Hernández Palmar, a Wayuu filmmaker from Venezuela, evolves from a non-political young man to an outspoken advocate for Indigenous film and video and a leading figure in Latin American Indigenous media. Graham is interested in the ways engagement with Indigenous media affects specific lives and subjectivities. As she points out, Hernández Palmar's example is important because, as an educated, urban Indigenous person, he represents an important sector of contemporary Indigenous reality that is generally overlooked. Through the process of "dialogic editing," Graham incorporates Hernández Palmar's voice into the chapter as she discusses ethnographic observations, interviews, and autobiographical narratives collected since 2005. She highlights their collaborative work in the making of the documentary film *Owners of the Water* (2009), the conceptualization of the Venezuelan International Indigenous Media Showcase (MICIV), and the laying of the groundwork for his work with the Venezuelan Ministry of Culture's National Cinema Foundation, Cinemateca. Graham concludes that Hernández Palmars's case exemplifies the cultural mediations, social relationships, and connections that Indigenous media open up from within and across local communities to global partnerships and collaborations.

In Chapter 5, Erica Cusi Wortham examines the complex issues of managing the digitization of vintage media in "Value and Ephemeral Materiality: Media

Archiving in Tamazulapam, Oaxaca." As with many Indigenous media projects initiated in the 1990s, there was a rush to film but never a corresponding effort to archive material that now languishes in substandard storage conditions. In the case of the highland Oaxacan village of Tamazulapam, Wortham writes that the local discourses about value, in this case what footage merits saving and restoring, position media within a regime of materiality that can challenge its worth as cultural heritage. She argues that it is precisely media's ephemeral value that matters most, a notion best captured by "conjuring what happens when you press PLAY" (97). Wortham describes how community dissatisfaction with community filmmakers' activities and products of the past resurfaces in the digitizing process. The conflict, she explains, seems to contradict the notion of embeddedness as typically understood in Indigenous media scholarship, which should key us into the fact that embeddedness, in some cases, must be achieved. The conflict, however, is mitigated by resituating media practices within the community through archiving. In other words, the process provides a second chance to reposition media as a participatory, collective endeavor. She concludes that exploring questions of value and ownership in the archiving process can create a dialogue and transparency about media making that was not perceptible to community members during the original production.

Chapter 6 returns to Kayapó filmmaking. Ingrid Ramón Parra, Laura Zanotti, and Diego Soares da Silveira's "Making Media: Collaborative Ethnography and Kayapó Digital Worlds" describes the co-creation of a research partnership with the community of A'Ukre located in Kayapó Indigenous Lands of the central Brazilian Amazon. The project aims for visual sovereignty through the creation of a media-making project and media center that provides

(1) on-site capacity to train community members in all aspects of film production,
(2) the ability to choose and maintain equipment and infrastructure used to produce films,
(3) a low barrier to entry software and affordable maintenance costs,
(4) data management platforms and storage capacity for lengthy films and extended raw footage,
(5) the production of films for and by community members that do not have to conform to outsider aesthetics and where Kayapó filmmakers have control over the aesthetics they wish to deploy, and
(6) the ability to distribute and circulate films in forms that are portable, secure, and easily shared.

The project, while aligning with earlier work such as that of Turner, also diverges in that it explicitly engages with gender and intergenerational shifts, recognizing the broader dynamics of heterogeneous communities and individual artistic expressions, while at the same time acknowledging shared sensibilities and goals of visual sovereignty.

The third section of the volume, "Sounds and Images," focuses on a collection of studies about radio, recordings on flash drives, and photographs. First is Chapter 7, Mario Murillo's "National Culture, Indigenous Voice: Creating a Counternarrative on Colombian Radio," which recounts the history of Indigenous radio in Colombia. Murillo notes that although national radio may reach most Colombians, it, along with television, has been used to systematically to exclude and marginalize Indigenous peoples by ignoring them or presenting them as backward, uncivilized, and an obstacle to economic development and progress. Within this context, he writes, the emergence of Indigenous radio over the last twenty-plus years is a critical manifestation of the Indigenous movement's open rejection of the hierarchical, largely European, individualist, and consumerist conception of the Colombian nation that has dominated broadcast media since the 1930s. Murillo shows how Indigenous communities use radio, as well as video, the internet, and social media, to promote their own cultural identity and community values, very often in direct contradiction to the centralist, top-down mandates of the dominant political and social classes. Yet, importantly, Indigenous media channels are not insular, nor designed to cut the community off from the rest of Colombian society. Rather, the medium is employed to establish an ongoing dialogue with the dominant society and articulate a vision about Indigenous people's fundamental concerns, organizing structures, and proposals for the country as a whole that are distinct and more nuanced than what is typically presented in the mainstream media. In this way Indigenous radio stations represent a fundamental break from the traditional broadcast models designed to create a unified national identity and a movement toward ones that recognize Colombia as a multicultural, pluri-ethnic society. Murillo concludes that Colombian Indigenous radio is emblematic of the generational struggle for communicative democracy, and one of the crowning achievements of the media justice movement in Colombia.

Chapter 8, written by Guilherme Orlandini Heurich and titled "The Shaman and the Flash Drive," examines the boom in popularity of digital recordings of shamans among the Araweté of the Brazilian Amazonian state of Pará. The recordings are stored on flash drives (also known as pin, travel, or USB drives) and played on small battery-powered radios with USB ports. Heurich charts the rapid spread of such devices once he and a young Araweté man named Majoro developed the idea of transferring recordings of shamanic songs to flash drives. Curious about how the songs are used and what restrictions on listening might exist, Heurich discusses Araweté shamanistic practices with a focus on how the shaman can serve as a conduit to bring deceased people back to sing. He notes a triangulation between body, radio, and voice: People should not have their voices reproduced while they are alive, and they should not be put inside a radio if they still have a body. This indicates that a dead person's voice is bodiless and the radio can serve as a pseudo-body to carry the voice of the dead. Heurich notes that years earlier an Araweté shaman commented to Eduardo Viveiros de Castro that "shamans are like radios," in the sense the words they sing are not their own (coming from dead others). Heurich works from this notion to explore the idea that a radio is like a shaman because both are carriers of others' voices and that both shamanic reproduction and mechanical reproduction are acts of quoting. A radio is a body with a voice other than its own, and in this sense it seems very similar to a shaman's performance. Yet shamans eventually die, and those relatives they once knew can no longer sing through them. Compared to a shaman's body, a radio can last a long time and carries the words of the dead regardless of whether it knew them or not. It is as if the radio has a perfect memory, but no capacity to bring the recently deceased to sing. Heurich ends his chapter with a question: If a flash drive radio can carry the voices of dead people long forgotten, what happens when the living hear the words of people their shamans can no longer bring to sing? This is a question he hopes to answer with future research.

Suzanne Oakdale in Chapter 9 ponders the relationships between photography and memory in "Kawaiwete Perspectives on the Role of Photography in State Projects to Colonize the Brazilian Interior." In the first part of the chapter she reviews the use of photography in Brazil's pacification expeditions in the twentieth century and how images were designed to signify and justify the "civilization" of generic Indigenous people and the productive occupation (that is, expropriation) of their lands. In the second part of the chapter she discusses Kawaiwete autobiographical accounts she collected in the Xingu Indigenous Park of central Brazil from men involved with government teams that "contacted" Indigenous groups as part of the pacification process of the early twentieth century. As these men recounted their experiences, she found they frequently paused to search their memories for the names of the photographers or spent time describing the experience of being photographed while working on these missions. What was rarely part of the conversation were the actual photographs, which the Kawaiwete did not possess. Oakdale highlights the stories of Tymakang and Sabino who, although clearly understanding photography to be a part of state coercion, still articulated accounts that in many ways paralleled the government's narrative of pacification and progress. Oakdale suggests, in this context, that the act of filming was as important as the representations produced, meaning the state attempted to produce a kind of social reality, not just to record it. She concludes that explorations into the use of media from the perspective of those photographed gives a greater appreciation for how national belonging is currently being configured by Indigenous Brazilians.

The last section of the volume focuses on television. In Chapter 10, Jamie Shenton's "As Seen on TV? Visions of Civilization in Emerging Kichwa Media Markets" focuses on how Kichwa women in the Amazonian community of Sacha Loma, Ecuador, perceive and negotiate mass-mediatized, "White, civilized" bodies and behaviors alongside essentialized, "uncivilized" representations of traditional Indigenous culture. Representations of Indigenous peoples, like those seen in music videos on TV or on postcards that Shenton has examined, are interpreted by the Kichwa women as uncivilized in terms of both cultural practices and the requisites of contemporary society (e.g., they do not pursue higher education). Mass media, in contrast, consistently represents proper womanhood with Whiteness, conventional attractiveness, and wealth. While Kichwa women grasp, criticize, and buy into these intended readings of mainstream bodies and behaviors, their understandings are also influenced by the foundational principles of productive sociality that their mothers and grandmothers have long found important (i.e., the ultimate goal of providing for one's family). That is, Kichwa women are incorporating new types of bodies and behaviors into their images of productive women, or women who "do" for others. In this way actresses in telenovelas and magazines are construed as unquestionably civilized, with their bodies and behaviors conforming to the standards of conventional Western beauty, as well as Kichwa cultural standards which privilege kin-centeredness since White actresses have money to provide for their families. Shenton concludes by noting the dynamic of change ("customizing") for the Kichwa in that the globalized images of individualized bodies and behaviors received through media regularly collide with images of communal preferences and obligations, such as the role of grandmothers making chicha beer.

In Chapter 11, Antonio La Pastina analyzes the representations of Indigenous peoples on Brazilian television in his "Reproducing Colonial Fantasies: The Indigenous Other in Brazilian Telenovelas." He begins by noting that although Indigenous people in Brazil make up only 0.4 percent of the country's population, they maintain an important historical and symbolic presence that is key to the country's self-imagining. Yet in telenovelas, which are prime-time serial-fictions that since the 1950s have constituted one of Brazil's most popular television genres, Indigenous peoples are consistently misrepresented, stereotyped, marginalized, and symbolically annihilated (i.e., groups are not represented as fully developed via conventions of absence, trivialization, or condemnation that diminish their social status). La Pastina analyzes the information available on telenovelas produced since 1950 and encounters several patterns of representation: few shows incorporated recurring Indigenous characters; few had Indigenous people as leading characters or their concerns as themes; Indigenous characters were often the result of interracial relationships (typically the father being White and the mother Indigenous); non-Indigenous actors in make-up typically portrayed Indigenous people; and Indigenous people spoke in broken Portuguese, were often infantilized, and were portrayed as part of a generic Indigenous society with no clear ethnic, cultural, or linguistic traditions. La Pastina notes that for over sixty years of telenovela production in Brazil, the few productions that included Indigenous characters presented then as inarticulate, comedic, oversexed, gullible, and violent, but also of good heart, naïve, docile, submissive, and passive. In sum, through television Indigenous people in Brazil remain at the margins of society and mostly absent from the main source of entertainment. This silencing and symbolic and de facto annihilation of the first inhabitants of Brazil continues.

For the last chapter we return for the third time to Kapayó media, but with a focus on television reception. In Chapter 12, "Kayapó TV: An Audience Ethnography in Turedjam Village, Brazil," Richard Pace, Glenn H. Shepard Jr., Eduardo Rafael Galvão, and Conrad P. Kottak investigate the role of television in daily life, as well as the reception of Brazilian media messages. Even though most people in the village of Turedjam watch television only an hour or less per day (and about one-third of the people in the village are non-viewers), and there are linguistic and cultural barriers to enjoying programming, the authors' media inventories indicate that television, both as device for watching commercial broadcasts as well as a monitor for DVD players, is the most utilized media technology in the village. Still, television's signification as a communication modality is ambiguous, with more than half of respondents in the authors' survey expressing only a neutral opinion about the medium (a far less enthusiastic opinion than comparable non-Indigenous rural populations expressed as measured by the authors' larger research project on media engagement throughout Brazil). Even among those who judge television positively, one-fourth do so because of the medium's usefulness for playing Kayapó film productions on DVDs. People express an interest in gaining knowledge of the outside world through televiewing, particularly by monitoring political events, learning Portuguese, and understanding Brazilian culture, but they also express a clear distrust toward the medium and its messages. Finally, the authors and Turedjam villagers themselves identify specific changes associated with the arrival of widespread in-home TV sets over the last five years, notably, the use of certain Portuguese language terms in discourse among the young, changes in clothing and hair styles, and challenges to adult authority by the youth. At present, these developments are seen as an inconvenience for older generations but not as insurmountable obstacles to Kayapó cultural well-being. Future media engagement, of course, is difficult to predict, but the trend is toward increasing exposure to television and other media, which will lead to changes that only future research will identify.

Conclusion

Looking through the three decades of Indigenous media literature for Latin America and comparing it to the collection of chapters in this volume, a reader might be struck by the consistency of a core of basic research questions. Obviously analyses of new media technologies have begun to enter the literature as they become available to Indigenous peoples, and studies of new groups engaging media are increasing, although not at a rate representative of all the change occurring. Yet thirty years into Indigenous media studies we are still struggling to define what makes Indigenous media Indigenous—or whether or not this should matter—and to what extent the struggle for visual or media sovereignty leads to political successes—from identity formation to self-determination.

A good example of this consistency is found in the edited volume from the International Symposium on Media and Indigenous Communities held at the Iberoamericana University in Puebla, Mexico, in 2013. In the introduction to the book, the organizers write that they conceived of the meeting as a space for group reflection on the lessons learned and the challenges faced as they deepened knowledge of Indigenous media. To serve as a guide, the organizers list ten sets of questions (Magallanes Blanco and Ramos Rodríguez 2016, 12). The first set includes, "What are the fundamental characteristics that permits media to be considered Indigenous?" followed by, "Can we or should we construct a definition that contributes to the theoretical development on these media?" The remaining questions cover the use of alternative theories and approaches (e.g., multiculturalism, postcolonialism, identity, cultural self-determination, sovereignty, ethnicity, racism, otherness, gender, representation, nationalism, autonomy, citizenship) and then ponder ethics, varying methods, the importance of folk or insider views (inside looking in), sustainability of production, distribution, reception, circulation, and praxis tied to self-determination. Most of these sets of questions find some parallel within the chapters in this volume—in fact some of the participants are the same.

But what about the future? Will questions on Indigeneity, embedded aesthetics, media sovereignty, and self-determination continue to dominate? Following the lead of Ginsburg in the next chapter of this book, there is much to study, and, through the process of ethnographic entanglements, there is a need to offer assistance with media logistics (expense of media, sustainability of projects, lack of digital infrastructure, obsolescence of technology, and problems of archiving material). Magallanes Blanco's and Ramos Rodríguez's (2016, 12) last set of questions from their symposium explores a future research agenda that they maintain will be shaped by the new realities of globalization, intense migration flows, the intrusive exploration of natural resources in Indigenous regions, and accelerated technological changes, among other factors. In other words, future studies of Indigenous media will struggle to "keep up" not only with rapidly involving technology, but with rapidly changing socio-economic-political environments.

Salazar's (2015) plea for more engaged scholarship and for "anthropologies otherwise" (as per Restrepo and Escobar 2005) urges researchers to keep pace with the defiant forms of political activism expressed through Indigenous media that are surging throughout the region. He is interested in the productive frictions that develop as the perspectives and practices of communications and media researchers, Indigenous cultural activists, and media producers "rub up against each other in relation to the complex processes of . . . making culture visible" (123). Ultimately, he insists, future research, especially ethnography studies, should move beyond the current emphasis on the epistemology of textual critique to the ontology of performing engaged research (139–40).

The collection of studies in this volume may not meet all the above goals for a future research agenda, but they are important steps in expanding the scope of Indigenous media studies into new areas and among more peoples. The contributions add to the existing body of literature on video production and circulation but also expand to examine the less charted realms of ethnographically based media reception, and, in particular, begin to explore the complexities of media ecology that seeks out the interconnections and intertwining of video, television, radio, the internet, and all manners of new technology arising.

Notes

1. The village of Turedjam, established in 2010, is located in the northern fringe of the Kayapó Indigenous Lands about thirty kilometers from the Brazilian town of Novo Ourilândia do Norte. Because of its proximity to Ourilândia, the village is connected to the town's electrical grid and receives electricity twenty-four hours a day.

2. National Science Foundation Grant 1226335, "The Evolution of Media Influence in Brazil: A Longitudinal and Multi-Sited Study of Electronic and Digital Media," Principal Investigator Richard Pace and Co-Principal Investigator Conrad P. Kottak. Also see Chapter 12 (Pace et al.) this volume.

3. The quantity and scope of studies on Indigenous media production, circulation, and consumption, as well as on Indigenous engagement with non-Indigenous media, varies greatly among geographic regions, cultural groups, and media type. For Latin America

there are a couple of compilations dealing at least in part with the region and covering a range of topics (Magallanes Blanco and Ramos Rodríguez 2016; Wilson and Stewart 2008). However, most studied by far is Indigenous video production—particularly in Mexico, Bolivia, Brazil, and Ecuador where there have been continual productions for several decades—and to a lesser extent Guatemala, Colombia, Peru, Chile, Venezuela, and Argentina, where the traditions are weaker (Salazar 2011). Key publications include, but clearly are not limited to: Aufderheide (1993, 1995); Córdova (2011, 2014); Corrêa (2004); Dias and Demarchi (2013); Gleghorn (2013); Graham (2016); Halkin (2008); Himpele (2008); Köhler (2004); Propios (2002); Rodriquez Ramos and Castells-Talens (2010); Salazar (2002, 2003, 2005, 2009, 2010, 2014, 2015, 2016); Salazar and Córdova (2008); Schiwy (2003, 2009); Smith (2006, 2012); Turner (1990, 1991a, 1991b, 1992, 2002), Video in the Villages (2004); Villarreal (2017); Wortham (2004, 2013); Zamorano (2009); and Zamorano and León (2012). Included in this mix are studies of video production institutions/programs, the history of video and videographers, and textual analyses of productions. What is lacking, however, are sufficient studies of distribution (see Himpele 2008 and Villarreal 2017).

A distant second to Indigenous video in terms of a critical mass of literature for comparative purposes are studies of community radio (Castells-Talens 2011; Murillo 2003; Herrera and Sierra 2016; Ramos Rodríguez 2005, 2016; Carillo Olano 2016, Nava Morales 2016). Falling far behind video and radio, both in terms of quantity and scope of research are studies of Indigenous engagement of television, cell phones, and the internet (from online content to cyber social networks—see Landzelius 2006; Monasterios 2003; Salazar 2003). Possibly the least studied subject matter that falls within a broad umbrella of Indigenous media studies are the impacts of non-Indigenous media upon Indigenous groups, as in engaging commercial television, movies on DVDs or other devices, and commercial radio (in this volume see Murillo, Chapter 7; Shenton, Chapter 10; and Pace et al., Chapter 12). The shortage of these types of studies is critical when trying to understand and contextualize an overall media engagement.

4. There have been other such endeavors, most notably for Latin America the symposium held in Puebla, Mexico, in 2013 that resulted in the publication of the edited volume *Miradas propias: Pueblos indígenas, comunicación y medios en la sociedad global* (Magallanes Blanco and Ramos Rodríguez 2016). Also see the Indigenous Media and Political Resistance in Latin America Conference held at Cambridge University in 2014 (*www.latin-american.cam.ac.uk/events/indigenous-media*).

5. As part of the same tour with Kiabieti, Turner also spoke at the University of Florida immediately following the InDigital Latin Ameria Conference, during which time a joint interview was recorded (see Pace and Shepard this volume).

6. For discussions of what constitutes an Indigenous population and Indigeneity see Wilson and Stewart (2008), Ginsburg (2011, 254); Wortham (2013, 10–11), and Graham and Penny (2014, 4–8).

7. All translations of Spanish and Portuguese by author unless otherwise noted.

Introduction ▲ 23

References

Abercrombie, N., and B. Longhurst. 1998. *Audiences: A Sociological Theory of Performance and Imagination*. London: Sage

Alia, V. 2010. *The New Media Nation: Indigenous Peoples and Global Communication*. New York: Berghahn Books.

Aufderheide, P. 1993. "Latin American Grassroots Video: Beyond Television." *Public Culture* 5 (3): 569–92.

———. 1995. "The Video in the Villages Project: Videomaking with and by Brazilian Indians." *Visual Anthropology Review* 11 (2): 83–93.

Bird, E. 2003. *The Audience in Everyday Life: Living in a Media World*. New York: Routledge.

Cardús i Font, L. 2014. *Indigenous Media: From Transference to Appropriation*. Anthrovision [Online] 2 (1). *anthrovision.revues.org/668*.

Carelli, V. 2013. "Video nas Aldeias: Una propuesta de seducción cultural." *Revista chilena de antropologia visual* 21: 51–63.

Carrillo Olano, A. 2016. "Radios communitarias como forma de resistencia a la homogeneización de la vida." In Magallanes Blanco and Ramos Rodríguez 2016, 195–214.

Castells-Talens, Antoni. 2011. "¿Ni indígena ni comunitaria? La radio indigenista en tiempos neoindigenistas." *Nueva época* 15 (January–June): 123–42.

Champutiz, E. 2013. "Productores audiovisulaes indígenas de Ecuador: Una práctica integral de cosmovivencia." *Revista chilena de antropologia visual* 21: 118–36.

Córdova, A. 2011. "Estéticas enraizadas: Aproximaciones al video indígena en América Latina." *Comunicación y medios* 24: 81–107.

———. 2014. "Reenact, Reimagine: Performative Indigenous Documentaries of Bolivia and Brazil." In *New Documentaries in Latin America*, edited by V. Navarro and J. Rodríguez, 123–44. New York: Palgrave Macmillan.

Corner, J. 2000. "'Influence': The Contested Core of Media Research." In *Mass Media and Society*, edited by J. Curran and M. Gurevitch, 376–97. London: Arnold.

Corrêa, Mari. 2004. "Video from the Villages." In *Mostra video nas Aldeias: Um olhar indígena*, edited by S. Bloch, 33–49. Rio de Janeiro: Centro Cultural Banco do Brasil.

CLACPI (Coordinadora Latinoamericana de Cine y Comunicación de los Pueblos Indígenas). 2013. "About Us" (website). *www.clacpi.org/pagina-ejemplo-2*.

Deger, J. 2006. *Shimmering Screens: Making Media in an Aboriginal Community*. Minneapolis: University of Minnesota Press.

Dias, D., and A. Demarchi. 2013. "A imagem cronicamente imperfeita: O corpo e a câmera entre os Mebêngôkre-Kayapó." *Espaço Ameríndio* 7 (2): 147–71.

Dowell, K. 2013. *Sovereign Screens: Aboriginal Media on the Canadian West Coast*. Lincoln: University of Nebraska Press.

Faris, J. 1992. "Anthropological Transparency: Film, Representation, and Politics." In *Film as Ethnography*, edited by P. Crawford and D. Turton, 171–82. Manchester, England: Manchester University Press.

García, J. 2013. "El video indígena, un poryecto de vida, una ideología, una actitud política." *Revista chilena de antropología visual* 21: 104–17.

García Espinosa, J. 1979. "For an Imperfect Cinema." *Jump Cut: A Review of Contemporary Media* 20: 24–26.

Ginsburg, F. 1991. "Indigenous Media: Faustian Contract or Global Village?" *Cultural Anthropology* 6 (1): 92–112.

———. 1993. "Aboriginal Media and the Australian Imaginary." *Public Culture* 5 (3): 557–78.

———. 1994. "Embedded Aesthetics: Creating a Discursive Space for Indigenous Media." *Cultural Anthropology* 9 (3): 365–82.

———. 1995. "The Parallax Effect: The Impact of Aboriginal Media on Ethnographic Film." *Visual Anthropology Review* 11 (2): 64–76.

———. 1999. "Shooting Back: From Ethnographic Film to Indigenous Production/ Ethnography of Media." In *A Companion to Film Theory*, edited by T. Miller and R. Stam, 295–322. Malden, MA: Blackwell.

———. 2011. "Native Intelligence: A Short History of Debates on Indigenous Media and Ethnographic Film." In *Made to Be Seen: Perspectives on the History of Visual Anthropology*, edited by M. Banks and J. Ruby, 234–55. Chicago: University of Chicago Press.

Gleghorn, C. 2013. "Reconciliation en Minga: Indigenous Video and Social Justice in Colombia." *Journal of Latin American Cultural Studies* 22 (2): 169–94.

Graham, L. 2016. "Toward Representational Sovereignty of Indigenous Media in the A'uwe-Xavante Communities of Etenhiritipa-Pimentel Barbosa." *Media & Communication* 4 (2): 13–32.

Graham, L., and G. Penny. 2014. "Performing Indigeneity: Emergent Identity, Self-Determination, and Sovereignty." In *Performing Indigeneity: Global Histories and Contemporary Experiences,* edited by L. Graham and G. Penney, 1–31. Lincoln: University of Nebraska Press

Halkin, A. 2008. "Outside the Lens: Zapatist and Autonomous Video-Making." In *Global Indigenous Media: Cultures, Poetics, and Politics*, edited by P. Wilson and M. Steward, 160–80. Durham, NC: Duke University Press.

Herrea, E., and F. Sierra. 2016. "Comunicación y pueblos indígenas en Colombia: Aputes sobre la necesidade de una política pública." In Magallanes Blanco and Ramos Rodríguez 2016, 45–58.

Himpele, J. 2008. *Circuits of Culture: Media, Politics, and Indigenous Identity in the Andes.* Minneapolis: University of Minnesota Press.

Köhler, Axel. 2004. "Nuestros antepasados no tenían cameras: El video como machete y otros retos de la video-producción indígena en Chiapas, México." *Revista chilena de antropologia visual* 4: 391–406.

Kottak, C. 2009 [1990]. *Prime-Time Society: An Anthropological Analysis of Television and Culture*. Walnut Creek, CA: Left Coast Press.

Landzelius, K., ed. 2006. *Native on the Net: Indigenous and Diasporic Peoples in the Virtual Age*. New York: Routledge.

La Pastina, A. 2005. "Audience Ethnographies: A Media Engagement Approach." In *Media Anthropology*, edited by E. Rothenbuhler and M. Coman, 139–48. Thousand Oaks, CA: Sage.

Magallanes Blanco, C., and J. Ramos Rodríguez. 2016. *Miradas propias: Pueblos indigenas, comunicación y medios en la sociedad global.* Puebla, Mexico: Universidad Iberoamericana Puebla.

Masayesva, V. 1995. "The Emerging Native American Aesthetics in Film and Video." *Felix* 2 (1): 156–60.

Moore, R. 1992. "Marketing Alterity." *Visual Anthropology Review* 8 (2): 16–26.

Monasterios, G. 2003. "Usos de internet por organizaciones indígenas de Abya Yala." *Communicación* (Cinero Gumilla de Estudios Venezolanos de Communicación) 22: 60–69.

Murillo, M. 2003. "Community Radio in Colombia: Civil Conflict, Popular Media and the Construction of a Public Sphere." *Journal of Radio Studies* 10 (1): 120–40.

Nava Morales, E. 2016. "Radio Totopo y comunalidad: Una experiendia de comunicación indigena en Oaxaca." In Magallanes Blanco and Ramos Rodríguez 2016, 215–32.

Oxford Bibliographies. 2014. s.v. "Indigenous Media," by P. Wilson, J. Hearne, A. Córdova, and S. Thorner, last reviewed April 28, 2017. *doi.org/10.1093/OBO/9780199791286-0229.*

Pace, R. 2009. "Television's Interpellation: Heeding, Missing, Ignoring, and Resisting the Call for Pan-National Identity in the Brazilian Amazon." *American Anthropologist* 111 (4): 407–19.

Pace, R., and B. Hinote. 2013. *Amazon Town TV: An Audience Ethnography in Gurupá, Brazil.* Austin: University of Texas Press.

Pearson, W., and S. Knabe. 2015. "Introduction: Globalizing Indigenous Film and Media." In *Reverse Shots: Indigenous Film and Media in an International Context* edited by W. Pearson and S. Knabe, 3–39. Waterloo, Canada: Wilfrid Laurier University Press.

Peterson, M. 2003. *Anthropology and Mass Communication: Media and Myth in the New Millennium.* New York: Berghahn Books.

Propios, C. 2002. "Vídeo indígena en México: Viejas demandas, nuevos desafíos." In *América Latina. Historia y sociedad. Una vision interdisciplinaria* edited by R. Piqué and M. Ventura, 573–86. Barcelona: Insitut Catalàde Cooperació Iberoamericana (Amer and Cat Número 7).

Raheja, M. 2007. "Reading Nanook's Smile: Visual Sovereignty, Indigenous Revisions of Ethnography, and 'Atanarjuat (The Fast Runner).'" *American Quarterly* 59 (40): 159–85.

———. 2010. *Reservation Reelism: Redfacing, Visual Sovereignty, and Representations of Native Americans in Film.* Lincoln: University of Nebraska Press.

Restrepo, E., and A. Escobar. 2005. "Other Anthropologies and Anthropology Otherwise." *Critique of Anthropology* 25 (2): 99–129.

Rickard, J. 2011. "Visualizing Sovereignty in a Time of Biometric Sensors." *South Atlantic Quarterly* 110 (2): 465–82.

Ramos Rodríguez, J. 2005. "Indigenous Radio Stations in Mexico: A Catalyst for Social Cohesion and Cultural Strength." *Radio Journal* 3 (3): 155–69.

———. 2016. "Radio, cultural e identidad: 10 tesis sobre la radio indigenista mexicana." In Magallanes Blanco and Ramos Rodríguez 2016, 179–94.

Ramos Rodriguez, J., and A. Castells-Talens. 2010. "The Training of Indigenous Videomakers by the Mexican State: Negotiation, Politics and Media." *Postscript: Essays in Film and the Humanities* 29 (3): 83–105.

Rodrígues, M. 2013. "Hacia un cine indígena como metáfora de la memoria de un pueblo y de su resistencia." *Revista chilena de antropología visual* 21: 64–79.

Rodríguez, C. 2001. *Fissures in the Mediascape: An International Study of Citizens' Media.* Cresskill, NJ: Hampton Press.

Ruby, J. 2005. "The Last 20 Years of Visual Anthropology – A Critical Review." *Visual Studies* 20 (2): 159–70.

Salazar, J. 2002, "Activismo indígena en América Latina: Estrategias para una construcción cultural de las tecnologías de información y comunicación." *Journal of Iberian and Latin American Studies* 8 (2): 61–79.

———. 2003. "Articulating an Activist Imaginary: Internet as Counter Public Sphere in the Mapuche Movement." *Media International Australia* 107 (1): 19–29.

———. 2004. "Imperfect Media: The Poetics of Indigenous Media in Chile." PhD diss., University of Western Sydney.

———. 2005. "Communication Rights in the 'Information Society': The Case of Indigenous Media in Latin America." *Revista Codigos* 2: 38–52.

———. 2009. "Indigenous Video and Policy Contexts in Latin America." *International Journal of Media & Cultural Politics* 5 (1/2): 125–30.

———. 2010. "Making Culture Visible: The Mediated Construction of a Mapuche Nation in Chile. In *Making Our Media: Global Initiatives toward a Democratic Public Sphere*, Vol. 1, edited by L. Stein, C. Rodriquez, and D. Kidd, 29–46. Cresshill: Hampton Press.

———. 2011. "Indigenous Media in Latin America." In *Encyclopedia of Social Movement Media*, edited by J. Downing, 254–57. Thousand Oaks, CA: Sage.

———. 2014. "Prácticas de auto-representación y los dilemas de la auto-determinación: El cara y sello de los derechos a la communicación Mapuche." In *Approximaciones a la cuestión mapuche en Chile, una mirada desde la historia y las ciencias sociales*, edited by C. Barrientos, 143–60. Santiago, Chile: RIL Editores.

———. 2015. "Social Movements and Video Indígena in Latin America: Key Challenges for 'Anthropologies Otherwise.'" In *Media, Anthropology and Public Engagement*, edited by S. Pink and S. Abram, 122–143. New York: Berghahn.

———. 2016. "Contar para ser contados: El video indígena como prática ciudadana." In Magallanes Blanco and Ramos Rodríguez 2016, 91–107.

Salazar, J., and A. Cordova. 2008. "Imperfect Media: The Politics of Indigenous Video in Latin America." In *Global Indigenous Media: Cultures, Poetics, and Politics*, edited by P. Wilson, M. Stewart, and A. Córodova, 39–57. Durham, NC: Duke University Press.

Sanjiné, I. 2013. "Usando el audiovisual como una estrategia de sobrevivencia y de lucha, de creación y recreación de un imaginario propio." *Revista chilena de antropología visual* 21: 32–50.

Schiwy, F. 2003. "Decolonizing the Frame: Indigenous Video in the Andes." *Framework* 44 (1): 116–32.

———. 2009. *Indianizing Film: Decolonization, the Andes, and the Question of Technology.* New Brunswick, NJ: Rutgers University Press.

———. 2016. "¿Hay un común posible?" In Magallanes Blanco and Ramos Rodríguez 2016, 17–44.

Shepard, G., Jr. and R. Pace. 2012. "Through Kayapó Cameras: Report from the Field. Knowledge Exchange." *Anthropology News* 53 (4): 18–19.

Smith, Laurel C. 2006. "Mobilizing Indigenous Video: The Mexican Case." *Journal of Latin American Geography* 5 (1): 113–28.

———. 2012. "Decolonizing Hybridity: Indigenous Video, Knowledge, and Diffraction." *Cultural Geographies* 19 (3): 329–48.

Spitulnit, D. 1993. "Anthropology and the Mass Media." *Annual Review of Anthropology* 22: 293–315.

Sreberny-Mohammadi, A., and A. Mohammadi. 1994. *Small Media, Big Revolution: Communication, Culture, and the Iranian Revolution.* Minneapolis: University of Minnesota Press.

Turner, T. 1990. *The Kayapó Video Project: A Progress Report.* Montreal: Revue de la Commission d'Anthropologie Visuelle (Université de Montréal).

———. 1991a. "Visual Media, Cultural Politics, and Anthropological Practice: Some Implications of Recent Uses of Film and Video among the Kayapó of Brazil." *The Independent: A Magazine for Video and Filmmakers* 14 (January/February): 34–40. *independent-magazine.org/archives/#1991.*

———. 1991b. "The Social Dynamics of Video Media in an Indigenous Society: The Cultural Meaning and the Personal Politics of Video-Making in Kayapó Communities." *Visual Anthropology Review* 17 (2): 68–76.

———. 1991c. "Representing, Resisting, Rethinking: Historical Transformations of Kayapó Culture and Anthropological Consciousness." In *Colonial Situations*, edited by G. Stocking, 285–313. Madison: University of Wisconsin Press.

———. 1992. "Defiant Images: The Kayapó Appropriation of Video." *Anthropology Today* 8 (6): 5–16.

———. 2002. "Representation, Politics, and Cultural Imagination in Indigenous Video: General Points and Kayapó Examples." In *Media Worlds: Anthropology on New Terrain*, edited by F. Ginsburg, L. Abu-Lughod, and B. Larkin, 75–89. Berkeley: University of California Press.

Video in the Villages. 2004. *Video in the Villages Exhibition: Through Indian Eyes.* Brasilia: Banco do Brasil.

Villarreal, G. 2017. *Indigenous Media and Political Imaginaries in Contemporary Bolivia.* Lincoln: University of Nebraska Press.

Weiner, J. 1997. "Televisualist Anthropology: Representation, Aesthetics, Politics." *Current Anthropology* 38 (2): 197–235.

Wilson, P., and M. Stewart, eds. 2008. *Global Indigenous Media: Cultures, Poetics, and Politics.* Durham, NC: Duke University Press.

Wortham, Erica. 2004. "Between the State and Indigenous Autonomy: Video Indígena in Mexico." *American Anthropologist* 106 (2): 363–67.

———. 2013. *Indigenous Media in Mexico: Culture, Community, and the State.* Durham, NC: Duke University Press.

Worth, S., and J. Adair. 1972. *Through Navajo Eyes: An Exploration in Film Communication and Anthropology.* Albuquerque: University of New Mexico Press.

Zamorano, G. 2009. "Reimagining Politics: Video and Indigenous Struggles in Contemporary Bolivia." PhD dissertation, City University of New York.

Zamorano, G., and C. León. 2012. "Video indígena, un diálogo sobre temáticas y lenguajes diverso." *Chasqui: Revista Latinoamericana de Comunicación* 120: 19–22.

Films

Amazon Tribe: "Video Is Our Bow. It's Our Weapon." 2015. Produced by J. Murphy. *National Geographic*, December 7. Online video, 3:37. Washington, DC: National Geographic Society. *video.nationalgeographic.com/video/news/151204-amazon-kayapo-video-warriors-vin*.

The Kayapó: Out of the Forest. 1989. Directed by Michael Beckham and Terence Turner. Disappearing World (Granada Television). Baseline. 1991, videocassette. Chicago: Films Incorporated.

The Kayapó: Indians of the Brazilian Rain Forest. 1987. Directed by Michael Beckham and Terence Turner. Disappearing World (Granada Television). Baseline. 2003, DVD. Newton, NJ: Shanachie Entertainment Corp.

Owners of the Water: Conflict and Collaborations over Rivers (Spanish: *Dueños del agua*; Portuguese: *Donos da agua*). 2008. C. Waiassé and D. Hernández Palmar, directors; L. Graham, executive producer. 2009, DVD. Watertown, MA: Documentary Educational Resources.

PART ONE

Overview

1

Indigenous Media from U-Matic to YouTube

Media Sovereignty in the Digital Age

By Faye Ginsburg

My chapter builds on more than twenty-five years of research and engagement with Indigenous media makers, encompassed in a book in progress entitled *Mediating Culture: Indigenous Media in a Digital Age.* In this chapter, I cover a wide range of projects from the earliest epistemological challenges of the video experiments in remote Central Australia in the 1980s (Ginsburg 1991; Michaels 1986) to the emergence of Indigenous filmmaking as an intervention into both the Australian national imaginary and the idea of world cinema (Ginsburg 2010; Collins and Davis 2005). I also address the political activism that led to the creation of four national Indigenous television stations in the early twenty-first century: Aboriginal People's Television Network in Canada; National Indigenous Television in Australia; Maori TV in New Zealand; and Taiwan Indigenous Television in Taiwan (Ginsburg 2011); and consider the questions of what the digital age might mean for Indigenous people worldwide with great technological as well as political creativity (Ginsburg 2008).

I draw on this knowledge to provide a broad context for contemporary Indigenous media in multiple locations, and to consider what connects and distinguishes these projects both concretely and theoretically. What kinds of opportunities and obstacles emerge from the shift to the digital for Indigenous media makers in many different locations and across generations? The uptake of media technologies by Indigenous producers—from the old analog format of U-Matic widely used in the 1980s to contemporary digital social media platforms such as YouTube and cell phones[1]—has often been motivated at least initially by a desire to "talk back" to structures of power that have erased or distorted Indigenous interests and realities and denied access to dominant media outlets. Many of the works and projects that have been produced might best be understood as forms of "cultural activism," a term that underscores the intertwined sense of both political agency and cultural intervention that people bring to these efforts to sustain and transform cultural practices in Aboriginal communities. These are activities that are linked to Indigenous efforts for rights to self-representation, governance, and cultural autonomy after centuries of assimilationist policies by surrounding states, part of a spectrum of practices of self-conscious mediation and mobilization of culture more generally that took on particular shape and velocity beginning in the late twentieth century.

Even as Indigenous media have evolved in sophistication and reach in many parts of the world, these central motivations continue to drive much of the work, whether created by people living in remote communities or urban centers. While cultural, linguistic, and historical circumstances certainly differ, Indigenous communities everywhere face similar circumstances wrought by colonial histories that often motivate their uptake of media. Additionally, the possibilities and constraints of the political economy and material conditions shaping contemporary digital media are important to keep in mind, given the lack of digital infrastructure in many remote areas. In this article, I want to focus on some key issues facing Indigenous media makers, including the expense and sustainability of media and the constant search for funding, the lack of digital infrastructure and its constant obsolescence, and issues of archiving and access according to the demands of both preservation and cultural protocols.

From the vantage point of the second decade of the twenty-first century, it is hard to imagine that just a little over two decades ago, some scholars were assuming that the uptake of media in Indigenous communities would be the death knell of "authentic cultural practices," despite considerable evidence to the contrary (Weiner 1997). The broader question this raised—what I called the Faustian contract in 1991—as to whether Indigenous (or indeed, minority or dominated subjects anywhere) can assimilate dominant media to their own cultural and political concerns or are inevitably compromised by their presence, haunted much of the research and debate on Indigenous media at that time. Happily, the uptake of media in Indigenous communities has gone well.

Before exploring particular cases, I would like to provide a brief overview of the current state of things and introduce some key concepts. Indigenous media work has become a particularly robust form of contemporary cultural production, expressive of longstanding concerns shared by Indigenous people across the planet to gain power over their representations. I think of this as media sovereignty, a term I am introducing to describe practices in which people are exercising the right and developing the capacity to control their images and words and their circulation. Here, I am drawing on a classic legal definition of sovereignty as having authority over an area, extending the usual reference of the word to political authority over a land and populace to consider the significance of having technical, cultural, political and creative control over media being produced by and about Indigenous lives. This is in dialogue with discourse emerging from native North American intellectuals since the mid-twentieth century. I build on the idea of "visual sovereignty" initially deployed by Tuscarora scholar, artist, and curator Jolene Rickard (2011) to characterize the interventions of Indigenous artists in the North American context that amplify in another register the legal-political assertion of sovereignty as a complex, expressive Indigenous visual imaginary.

More recently, Seneca scholar Michelle Raheja expanded on the term and its genealogy, elaborating on the term and giving it further recognition in her important 2011 book, *Reservation Reelism: Redfacing, Visual Sovereignty, and Representations of Native Americans in Film* (Raheja 2011). In it she shows how "video-makers and cultural artists are . . . interrogating the powers of the state, providing nuanced and complex forms of self-representation, imagining a futurity that militates against the figure of the vanishing Indian, and engaging in visual sovereignty on virtual reservations of their own creation" (2011, 240). Raheja acknowledges a genealogy that includes the influence of Tewa/Dine (Santa Clara Pueblo) writer and filmmaker Beverly Singer's notion of "cultural sovereignty" that she uses to describe Native American filmmakers' strategies that rely on trust "in the older ways and adapting them to our lives in the present," an idea she developed in her 2001 book, *Wiping the Warpaint off the Lens* (Singer and Warrior 2001, 5).

From small-scale video and local radio, to digital projects, archival websites, and cell phone films, to national Indigenous television stations and feature films, Indigenous media makers have found opportunities for cultural creativity of all sorts, increasingly on their own terms. Some are directly engaged with political actions; more frequently, the projects are forms of cultural activism. They often support the maintenance or even revival of ritual practices and local languages as well as historical knowledge while building forms of cultural expression that frequently serve to repair fraying intergenerational relationships, bringing much needed sources of productive activity and at times income into communities that habitually suffer from poverty, anomie, and political disenfranchisement. I wanted to give you a sense of the remarkable range of work across a range of technologies and community or institutional bases encompassed by the term Indigenous media.

- Small-format local productions, originally produced in analog video beginning in the 1980s, and now on digital formats
- The creation of local and regional television over the last two decades, facilitated initially by the launch of communication satellites over remote areas as with CAAMA radio and video in Central Australia and Inuit Broadcasting in Canada; and now by digital possibilities as inaugurated in 2009 with Isuma TV in Nunavut, Canada, by Igloolik Isuma

- The emergence of the aforementioned Indigenously run national television stations since 1999 with the debut of
  — Aboriginal People's Television Network in Canada (1999)
  — Maori TV in New Zealand/Aoteoroa (2003) (and a second channel for Maori speakers in 2007)
  — Taiwan Indigenous Television in 2005
  — National Indigenous Television (NITV) in Australia (2007)
  Together, these stations have formed the World Indigenous Broadcasting Network.[2]
- The production of—by now—over one hundred Indigenously directed feature films worldwide that have contributed to Indigenous film taking its place as a form of world cinema on the global stage, circulating through prestigious mainstream venues, such as Cannes, the Toronto International Film Festival, and the Sundance Film Festival, that showcase work and in some cases help support its development. A number of Indigenously directed films have picked up major prizes, which serve as important forms of cultural capital that can be turned into resources to continue to support the work. Feature films also are part of a lively circuit of Indigenous film festivals worldwide. Two key organizations that serve as showcases and important Indigenous transnational meeting grounds are imagineNative in Canada, and the Latin American CLACPI: Coordinadora Latinoamericano de Cine y Comunicación de los Pueblos Indígenas.

These and other projects raise important questions, bringing us back to some of the basic issues about representation and the materiality of different platforms including concerns about the increasing stratification of broadband access as well as media practices that are dependent on literacy-based, corporately designed computer interfaces. As an example of a creative workaround, Isuma TV and its latest retooling, the Nunavut Independent TV Network (NITV), exploit the possibilities of the digital for providing alternative ways of circulating Indigenous media around the world among communities whose very remoteness has made such access difficult through conventional means of distribution, a project they call Digital Indigenous Democracy.[3]

Finally, Indigenous archives based on decades of community-based work as well as the return and repatriation of ethnographic and other kinds of films and photographs made in earlier, often colonial/settler eras are an increasingly important and exciting social practice enhanced by mindful use of digital technologies. These are often created through deeply collaborative, creative partnerships with technically skilled non-Indigenous fellow travelers, as they together imagine and invent new ways to build in cultural protocols, such as restrictions on viewing images of people who have died and use of non-alphabetic language, as in the groundbreaking work of the Ara Irititja project in Australia.[4] In the next section, I focus on the question of archives and the sense of crisis and creativity shaping some contemporary projects that are addressing the need to sustain and preserve this work for the communities that made them, a crucial aspect of media sovereignty that, in my view, has been insufficiently addressed.

Archival Exposure

For many "legacy" Indigenous media organizations, such as the Kayapó Video Project catalyzed by Terry Turner (2006), questions of sustainability loom large, given scarce labor and resources along with the ravages of tropical, desert, or Arctic environments. This is made even more complex with the shift to digital platforms as the hyper-capitalist imperatives of planned obsolescence that shape contemporary computer technologies render certain kinds of formats and software outdated over shorter and shorter periods of time, with associated costs for purchasing newer versions constantly looming. This is something we have all experienced when we attempt (or are required to install) so-called upgrades to operating systems, only to discover, to our frustration, that the programs we have been using for years can no longer function, an experience the industry calls "lack of backward compatibility."[5] If this is difficult to deal with for those of us in first world academic settings who have ready access to technology support and funding, the consequences of the shift to digital infrastructures in remote areas of the Indigenous world can be far more troubling, although such challenges are often met with considerable creativity.

Consider the consequences of the constant change in digital platforms for the sustainability of valuable Indigenous media collections from Latin America and elsewhere that in some cases now reach back over more than two decades. The question of archiving a rich array of cherished material looms large everywhere. Projects such as the Indigenous Latin American Digital Media Archive, which Erica Wortham (2013) has proposed, are important efforts to respond to that crisis. Such work calls attention to the need to look after this material and shows the circuits of connection that have been built over two decades, as supportive partnerships are created with groups across the globe, from Isuma TV in the Arctic to the Indigenous Australian platform Mukurtu, a free, mobile, and open source project originally built with Indigenous communities in central Australia to manage and share digital cultural heritage in culturally and ethically relevant ways, fostering relationships of respect and trust.[6]

Even the Film & Video Center at the National Museum of the American Indian (NMAI), one of the most visible and robust institutions supporting and showcasing Indigenous media from across the Americas for over thirty years, has not been immune to budget cuts that threaten the preservation of the valuable Indigenous media from across the Americas that they have gathered. Their extraordinary collection reflects works shown at programs, showcases, conferences, and festivals at the NMAI; it is now at great risk due to cuts in federal funding for all national cultural institutions, forcing the museum to make Solomonic choices between the preservation of traditional objects and the legacy of Indigenous film and video holdings.

Fortunately, NYU's longstanding alliance with the museum's Film & Video Center created an opportunity. When NMAI Film & Video Center director Elizabeth Weatherford called me, despondent over the pending fate of their media collection, we held an emergency meeting with a range of expert allies to alert them to the gravity of the problem. This group included our library's collection development staff, people dedicated to the expansive growth of licensed electronic resources and the rescue of valuable collections at risk. We are moving forward with them on a plan to care for this collection through the support of a Mellon Foundation grant that we are currently writing to acquire this material in trust with the museum. While this circumstance arose from a crisis precipitated by national austerity measures, it also offers us the opportunity, in the age of YouTube, to upgrade materials to contemporary formats that were first recorded on older ones such as 16 mm, VHS, or the even older U-Matic, once the state-of-the-art analog electronic format until the 1990s.

Such a relocation of materials to a new site necessitates more than technological transfers. If we are to respect the framework of media sovereignty, this will require a rekindling of social relations with the many media makers and their communities represented in the NMAI collection, from Igloolik Isuma in the Arctic to the work of Mapuche filmmakers such as Jeannette Paillán from southern Chile, in order to renew and extend permissions to hold their work in a new location, and, if appropriate, make it available as a study collection. We also are working with faculty developing creative solutions for the dilemmas of digital archives and the possibilities for traditional knowledge license and labels as alternatives to copyright controls developed for corporate purposes, as the Local Contexts project is doing.[7] These kinds of projects offer opportunities that we need to keep in mind—especially those of us who can act as allies in mobilizing the resources available in our institutions when our Indigenous colleagues outside the academy face challenges. Renewing permissions and relationships, and making a wide range of Indigenous media work available for source communities and for teaching and research are important outcomes, and also demonstrate how those of us in universities can use our available resources to support Indigenous media makers in the digital age, not only through showcasing work but also by providing the financial and infrastructural support that can contribute to the preservation of Indigenous media archives for future generations.

Let me offer another example of creative efforts at Indigenous archiving of media of another sort. Ara Irititja—which translates from the Pitjantjatjara language as "stories from long ago"—was created by Ngaanyatjarra, Pitjantjara, and Yankunytjatjara people in central Australia by Indigenous producers, known collectively as Anangu, along with their non-Indigenous supporters (Srinivasan et al. 2010). Inaugurated in 1994, the project has been dedicated to repatriating "lost" material—artifacts, photographs, film footage, and sound recordings—taken and then taken away by visitors to these lands, including missionaries, school teachers, anthropologists, and government workers. Despite their potential great value for Anangu, most of these items had been removed and placed in archives of public institutions or in family photo albums, old suitcases, or boxes stored in closets and under beds. Now, more than two decades after its founding, Ara Irititja staff members have tracked down hundreds of thousands of films and photos. Given the harsh environmental conditions of desert life, fragile materials cannot be physically held in remote settlements but are carefully maintained by supporters in the South Australia Museum. However, they are all digitally returned using a purpose-built knowledge management system. As the Ara Irititja website explains:

> Anangu are passionate about protecting their [recently discovered] archival past, accessing it today and securing it for tomorrow. Anangu have managed complex cultural information systems for thousands of years, restricting access to some knowledge on the basis of seniority and gender, priorities that have been built into their cultural lives for millennia, and that now shape the design of their digital archive. In the past, Anangu were photographed and their knowledge recorded and published without any negotiation. Today, Anangu are careful to determine how their history and culture are presented to the world-wide audience.[8]

The interface was designed to be easy to use for people who might not be literate in English as a first language, using large icons familiar to communities, minimizing trouble for populations with high rates of eye problems, and little familiarity with computer tools. The software was adapted to restrict access to sensitive materials, such as images of people recently deceased (as these tend to cause distress to Anangu). Additionally, separate databases were created to protect the privacy concerns surrounding both men's and women's materials. These functions facilitated the development of multivocal, Anangu-centered histories and resulted in the unique attributes of the initial software.

Since 2012, a convergence of circumstances has revolutionized the project's potential: adequate infrastructure for high-speed connections has reached many communities on their lands; young people have grown up using the internet as a communications tool; and the Ara Irititja team received funding to build new software to be shared on a network. The new, browser-based, cross-platform, multimedia knowledge management system was launched in 2010 incorporating all the functions of the old software and adding many new features. These include individual profiles for every person, plant, animal, thing, place, and collection in the archive, expanding the original Ara Irititja software into a comprehensive tool for preserving and reproducing traditional cultural knowledge. The program is now accessible only to people who can log in with individual passwords, which makes information entry and editing much more accountable and archivally rigorous. Finally, the new system is delivered using the web but via a private intranet adhering to strict Anangu privacy imperatives. In response to the fundamental question "How long will Ara Irititja last?," the website has a compelling statement I suspect applies to many Indigenous communities, although optimism about technology's promise for preservation must be taken with a grain of salt.

> From the late 20th Century, Anangu have become overwhelmed by cultural globalisation through national and international media. This has caused widespread concern among the elders . . . about the transmission of culture and language under contemporary conditions. In 2015, this issue is critical. The senior Anangu who carry the culture are ageing and many are in failing health. When they are gone, the knowledge dies with them. [Ara Irititja's management system] provides a means for this knowledge to be passed on through the use of contemporary technology . . . and can provide this forever.[9]

Let me turn to a third case in which early analog Indigenous media projects made as first experiments in Australian Aboriginal television are being repurposed and made newly accessible on the digital platform of Australian National Indigenous Television (NITV), the fourth such station in the world to be created as a national Indigenous broadcaster. NITV began in 2007 in the town of Alice Springs in Central Australia. It had barely two hours per week of dedicated Aboriginal programming being broadcast across the nation when it began "beaming across the bush" as a channel made by, for, and about Aboriginal people, with a staff of twenty-five. It was the culmination of a quarter century of campaigning on the part of Indigenous Australians for the right to have their languages, cultures, and concerns reflected within the nation's mediascape, building on the work that began in the late 1980s with groups I initially studied in Central Australia such as Warlpiri Media, Ernabella Video and Television, and the Central Australian Aboriginal Media Association (CAAMA). In

2012, NITV moved from Central Australia to Sydney and was incorporated into SBS, the second of Australia's public service broadcasters, making it a free-to-air channel.

Two years ago, to supplement their popular Indigenous sports and news programming, and the broadcasting of Indigenous films, NITV acquired over 180 episodes of a series called *Nganampa Anwernekenhe* ("ours" in Pitjantjatjara and Arrernte languages) that began over twenty years ago as half-hour video oral histories with mostly older, traditional Indigenous Australians living in remote areas of Central Australia. These short films were a staple of Alice Springs–based CAAMA's broadcasting in the 1990s, made by younger Aboriginal Australians from that region, often relatives of the elders they filmed. Many have gone on to become some of Australia's most prominent Indigenous filmmakers, including Rachel Perkins, Warwick Thornton, Beck Cole, and others. The original series was, for many years, the only Aboriginal program produced by and broadcast primarily to Aboriginal people in their own languages (with English subtitles for those who don't know the languages). CAAMA taught a particular style of documentary production, what they call "respectful listening," that permits the subject's voice to shape the narrative and takes the time necessary during production to allow that to occur (Ginsburg 1991). The result is an invaluable video archive about Indigenous lives lived over the last century in remote Central Australia, strong cultural leaders who often had no contact with "whitefellas" until they were young adults. NITV's efforts to digitize this early analog work, originally shot in U-Matic, and make it available on new platforms to a national audience gives these remarkable if under-valued works new significance, amplifying the work of CAAMA and its important early enactment of media sovereignty in the late twentieth century. On NITV, the works are further enhanced by the introduction provided by Warwick Thornton, now one of Australia's most recognized filmmakers and artists, who got his start working on the Nganampa series in Alice Springs twenty years ago (NITV 2015).

It's important to keep in mind that in two of the key locales for the initial formation of Indigenous media—Canada and Australia—the media first developed in response to the entry of mass media into the lives of First Nations people through the state's imposition of satellite-based commercial television over remote regions where more traditional populations lived, beginning in Canada in the late 1970s and in Australia in the 1980s. Remote Indigenous communities vigorously opposed the "dumping" of mainstream media into their lives, insisting on the opportunity to shape their own media to meet local concerns. At the same time, the increasing availability of inexpensive, user-friendly, small-format analog video and small satellite dishes presented an opportunity for these groups to produce their own work; some Indigenous activists imagined their work, metaphorically, as a shield of local manufacture that might fend off the invasion of these other signals from the dominant culture (Ginsburg 1991). This happened with the early foundational case made famous by activist researcher Eric Michaels, when he was hired to study the impact of media on Indigenous people living in the Central Desert of Australia. In the 1980s, he worked with Warlpiri people to help them develop their own analog video practices and low-power television—what he called "the aboriginal invention of television in Central Australia" (also the title of his 1986 book)—created as an alternative to the onslaught of commercial television via satellite. Thus, they provided a kind of natural laboratory for understanding the possibilities of radically different media practices that are "off the grid" of most media scholarship or research addressing Indigenous lives (in which media practices are still too easily regarded as either epiphenomenal or insufficiently traditional).

The significance of "embedded aesthetics" in Indigenous media being produced in traditional Aboriginal communities is still underappreciated. I created this phrase in 1994 to call attention to a system of evaluation that refuses a separation of textual production and circulation from broader arenas of social relations (Ginsburg 1994). This is evident, for example, in Kayapó video with the valorization of the temporal dimensions of ritual, and qualities enhanced by repetition, amplified from embodied performance to its doubled presence on video. With embedded aesthetics, the quality of a work is assessed according to its capacity to represent, embody, sustain, and even revive or create certain social relations both on- and off-screen, respecting longstanding protocols appropriate to the group making the work. Indigenous media, then, can be seen as a new kind of object operating in a number of domains as an extension of collective self-production in ways that enhance Indigenous regimes of value. As another instance of this complex sense of embedded aesthetics, anthropologist/artist Jennifer Deger's work with Yolngu media makers at the community of Gapuwiyak in Arnhemland in northern Australia focuses on what one might call an Indigenous (Yolngu) theory of "media effects." As she explains in her book *Shimmering Screens* (2006), traditional concepts of the impact of revelation, witnessing, and showing are constitutive of identity, a kind of active viewing that empowers and catalyzes ancestral power, rendered evident to knowledgeable viewers, even if it is not actually visible to non-Yolngu audiences.

Most recently, the Yolngu Miyaarka Media Collective from Gapuwiyak that Deger is part of has created a traveling media exhibition called *Gapuwiyak Calling*.[10] The exhibit features a number of distinct genres of Yolngu phone-media. They include phone-art collages featuring giant green frogs and dreadlocked babies; cut and pasted family photographs uniting the living and the dead in flashing gif files; funny videos featuring fragments of mainstream television and movies re-voiced with Yolngu jokes in Yolngu languages; young men dancing in blue grass skirts ordered from the internet to a remix of the 1980s Eurythmics hit "Sweet Dreams";

and a charming thirty-minute film, *Ringtone* (2014), about the variety of ringtones in use in Gapuwiyak, from ceremonial songs to gospel and hip-hop.[11] Although much of the content is deliberately playful, incorporating ostensibly "foreign" sound and image elements accessed via the internet connections on their phones, the Yolngu media makers nonetheless see the exhibition as an opportunity to assert enduring and meaningful connections between generations of Yolngu kin living through times of enormous social stress and change. Structured according to a Yolngu poetics, the exhibition takes motif and meaning from the actions of Mokuy, an ancestral trickster spirit who lives in the forests of Arnhem Land. (Note: The NITV news team did a story on *Gapuwiyak Calling* exhibition's debut at the University of Queensland in Australia, showing how the routines of television news have been incorporated into Indigenous television while delivering a story about Indigenous media from remote communities with a far more distinctive aesthetic.[12])

For my final case, I would like to consider a recent experiment in Indigenous media from the Arctic, the latest venture in the longstanding and always groundbreaking work of the remote Nunavut-based Inuit media collective, Igloolik Isuma. This group is perhaps the most well-known of Indigenous media organizations in the world through the global success of their prize-winning 2001 film, *Atanarjuat The Fast Runner*, the first of their three extraordinary Inuit feature films, created through their distinctive community-based production process.

The group formed in 1990, turning video technologies into vehicles for cultural expression of Inuit lives and histories, another formation catalyzed as a counterpoint to the introduction of mainstream satellite-based television into the Canadian Arctic. Headed by Inuit director Zacharias Kunuk, Isuma engages Igloolik community members while Brooklyn-born filmmaker and Isuma partner Norm Cohn, when not in residence up north, leads a tech support team in Montreal. Frustrated by the difficulty of showing their work to other Inuit communities, in 2008 they created an innovative alternative for Indigenous distribution, Isuma TV, a free internet video portal for global Indigenous media, available to local audiences and worldwide viewers.

In 2009, Isuma inaugurated the Nunavut Independent Television Network on Isuma TV, a digital distribution project bringing a low-speed version of Isuma TV into remote Nunavut communities where the bandwidth is inadequate to view even a single YouTube video. This workaround allows films to be uploaded from anywhere and rebroadcast through local cable or low-power channels, or downloaded to digital projectors. The platform currently carries over five thousand films and videos in more than seventy languages across more than eight hundred user-generated channels, including many works from Indigenous producers in Latin America such as the Brazilian Indigenous media group Video nas Aldeias. This important intervention makes evident the unanticipated possibilities presented to Indigenous cultural activists at moments of media innovation, and the enormously creative use made of these transforming technologies. In a conversation on January 6, 2009, Norm Cohn explained to me:

> We saw the historical technological "moment of opportunity" for the internet, the way we saw the analog video moment in 1980, and the Atanarjuat digital/ film moment in 1998: the brief window in the technology of communication where marginalized users with a serious political and cultural objective could bypass centuries of entrenched powerlessness with a serious new idea at a much higher level of visibility than usual in our top-down power-driven global politics. In 2007, internet capacity allowed us to end-run the film industry entirely and launch a video website that could take aspects of YouTube to a much higher level of thematic seriousness, and see what happens.

In spring of 2015, Isuma kicked off a new project—an online film festival— showcasing Inuit and other Aboriginal-produced works, including the world premieres of director Zacharias Kunuk's documentaries *My Father's Land* and *Coming Home*. The first festival ran from March 2 through April 1, 2015, and was envisioned as a regular (if not annual) event to showcase Indigenous media.

Rethinking the Digital Age

In conclusion, how might we understand what the circumstances are for Indigenous communities in remote regions of the world where access to broadband and cellular networks is difficult or even nonexistent? As one scholar queried in 2006: "Can the info-superhighway be a fast track to greater empowerment for the historically disenfranchised? Or do they risk becoming 'roadkill': casualties of hyper-media and the drive to electronically map everything?" (Landzelius 2007). The recent developments I have discussed offer some insight into what the digital age actually means for Indigenous media makers in a variety of locations, and how new technologies are being both decolonized and indigenized, from the design of archives, hardware, and software, to the questions raised about protocols of viewing, as in the Ara Irititja case. While Indigenous access to digital platforms is certainly uneven, we have ample evidence for the creative uptake of new technologies in Indigenous communities on their own terms, furthering the development of political networks and the capacity to extend their traditional cultural worlds into new domains. This, I suggest, is the basis for media sovereignty in the digital age.

Indigenous digital media raise important questions about the politics and circulation of knowledge at a number of levels; within communities this may be about who has had access to and understanding of media technologies, and who has the rights to know, tell, and circulate certain stories and images. Within nation-states, these media are linked to larger battles over cultural citizenship, racism, sovereignty, and land rights, as well as struggles over funding, airspace and satellites, networks of broadcasting and distribution, access to archives, and digital broadband services that may or may not be available to Indigenous communities. Norm Cohn, speaking from his experiences with Igloolik Isuma over three decades, articulates the dilemmas posed by this infrastructural stratification while embracing the opportunities to indigenize new digital technologies under circumstances of radical difference.

> At present, Inuit and other Indigenous people are on the brink of being left out of the most important new communication technology since the printing press. Almost everything in the 21st century will be conducted at least partly by internet. Being left off, even for another decade or two, is like a linguistic, cultural, and economic death sentence. Isuma's commitment to create IsumaTV even in the face of these disadvantages is our recognition of how access to the internet cannot be 'negotiable' for Indigenous communities struggling to survive. This is particularly the case since the new 2.0 multimedia internet actually offers a practical tool especially suitable for oral cultures in remote regions. Unlike the literary medium of print, or the 1.0 print-based internet which is all about reading, in which oral cultures traditionally have been disadvantaged by participating in their second languages, the 2.0 audiovisual internet advantages people using sophisticated aural and visual skill-sets in their own first languages.[13]

Cohn's words underscore how Indigenous media projects formed over the last decades are now positioned at the conjuncture of a number of crucial historical developments, including the circuits opened by new media technologies such as digital circuits, satellites, compressed video, cyberspace, and cellphones, as well as their links to ongoing legacies of Indigenous cultural activism worldwide. Now, this work is increasingly being produced by a generation comfortable with media and concerned with making their own distinctive representations as a mode of everyday cultural creativity and social action.

I conclude on a note of cautious optimism. The evidence of the growth and creativity of Indigenous media over the last two decades, whatever problems may have accompanied these developments, is nothing short of remarkable, whether working out of grounded remote communities, urban Indigenous enclaves, or broader regional, national, or transnational bases. While Indigenous media activism alone certainly cannot unseat the power asymmetries which underwrite the profound inequalities that continue to shape the world, their

media interventions raise important issues and images about their past legacies, present lives, and cultural futures. These are on a continuum with broader
issues of self-determination, cultural rights, political sovereignty, and environmental degradation, and may help bring some attention to these profoundly
troubling and interconnected concerns.

Indigenous media have grown more robust over the last two decades, in
part through the increasing convergence of media forms that blur the boundaries marking television from film from web-based work or phone-made media.
This remarkably diverse array of works suggest that the emergence of media
sovereignty—the synthesis of command over media technology linked with
new and ongoing forms of collective self-production and control over circulation—has much to offer Indigenous communities as they redefine their lives to
themselves, the world, and future generations.

Notes

Although this material was original presented as the keynote address at the InDigital
Conference in 2015, it has subsequently been published under the same title in
Sociologia e Antropologia (Ginsburg 2016) and is reprinted here with permission from
the journal.

1. For information on the history of U-matic video, once the industry standard until the
   1990s, please see *en.wikipedia.org/wiki/U-matic* (accessed July 8, 2016).
2. For more information on the World Indigenous Broadcasting Network, see *www.wibn
   .org*.
3. For discussion of this project, see my May 4, 2009, piece and the commentary in
   response to it as part of a media commons discussion on Indigenous media for the
   web-based *In Media Res*, "Beyond Broadcast: Launching NITV on Isuma TV,"
   *mediacommons.futureofthebook.org/imr/2009/05/01/beyond-broadcast-launching-nitv-and-
   isuma-tv*.
4. As their website explains, *ara irititja* means "stories from a long time ago" in the language
   of Anangu (Pitjantjatjara and Yankunytjatjara people) of Central Australia. The aim of Ara
   Irititja is to bring back home materials of cultural and historical significance to Anangu.
   These include photographs, films, sound recordings, and documents. Ara Irititja has designed
   a purpose-built computer archive that digitally stores repatriated materials and other
   contemporary items. Anangu are passionate about protecting their archival past, making it
   accessible today, and securing it for the future. See *www.irititja.com*.
5. Bos, Bert, "What Is a Good Standard: An Essay on W3C's Design Principles—
   Backwards Compatibility," *www.w3.org/People/Bos/DesignGuide/compatibility.html*
   (March 6, 2003).
6. Please see "Our Mission," Murkutu CMS 2.0, *mukurtu.org/about* (accessed July 8, 2016).
7. Please see "Local Contexts," *www.localcontexts.org* (accessed July 8, 2016).
8. See "Welcome to Ara Irititja," *www.irititja.com* (accessed July 8, 2016).

9. "How long will Ara Irititja last?" *www.irititja.com/challenges/index.html* (accessed Nov. 8, 2017).
10. "*Gapuwiyak Calling*: Phone-Made Media from Arnhem Land," Miyarrka Media, *miyarrkamedia.com/projects/gapuwiyak-calling* (accessed July 8, 2016).
11. "Ringtone," Miyarrka Media, *miyarrkamedia.com/projects/ringtone* (accessed July 8, 2016).
12. I invited the show to be installed in October 2014 for the Margaret Mead Film Festival at the American Museum of Natural History in New York City. Miyaarka Media brought over their cell phone–made media and some of the key members of the collective to install the show and present their work.
13. Norman Cohn, "Hi-Speed Video in Low-Speed Communities," May 13, 2009, comment on Ginsburg 2009. *mediacommons.futureofthebook.org/imr/2009/05/01/beyond-broadcast-launching-nitv-and-isuma-tv#comment-1489.*

References

Collins, F., and T. Davis. 2005. *Australian Cinema after Mabo*, New York: Cambridge University Press.

Deger, J. 2006. *Shimmering Screens: Making Media in an Aboriginal Community.* Minneapolis: University of Minnesota Press.

Ginsburg, F. 1991. "Indigenous Media: Faustian Contract or Global Village?" *Cultural Anthropology* 6 (1): 92–112.

———. 1994. "Embedded Aesthetics: Creating a Discursive Space for Indigenous Media." *Cultural Anthropology* 9 (3): 365–82.

———. 2008. "Rethinking the Digital Age." In *Global Indigenous Media: Cultures, Poetics, and Politics*, edited by P. Wilson and M. Stewart, 287–305. Durham, NC: Duke University Press.

———. 2009. "Beyond Broadcast: Launching NITV on Isuma TV: Curator's Note." *In Media Res*, May 4. *mediacommons.futureofthebook.org/imr/2009/05/01/beyond-broadcast-launching-nitv-and-isuma-tv.*

———. 2010. "Peripheral Visions: Blak Screens and Cultural Citizenship." In *Cinema at the Periphery*, edited by D. Iordanova, D. Martin-Jones, and B. Vidal, 84–103. Detroit: Wayne State University Press.

———. 2011. "Native Intelligence: A Short History of Debates on Indigenous Media and Ethnographic Film." In *Made to Be Seen: Perspectives on the History of Visual Anthropology*, edited by M. Banks and J. Ruby, 234–55. Chicago: University of Chicago Press.

———. 2016. "Indigenous Media from U-Matic to YouTube: Media Sovereignty in the Digital Age." *Sociologia e Antropologia* 6 (3): 581–99.

Landzelius, K., ed. 2007. *Native on the Net: Indigenous and Diasporic Peoples in the Virtual Age.* New York: Routledge.

Michaels, E. 1986. *The Aboriginal Invention of Television in Central Australia, 1982–1986.* Canberra: Australian Institute of Aboriginal Studies.

NITV. 2015. "'Nganampa Anwernekenhe' on tonight at 6.30pm on #NITV," Facebook, January 6, *www.facebook.com/NITVAustralia/posts/10152647447707005.*

Raheja, M. 2011. *Reservation Reelism: Redfacing, Visual Sovereignty, and Representations of Native Americans in Film*. Lincoln: University of Nebraska Press.

Rickard, J. 2011. "Visualizing Sovereignty in a Time of Biometric Sensors." *South Atlantic Quarterly* 110 (2): 465–82.

Singer, B., and R. Warrior. 2001. *Wiping the War Paint Off the Lens: Native American Film and Video*. Minneapolis: University of Minnesota Press.

Srinivasan, R., K. Becvar, R. Boast, and J. Enoteet. 2010. "Diverse Knowledges and Contact Zones within the Digital Museum." *Science, Technology & Human Values* 35 (5): 735–68.

Turner, T. 2006. "Anthropology as Reality Show and as Co-production: Internal Relations between Theory and Activism." *Critique of Anthropology* 26 (1): 15–25.

Weiner, J. 1997. "Televisualist Anthropology: Representation, Aesthetics, Politics." *Current Anthropology* 38 (2): 197–235.

Wortham, E. 2013. *Indigenous Media in Mexico*. Durham, NC: Duke University Press.

PART TWO

Indigenous Video and Videographers

2

Kiabieti Metuktire and Terence Turner

A Legacy of Kayapó Filmmaking

By Richard Pace and Glenn H. Shepard Jr.

An iconic scene from the film *Kayapó: Out of the Forest* (1989) shows a group of Indigenous Brazilians in full ceremonial regalia attending the Brazilian Congress during the 1988 ratification of a new constitution enshrining Indigenous peoples' rights. Some of these images, and others throughout the film, were captured by Kiabieti Metuktire, one of Brazil's first Indigenous filmmakers.[1] Kiabieti learned his filmmaking skills in the late 1980s and early 1990s, particularly through the Kayapó Video Project organized in part by anthropologist Terence Turner.[2] By virtue of Kiabieti's long-time friendship and collaboration with Turner, his ongoing dedication to training other Kayapó Mebêngôkre filmmakers, and his video images themselves, he may be considered a foundational figure in Indigenous film in Brazil and the broader academic study of Indigenous media.

Kiabieti first met Turner in the mid-1980s during the production of *The Kayapó: Indians of the Brazilian Rain Forest* (1987) when Turner was working as an anthropological consultant for the BBC and Granada International Films. They met for the last time in March of 2015, eight months before Turner passed away at age seventy-nine, when Kiabieti traveled to the United States with two younger Kayapó videographers, Bepunu and Krakrax, to participate with Turner and the authors in public presentations of Kayapó films at the InDigital Latin America Conference in Nashville, Tennessee, and at the University of Florida in Gainesville. These two presentations turned out to be Turner's last public appearances.

On Kiabieti's final day in Gainesville, we filmed an interview in Turner's hotel room. We asked both men to reflect on their thirty-year-long collaboration and their involvement with Indigenous media. In this chapter, we present highlights from this interview and from the recordings of their public presentations in Nashville and Gainesville. We also include observations made by Kiabieti and his younger Kayapó companions during their travels to various destinations in the southeast US, including Cherokee, North Carolina, and

Disney World in Orlando, Florida. This commentary reflects on three decades of the Kayapós' evolving engagement with film, digital media, and modernity.

The Interview: Kayapó Film across Three Decades

Kiabieti was dressed in hybrid formality, his blue jeans and long sleeve shirt contrasting with colorful beadwork and a green parrot-feather headdress, while Turner looked the epitome of the retired college professor with an open-collar Oxford, no tie, rolled-up sleeves, and dark cotton pants. The two had just spent several hours reviewing footage spanning three decades, and Turner was excited to encounter new interpretations provided by Kiabieti about animal transformations and the process of mythic representation in footage of a *Pád* anteater ceremony from the 1980s. The interview shifted freely between English, Portuguese, and Mebêngôkre, the Kayapó language.

We began by asking them about Kiabieti's early training and the origins of the Kayapó Video Project. Kiabieti told us about his initial encounter with the BBC/Granada film crew, who ultimately donated a video camera to his village. He began making films of Kayapó ceremonies, especially men's naming ceremonies, called *mebiok*. He recalled:

> I filmed the *mebiok* of the son of Wywy, a relative of my son. And then I began filming political meetings, for example the big trip the Kayapó leaders made to inspect the Tucuruí dam on the Tocantins River. After that I filmed the big rally in Altamira against what became the Belo Monte Dam. This involved a lot of travel outside my village, so I was making films on the road.

Turner, whom Kiabieti referred to by his Kayapó name, Wakampy, provided more details about the initial training Kiabieti (Kinh) received in 1987, and his ongoing role in the Kayapó Video Project:

> On the film crew there was an excellent cameraman, along with the other members of the crew, who were very supportive of Kinh and one or two other young Kayapó of the village who were very interested in the process of using the camera. The cameraman showed him how to use it and how to hold it. That was his start. When I came back with the Granada International film crew to film the Altamira Rally, I made as a condition that we offer to bring a camera to Kinh's village to become the property of the people in the village for their communal use. But there had already been a couple of people training the Kayapó in video by then. There was a group of Brazilian film students that came and [also] left a camera.
>
> So they had been given cameras and shown how to use them by visiting

camera people. They kept one or two of the cameras around and they kept using them. That was really the beginning of the Kayapó Film Project. The next year was the big Altamira Rally against the dam. Kinh was there filming that with the camera that the Granada film crew had brought as a present. Things just went on from there. We [formally] started the Kayapó Video Project in the aftermath of that big rally in Altamira. Kinh was the main camera person. He was the person, above all, who could show young Kayapó people how to use the camera. He taught a number of people. They were contemporaries of his, like Wywy for example and the Gorotire young chief Kuahi. There were several others who became interested in using the camera as a way of climbing the latter of prestige in the village. It was kind of a step toward leadership for some. For others, who didn't have those ambitions, it was an instrument for registering and preserving lore—their traditional knowledge, their culture. Or, as they call it, *krukaja*, which is a "thing that takes a long time to tell."

In his comments to audiences in Nashville and Gainesville, Kiabieti described the difficulties he encountered in continuing to make videos once the Kayapó Video Project ended. Outside support to obtain updated cameras, computers, editing software, and ongoing training was sporadic, and film production in some villages was abandoned for long periods of time. Kiabieti, too, was unable to work on occasion because there was no camera, computer, or editing software available. He persisted, however, sometimes filming with damaged or outdated equipment. Indeed his main request from the 2015 trip to the US was that funds be raised to purchase a spare camera for his village: they only had one camera, and it was being used at that time elsewhere to record a blockade of the Transamazon Highway to protest the Brazilian government's broken promises. Kiabieti also complained that in all his years of filming, he was never paid for his work. As a result, he could never invest in his own personal equipment or training. Even today it is rare for Kayapó videographers to receive any form of compensation for their work beyond production credits and a certain degree of local prestige.

When asked about the younger generation of Kayapó filmmakers, including Bepunu and Krakrax, who showed their work at the conference in Nashville, Kiabieti observed:

I see the youth advancing. Today the youth have more experience with technology, more memory [storage space], because they have all this technology from the Whites. . . . I saw the films of the young men yesterday [Bepunu and Krakrax] and I liked them. But I felt sad because I never had the same support. I am older than them, but never had support or help like they have with their project. But I am very happy with their work. This is our task, taking our message to other places, exchanging our messages with films, not forgetting our culture.

Without images, without equipment, without technology, a person cannot see how the dance is done, how the festival and music are, how the culture of the other looks. If you lose your culture, you can end up picking up other cultures that are not yours. So showing our films to our relatives is an important way of seeing if these dances and music and culture are being maintained. For this reason, today we use computers and laptops to maintain more of our culture.

Turner reflected on the striking persistence of Kayapó filmmaking in the three decades since his initial project:

Well you know when we were doing this I had no idea that it was going to be more than a sort of curiosity or perhaps a recreation for the Kayapó. I didn't know that it would take on any real importance for them or [become] something that they would want to keep going on their own without constant inputs from people like me. But that is what happened. My field grant ran out and I went back and worked on articles and things like that back in the States and I was not replaced by others in the next year. . . . There wasn't a constant succession of foreign presence who were video technologists or people who could teach video stuff, or fund it. But instead the Kayapó kept managing to acquire video cameras to replace the ones that broke down. They kept shooting video material. They kept building up their archive of their video shooting and they never let go. They never stopped. And that makes me feel good. I mean it caught on with them.

Through Kayapó Cameras

During our travels with Kiabieti, Bepunu, and Krakrax, we encountered a number of Brazilian tourists who, suspecting that the trio was from Brazil, would approach and ask a remarkably predictable, almost scripted set of questions showing a paternalistic attitude and a persistent cultural bias. One such interaction we observed went as followed [translated from Portuguese]:

"Are you Brazilian?"

—"Yes, we are Kayapó."

"But you speak Portuguese?"

—"Yes we speak Portuguese."

"But you are Indians?"

—"Yes, we are Kayapó."

"But you live in villages in the jungle and hunt for animals?"

—"Yes."

"But you have cameras?"

—"Yes, we are filmmakers."

"Ah, so you used to be Indians."

—"No, we are Kayapó."

We asked Kiabieti and Turner about these encounters; Kiabieti responded first:

I use glasses which are from the Whites, but I keep my traditions, I still speak my language. I sing in my language, my music. I don't use the language of the Whites except when I need to. I don't forget my language. I don't forget my dances. I don't forget my culture. I only use this kind of clothing where it's cold, or when there is a lot of sun.

Turner answered next with characteristic bluntness, "I'd say: *bullshit!* Of course they are Indians, of course they are themselves." Going beyond questions of mere cultural identity and authenticity, Turner (2002, 1992, 1991a, 1991b, 1990) has written extensively about what he calls a Kayapó film "symbolic strategy." In the interview, he summarized these thoughts as follows:

Unquestionably, there is something particularly Kayapó [in their way of making films]. . . . They have their own way of organizing . . . the process, which in this case is a process of coming to life, becoming a social being. [This is accomplished in] several ways. One is selecting what to shoot. You know what is important because you know what comes after what in the process of ritually regenerating, replacing social relations for which the ceremony is held. You film those things in that order. And also as an editor, you divide up your film in episodes that correspond to the main bundles of ritual activity. That's your organizing grammar, so to speak, of the film that you turn out. So you produce a film that consists of episodes that are the main units, each one embodying the structure of the whole thing that you're reproducing. The film becomes a string of those episodes, but that is what the ritual itself is, a string of those episodes. And the ritual as a string of those episodes embodies the structure of the social relations that it reproduces. It all fits together; . . . for them, filming the ceremonies that reproduce their own culture is in itself part of the process of reproducing their own culture. It's like an aspect of the same activity. And that is not the way most [Western] film editors think of their activities. There may be some overtones of that, but for the Kayapó it is the whole show, it is the main thing.

The "organizing grammar" Turner identifies derives from deeply rooted Kayapó concepts about truth and beauty, contributing to a unique Kayapó film aesthetic that is revealed throughout the entire media-making process: from choosing the subject matter to framing, camera movements, editing conventions, and audience engagement (Shepard and Pace 2012). "Truth" for the Kayapó consists of the beliefs, knowledge, and traditions that are passed on by successive generations from ancient times to the present, often in the form of songs and dances that shamans learned from mythical animals. These truths are transmitted through recurring patterns of ceremony and ritual, organized sequentially, which communicate the core or essence of Kayapó culture and thereby reproduce human society: "The perfection of such socialized forms through repeated performance embodies the supreme Kayapó value, at once social, moral and aesthetic, of 'beauty'. . . the ideal of completeness-and-perfection" (Turner 1992, 9).

When applied to videos, these same essential qualities of truth and beauty guide the filmmakers to record cultural performances, particularly ceremonies, rituals, and political meetings (Bessire 2009; Turner 2002, 82; Boyer 2006, 49). In addition to influencing the choice of material, these aesthetic principles can also be seen to govern camera position, focal length, framing, and point of view. Productions made by Kayapó filmmakers spanning decades and dozens of villages all seem to share the same set of unwritten rules regarding inclusiveness of all ritual participants, conventions for filming body decoration and nudity, and the avoidance of time compression as much as possible. No voice-over, commentary, narration, or subtitles are used, since the intended audience is Kayapó. However title, date, and production credits are usually included at the beginning of each work. Flashy effects for introductions and transitions are increasingly popular among the younger generation of videographers.

Kiabieti and other Kayapó filmmakers have developed this aesthetic by following their own internalized cultural models, but also in response to the demands of Kayapó audiences who are very vocal about what they expect to see. Younger Kayapó cameramen like Bepunu and Krakrax from far-flung regions remain true to the same filmmaking aesthetic a quarter century after Turner (1990, 1992) first described it. Yet there has been no direct contact between these successive generations of Kayapó filmmakers, nor has there been an overarching video training project that has reached all of these distant villages. The younger generation of videographers have had little or no contact with these earlier productions due to problems of archiving and preservation and the limited circulation of videos and other media until very recently (see Turner 1992). Indeed, Kiabieti had never met either Bepunu or Krakrax prior to this trip. More strikingly, this "Indigenous" Kayapó film aesthetic appears to remain constant even in the face of ever-growing exposure to commercial television and a wide range of Brazilian and foreign films on

DVD. Kayapó filmmakers admit to watching outside film productions with special attention, given their technical understanding of the art, but they do not appear compelled to mimic these foreign genres or filming conventions.

Turner's writings, Kiabieti's comments, and our own observations all re-affirm what Worth and Adair (1972) first contended in their book *Through Navajo Eyes*: Indigenous worldviews will create distinctive visual languages on film. In addition, studies of Indigenous filmmaking aesthetics remain relevant for contemporary Amazonian anthropology given its intense interest in notions of "cosmological perspective" (Viveiros de Castro 1996).

It's a "Small World"

As noted above, Kiabieti and his Kayapó fellows were confronted with cultural prejudice during several interactions with Brazilian tourists who questioned their "Indigeneity." Yet our Kayapó guests revealed their own conceptions and qualms about Indigenous authenticity during a brief visit to Cherokee, NC, as we drove from Nashville to Florida. We took a tour of the well-known Museum of the Cherokee Indian, but Kiabieti was not satisfied with such secondhand contact: "This is a nice museum, but where are the actual Cherokee?" So at random we went to a local craft shop and asked if we could speak to someone of Cherokee descent. We were introduced to a local finger-weaver. As we translated, Kiabieti asked the woman about her family and traditions. She gave her English name but Kiabieti asked for her Cherokee name. She could not quite remember it, so she went back to her office to retrieve a plaque from her desk and proceeded to pronounce, in halting syllables, the traditional name written there.

Kiabieti was stunned. While she returned to her office to replace the plaque, he shook his head and warned his two Kayapó companions to never let this happen to them. Names are a fundamental aspect of Kayapó identity, and indi-viduals may have a dozen or more names that they earn in elaborate ceremonies, including the *mebiok* ceremonies Kiabieti began filming as a novice videographer. Individuals who are rewarded with great names are considered complete, fully formed, beautiful, and powerful (Turner 2003, 21; Fisher 2003, 118; Lea 2012). Filming such a ceremony is an affirmation of the authenticity of the names ac-quired. Without their names, and, needless to say, without their language, tradi-tions, ceremonies, and culture, they would simply cease to be Kayapó.

At the opposite end of the spectrum of cultural experiences, we took our three Kayapó guests to Disney World's Magic Kingdom in Orlando, giving them a chance to turn the camera around and film the great American cliché. Even though Dis-ney World is a popular tourist destination for Brazilians, only Bepunu was vaguely familiar with the company name, which he recognized, together with the iconic Magic Kingdom castle, from the opening credits of Disney films. We observed which attractions the Kayapó videographers chose to film and which parts they ignored. Although none of the Kayapó had yet edited their footage at the time of this writing, Kiabieti described to us what he intended to do. He thought the most interesting aspect to show to the audience back home would be all the people at the park. So his plan was to film all the different types of people and the sheer numbers of them. He realized he was going to have a hard time explaining the practice of waiting in long lines for rides: this made no sense to him because, after long waits of twenty to forty minutes, the rides lasted only a few minutes.

The only attraction that all three Kayapó videographers found interesting was the Jungle Cruise boat ride, with its kitschy, fiberglass, animatronic jungle animals. Kiabieti explained that the Kayapó love to hunt, so these unusual animal specimens would be appealing to the home audience. He was so excited filming the mechanical creatures that the boat operator had to twice ask him to sit down, per park rules. None of the other attractions stimulated much enthusiasm from them. They watched with a mixture of curiosity and bewilderment but mostly showed little interest in filming.

The worst ride for Kiabieti was the Haunted Mansion. His only comment after finishing the ride was "Very ugly." In Kayapó cosmology, the essence or soul of the dead—referred to as *karon*, or image, the same word used to refer to film images—is to be avoided except in certain ceremonial contexts (Bamberger 1974, 368; Fisher 2003, 125, 130). Especially dangerous are the karon of the recently departed who may search out their living relatives and try to escort their own karon away with them (Fisher 2003, 131). The fear of meeting the karon of a recently departed Kayapó is so strong that the deceased owner's personal possessions are destroyed, given away, discarded, or piled on the grave, to avoid the attractive power such valuable items have. Objects typically given this treatment include pets, garden plants, utensils, weapons, body ornaments, and even cameras and televisions (see Bamberger 1974, 368). Given this cultural context, the Haunted Mansion with its ghouls, skeletons, and joking spectral apparitions made no cultural sense: not funny or entertaining in the least. Bepunu later got a headache, which he blamed on the ugly apparitions at the Haunted Mansion.

After only three hours in the park, our Kayapó guests were ready to leave. Having fond childhood memories of this particular attraction, Shepard insisted that the group take one last ride: It's a Small World. On its surface, the attraction, with its display of cultures and languages (however selective and stereotyped) from around the world would provide an opportunity to reflect on Americans' view of cultural diversity. However, to the Kayapó videographers, the ride was uninspiring and merited only a few short shots. While the Kayapó were mostly bored by the colorful dancing dolls intoning that insipid melody in numerous world languages, we, now with our adult sensibilities, cringed at the cultural stereotypes and childish vision of diversity superimposed on underlying universal humanity.

Farewell to Wakampy

Terence Turner passed away on November 17, 2015. His long friendship and collaboration with Kiabieti helped create a lasting tradition of filmmaking among the Kayapó of Brazil and was fundamental to the emergence of the field now known as Indigenous media studies (Ruby 2005, 164; Wortham 2013, 5). Turner's legacy lives on through his numerous students and through many others influenced by his writings. Meanwhile, Kiabieti continues to produce videos. His work was recently recognized by the United Nations Equator Initiative and featured in the 2015 National Geographic clip *Amazon Tribe: "Video Is Our Bow."* Upon learning of Turner's death, Kiabieti posted on Facebook, "A great warrior and friend, *Wakampy*, has passed away." We present these memories of their final encounter as a tribute to both men's enduring legacy.

Notes

1. A young Kiabieti appears as the unnamed Kayapó video maker in Freya Schiwy's (2009, 3) book *Indianizing Film.* A note on nomenclature: In the Spanish-language literature the subgenre is referred to as Indigenous video (*vídeo indígena*) while in the Portuguese literature it is Indigenous film or cinema (*filme indígena* or *cinema indígena*) and practitioners are commonly referred to as filmmakers or cinematographers (*cineastas*) more often than video makers or videographers. In this essay we use these terms interchangeably.

2. The Kayapó Video Project was a collaboration between Terence Turner and filmmaker Vincent Carelli, then of Centro de Trabalho Indigenista (Indigenous Work Center) or CTI. Carelli went on to found Video nas Aldeias (Video in the Villages, see *www.youtube.com/ user/VideoNasAldeias*), the most influential Indigenous media production center in Brazil.

References

Bamberger, J. 1974. "Naming and the Transmission of Status in a Central Brazilian Society." *Ethnology* 13: 363–78.

Bessire, L. 2009. "From the Ground, Looking Up: Report on the *Video nas Aldeias* Tour." *American Anthropologist* 111 (1): 101–3.

Boyer, D. 2006. "Turner's Anthropology of Media and Its Legacies." *Critique of Anthropology* 26 (1): 47–60.

Fisher, W. 2003. "Name Rituals and Acts of Feeling among the Kayapó (Mebengokre)." *Journal of the Royal Anthropological Institute* 9: 117–35.

Lea, V. 2012. *Riquezas intangíveis de pessoas partíveis: Os Mēbēngôkre (Kayapó) do Brasil Central.* São Paulo: EDUSP.an

Ruby, J. 2005. "The Last 20 Years of Visual Anthropology—A Critical Review." *Visual Studies* 20 (2): 159–70.

Shepard, G., Jr., and R. Pace. 2012. "Through Kayapó Cameras: Report from the Field. Knowledge Exchange." *Anthropology News* 53 (4): 18–19.

Schiwy, F. 2009. *Indianizing Film: Decolonization, the Andes, and the Question of Technology.* New Brunswick, NJ: Rutgers University Press.

Turner, T. 1990. *The Kayapó Video Project: A Progress Report.* Montreal: Revue de la Commission d'Anthropologie Visuelle (Université de Montréal).

———. 1991a. "Visual Media, Cultural Politics, and Anthropological Practice: Some Implications of Recent Uses of Film and Video among the Kayapó of Brazil." *The Independent: A Magazine for Video and Filmmakers* 14 (January/February): 34–40. *independent-magazine.org/archives/#1991.*

———. 1991b. "The Social Dynamics of Video Media in an Indigenous Society: The Cultural Meaning and the Personal Politics of Video-Making in Kayapó Communities." *Visual Anthropology Review* 17 (2): 68–76.

———. 1992. "Defiant Images: The Kayapó Appropriation of Video." *Anthropology Today* 8 (6): 5–16.

———. 2002. "Representation, Politics, and Cultural Imagination in Indigenous Video: General Points and Kayapó Examples." In *Media Worlds: Anthropology on New Terrain*, edited by F. Ginsburg, L. Abu-Lughod, and B. Larkin, 75–89. Berkeley: University of California Press.

———. 2003. "The Beautiful and the Common: Inequalities of Value and Revolving Hierarchy among the Kayapó." *Tipití* 1 (1): 11–26.

Viveiros de Castro, E. 1996. "Os pronomes cosmológicos e o perspectivismo Ameríndio." *Mana* 2 (2): 115–44.

Worth, S., and J. Adair. 1972. *Through Navajo Eyes: An Exploration in Film Communication and Anthropology.* Bloomington: Indiana University Press.

Wortham, E. 2013. *Indigenous Media in Mexico: Culture, Community, and the State.* Durham, NC: Duke University Press.

Films

Amazon Tribe: "Video Is Our Bow. It's Our Weapon." 2015. J. Murphy, producer. *National Geographic*, December 7. Online video, 3:37. Washington, DC: National Geographic Society. *video.nationalgeographic.com/video/news/151204-amazon-kayapo-video-warriors-vin.*

The Kayapó: Out of the Forest. 1989. Directed by Michael Beckham and Terence Turner. Disappearing World (Granada Television). 1991, videocassette. Chicago: Films Incorporated.

The Kayapó: Indians of the Brazilian Rain Forest. 1987. Directed by Michael Beckham and Terence Turner. Disappearing World (Granada Television). Baseline. 2003, DVD. Newton, NJ: Shanachie Entertainment Corp.

3

Wallmapu Rising

Re-envisioning the Mapuche Nation through Media

By Amalia Córdova

During the Closing Night and Awards Ceremony of the Twelfth International Film and Video Festival of Indigenous Peoples held in the Chilean city of Temuco, Mapuche singer/songwriter Daniela Millaleo closed the festivities with a song in honor of photojournalist Felipe Durán, detained two months earlier on September 22, 2015. While Mapuche art becomes fashionable and is increasingly visible in the museums, galleries, and airport shopping centers of Chile and Argentina, Mapuche communicators still routinely face threats and persecution.[1]

With an assertive discourse that has flourished over the years, the demands of various ethnic groups in Chile, particularly the Mapuche, embody the struggle against the dominant neoliberal model and the failure of public policies of democratic governments that diminish the already limited opportunities for participation and inclusion of Indigenous peoples on the national stage. By infusing new and evolving media communications with traditional practices and grassroots organizing, Mapuche-produced media, as with many Indigenous media projects, question notions of citizenship and support historical claims to sovereignty and territorial unity.[2]

Wallmapu, or the Mapuche Nation's traditional territory, encompasses the southern reaches of Chile and Argentina, countries where aboriginal peoples are still stigmatized and relegated to marginal sectors of society.[3] This mentality began to be audiovisually challenged in the mid-1990s, when Mapuche activists took up video cameras to record their histories and to document protests against extractive multinational incursions in the region. Today we see an increase in dedicated Mapuche filmmakers, journalists, and artists working in video and new media to express their visions and strengthen their culture, denounce the ongoing violations of their rights, and link dispersed, remote communities with the growing number of Mapuche migrants living in Chilean cities and abroad.[4]

In this chapter, I describe important productions by independent Mapuche women directors Jeannette Paillán and Jennifer Silva (a.k.a. JAAS) as case studies that illustrate how a rich body of work on the contemporary Mapuche experience is taking shape, displacing the cinematic focus on genre and mass audience expectation. Rather than seek out an "Indigenous aesthetic," as many would like to see established, I focus on the rooted aspects and on the creative innovations these directors have deployed to shape works that enjoy a certain popularity, and exercise an effective impact on a determined constituency. I consider these works exceptional in that they are pioneering and groundbreaking, though they may not be well-known outside specific circuits of Indigenous cinema. I discuss these "other" uses of Indigenous video productions; how they are being used to rethink indigeneity, rewrite history, and question assumptions on the practice of individual filmmaking. I propose that works such as these hybrid documentary practices offer counter-representations of the past and facilitate understanding of contentious, ongoing issues misrepresented or missing from the mainstream, public arenas of national debate.

Hybrid Documentary for Advocacy

The documentary has proven to be by far the weapon of choice for recording subaltern histories, contesting multinational extraction and development projects, and denouncing human rights violations on Native lands and bodies. The very real need to document these abuses in order to raise awareness often translates into expository shorts echoing newsreel-style reportage and longer works without artistic ambitions, produced under the auspices of nongovernmental organizations or other external agencies. While they may cover diverse topics, these works may present a similar and rather indistinct look and feel. Both time and funding constraints obviously affect the final outcome, and the directors seldom have formal film training; they often work collectively or in partnership with funding agencies or nonprofit organizations.

The reliance on others and the commitment to sustainable filmmaking leads to projects grounded in community accountability and infused with a community's pressures and interests; what Ginsburg has called "embedded aesthetics" (1994). These works, which can use unconventional film styles such as static shots of lengthy speeches in an Indigenous language, become more geared to the local audience rather than one trained on mainstream cinemas, more in line with "imperfect media" practices proposed by Salazar (2004). Fictional works are less common, often based on traditional stories, involving collective memory and consultation with elders to verify the accuracy of the working version of the tale. In addition, important works have been produced under duress, even overnight, when human rights are at stake.

Precisely for these reasons, highly innovative and creative self-produced works stand out. Mapuche filmmaker Jeannette Paillán's first video, the poetic video essay *Punalka: El alto Biobio* (Punalka: The upper Bío-Bío, 1995), was made with Lulul Mawidha, the group she formed to contest the building of a major hydro-electric dam in Pehuenche territory. Hip-hop artist Jennifer Silva's music video *Newen* pioneered the use of the Mapuche language, Mapuzungún, in the urban centers of the southern cone. These works are made with extremely low budgets but with a degree of creative freedom, shot in Indigenous languages yet with multiple audiences in mind. While the local community may be the primary audience, there is an underlying intent to reach potential allies for the local griev-ances they are denouncing. In some cases, these audiences are one and the same, if we consider the internalized colonialism that affects Indigenous communities.

These works are made with an urgency to be widely viewed, screening at a range of venues such as local meetings, academic conferences, human rights courts, and specialized festivals, to name a few. Such is the case of Paillán's *Punalka* and a host of other works that have been distinguished at festivals for their powerful delivery of critical issues. Several Indigenous directors have come to light with at least one short film that screens through the Indigenous festival circuit. A few of these directors go on to make second and third films. The real rarity is the Indigenous-produced feature film, narrative, or documentary. For Indigenous "rising" directors, making a few acclaimed shorts and winning prestigious awards may help to garner the funds to make a feature film, but that recognition does not guarantee its distribution, as might be expected in the more traditional art-house festival circuit.

The fact that the overwhelming majority of works produced by Indigenous media projects are documentaries has drawn the attention of ethnographic and documentary film festivals. As documentary film programmers know, the docu-mentary is already at a disadvantage as a film genre, from funding to screening. Fortunately, videos that have tackled complex issues of multinational encroach-ment on Indigenous rights have grown from urgent reportage to a solid body of documentary works that benefit from exhaustive research and know how to engage audiences, garnering diverse awards at international film festivals. These festivals and the funding agencies linked to them have opened up to this kind of work, reaching out to specialized programmers and producers to ensure their representation, often through the programming of Indigenous-themed side-bars, both in and out of competition.[5]

Framing Resistance

During the socialist Salvador Allende's presidential period (1970–1973), Indig-enous struggles became part of a broader human rights campaign within an in-creasingly polarized political scenario. However, starting in 1990 and through Chile's transitional democratic governments, promises to the Indigenous movement faded into the background despite efforts at organizing Indigenous demands. The independent organization Consejo de Todas las Tierras (Council of all lands, founded in 1990) attempted to unify an emerging Indigenous rights movement outside the government, putting pressure on the elected coalition government of Patricio Aylwin (1990–1994). Aylwin formed a special committee of Indigenous peoples, passing the first "Indigenous Law" of 1993 (Ley 19.253), a nod to Indigenous demands that established basic rights for Indigenous peoples. In 1996, as part of the law, a state-run Indigenous bureau was launched, the National Indigenous Development Corporation (Corporación Nacional de Desarrollo Indígena, CONADI), to support public policies regarding restitution and protection of lands and waters, and to some extent foment educational and cultural development initiatives for nine recognized ethnic groups—Aymara, Atacameño/Likanantai, Colla, Quechua, Diaguita, Mapuche, Rapa Nui, Kawésqar and Yagán.[6] However, this entity does not recognize Indigenous peoples or their traditional organizations as such; it only acknowledges them as ethnically distinct. Most notably, it doesn't recognize their political rights—to self-representation or traditional justice systems—or territorial rights, such as management and protection of natural resources. The four consecutive center-left coalition governments that followed Aylwin's administration consolidated the neoliberal policies of the Pinochet regime, allowing lumber and hydroelectric companies to aggressively implement development plans on Indigenous territory.

In response, the affected Mapuche communities organized on several fronts, protesting specific regional mega-projects and garnering international support. In 1997, Endesa, the largest electric company in Latin America, began building a massive hydroelectric complex called Ralco in the upper Bío-Bío River, a traditional territory of the Pehuenche people. Several films have been produced about its impact. The first one, *Punalka: El alto Biobio* (1995) was a poetic documentary by Mapuche journalist Jeannette Paillán, shot when the dam was under construction. Non-Mapuche directors have followed the case, producing *Ralco* (1999, by Esteban Larraín), *Üxüf xipay* (The plunder, 2004, by Dauno Tótoro) and *El velo de Berta* (Bertha's veil, 2004, by Esteban Larraín with Jeannette Paillán), which unveil the Chilean government's support for the dam and disregard for Mapuche rights. The Spanish films *Apaga y vámonos* (Switch off, 2005, by Manel Mayol) and *Ralco, un mal negocio / Ralco, a Bad Business* (2008, by Nicolás García and Xavier Vaqué) take the case further, establishing the transnational links of the Spanish capital behind the project.

The Poetics of *Punalka*

Resistance to the construction of the Ralco dam has become emblematic of the struggle of Indigenous peoples in the southern Andes. Even before actual construction of the dam began, Pehuenche resistance and displacement catalyzed a broad front of opposition to the project, which generated both national and international media coverage. The mobilization against Ralco, beginning in 1997, marked a turning point for the Mapuche political movement. Several regional fronts emerged to protest other development projects, such as lumber extraction, industrial fishing, and water privatization, that encroached on traditional Indigenous lands and rights and whose profits benefitted foreign companies and individual Chilean investors. A new movement took shape with the formation in 1998 of the Coordinadora Arauco-Malleco (CAM, a coordinating body for communities in the Arauco and Malleco regions) in Tranaquepe, which was active in the areas of Tirúa, Contulmo, and Cañete, and in Temucuicui, a community that declares itself autonomous and even has a website of its own.[7]

As conflicts over Mapuche territory and sovereignty escalated, a number of documentaries were made in defense of the Mapuche, particularly regarding the impact of the Ralco megaproject.[8] The first one was *Punalka: El alto Biobio* (1995), the aforementioned documentary video shot on U-matic by Mapuche journalist Jeannette Paillán, of Pehuenche origin. Narrated through a poem in Mapuzungún by Mapuche poet Leonel Lienlaf, the film is about the river's spirit and is both a prayer and a call to action to protect the threatened river. Through this short film, Paillán became the first internationally recognized Indigenous video-maker from Chile, a remarkable feat for an Indigenous woman without formal film training. The video screened at the VI Festival Latinoamericano de Cine de los Pueblos Indígenas in Guatemala (1999) and at the Smithsonian Institution's 1997 Native American Film + Video Festival in New York City. However, this did not protect her from suffering beatings and having her camera confiscated while covering protests. Paillán later directed *Wallmapu* (2003), a historical documentary on Mapuche territory from a Mapuche point of view, which won a Special Mention of the Jury for Best Historical Research at the 2003 Human Rights Festival in Santiago del Estero, Argentina, and a short fiction, *Perimontún* (2008), about identity loss, shot when Paillán was on a Ford fellowship studying film in Spain.

Paillán has also gained prominence as a leader of the *video indígena* movement, mainly through her participation in the Latin American Coordinator of Indigenous Peoples' Film and Communication (CLACPI, Coordinadora Latinoamericana de Cine y Comunicación de los Pueblos Indígenas). In 2004, she headed the CLACPI festival's eighth edition, the International Festival of Indigenous Peoples' Film and Video in Santiago, Chile, and in 2008 she was honored in Spain for her tireless defense of Indigenous peoples' culture and patrimony with the City of Córdova Award to Communication Solidarity, a distinction first awarded to writer Eduardo Galeano in 2006. Paillán was elected General Coordinator of CLACPI in 2008, and in 2012 was re-elected for a second term. In 2013, she was recognized with the Premio Bartolomé de las Casas Award, as a representative of CLACPI, for "the dissemination of Indigenous cultures in diverse international instances, allowing Indigenous peoples to express their own worldview, particularly with regards to defending Mother Earth and affirming the rights of Indigenous peoples."[9] This is an annual award offered by the Spanish Secretariat of International and Ibero-American Cooperation, of the Ministry of Foreign Affairs and Cooperation, in conjunction with Casa América, to distinguish outstanding individuals or organizations in the defense of the rights of Indigenous peoples. Paillán and a team of supporting broadcasters, journalists, and producers also organized the Twelfth Festival Internacional de Cine y Video de los Pueblos Indígenas, the first CLACPI festival to be presented not by a nation-state (i.e., Argentina and/or Chile) but convened by an Indigenous nation's traditional territory, in this case the ancestral Mapuche territory of Wallmapu.[10]

At the same time, a broader Mapuche social movement has taken root across Chile and Argentina. For years, Mapuche activism was largely ignored by local and national media, but when it was covered, it was actually charged with promoting acts of violence and outright secession from Chile. Acts of physical repression and legal persecution of Mapuche leaders are regularly denounced by human rights observers such as Amnesty International and Observatorio Ciudadano (Citizen Watch). Chile's mainstream print media in particular perpetuates a violent image of the Mapuche, going as far as to insinuate that there are links between Mapuche rights movements and worldwide terrorist organizations including al-Qaeda, ETA, and even FARC.[11] This climate seeks to warrant the excessive use of force in any situation regarding Mapuche demonstrations. As a result of widespread, violent persecution and murky court procedures, several young leaders have been killed or forced into hiding.[12] In all cases, the Mapuche protesters were proven to be unarmed, and no members of the police forces were killed.

Most prisoners held under an anti-terrorist law dating from the Pinochet regime are Mapuche.[13] Their trials are also tainted by false testimonies and anonymous witnesses, as expressed eloquently in the documentary *El juicio de Pascual Pichún / Besieged Land* (2007), by María Teresa Larraín, which juxtaposes the perspectives of the prosecution and the defense during the trial of a respected Mapuche traditional leader, or *lonko*, Pascual Pichún, now deceased. The number of political prisoners jumps to a hundred if one considers prosecutions under other laws, in addition to innumerable false arrests. In an effort to protest the law and bring awareness to their plight, three prisoners processed under the anti-terrorist law engaged in prolonged hunger strikes in 2007, drawing national media attention. Many were hospitalized while awaiting a response from the government of Michelle Bachelet, including Patricia Troncoso, who holds the record for the longest hunger strike in Chile over the last twenty years, for a total of 112 days. Through the mediation of the Catholic Church and with pressure from human rights organizations, the strikes were suspended in January of 2008. Although the more conservative government of Sebastián Piñera met in 2010 with Mapuche leaders to discuss the law and revise the terms of the sentences, there continue to be prisoners on hunger strike on and off in the jails of Wallmapu, regardless of the politics of the current government.

Non-Mapuche journalists, filmmakers, and communicators have also been harassed, arrested, and even deported over the mere fact of being sympathetic to the Mapuche cause. Chilean filmmaker Elena Varela was arrested by over twenty armed policemen on May 7, 2008, in her house in Lican Ray, in southern Chile. She was producing two films at the time of her arrest, one exploring the perceptions of local Mapuche communities to the repression suffered at the hands of the Chilean state in their attempt to recover seventeen thousand hectares of historically Mapuche-held territory from lumber companies. She received funding from the national Production Development Corporation (CORFO, a state agency), and from the national film fund Fondo de Fomento Audiovisual, of the National Council on the Arts, a peer-reviewed government granting agency. Varela was not allowed to speak to anyone for the first twenty-four hours of her arrest. The national media supported the investigation's thesis that her production company used state film funds to support terrorist actions. All of her audiovisual and written material such as scripts, diaries, log books, and archival interviews of ex-political militants (Mapuche and others), including political prisoners and leaders, were seized by the Investigations Police of Chile. Varela spent four months in solitary confinement as the case gained national and international attention from groups such as the Chilean Association of Documentarians, Amnesty International, and dozens of other human rights organizations worldwide who feared the information contained in her tapes might be used by Chilean security forces against Mapuche activists and the film's collaborators. Eventually some twenty tapes were returned to Varela, and she was able to shoot once a week while under house arrest. In the trial that took place nearly two years later, Varela was found innocent of all charges. She was released on April 22, 2010, and finally completed the two-hour documentary *Newen Mapuche* (2010, Chile), which includes the harrowing story of her arrest.[14]

Newen/Calling on the Power of the Land

Jennifer Andrea Aguilera Silva (whose artistic name is JAAS) grew up in the southern section of Santiago, Chile. Her working-class family never brought up their Mapuche heritage, a very common phenomenon in large cities where such ancestry is actually considered to cause setbacks and be a source of shame. She became involved in the somewhat marginal hip-hop scene in her early twenties, working with a music producer in the late nineties. As a result of her experimental artistic drive and a renewed interest in her native heritage, she produced an extraordinary song and music video called "Newen," a Mapuche term for life-force.[15]

JAAS never formally learned how to speak Mapuzungún, the language of the Mapuche people. She started to listen to local bilingual Mapuzungún-Spanish radio programs such as *Wixage anai* (Wake up and rise up, produced by the collective Jvken Mapu), and taught herself the basics. She sought out Mapuche community activists in Santiago such as radio producer Freddy Treuquil who negotiated the terms of the shoot in the *lof*, or Mapuche community. Freddy's brother José was a leader in a community near Valdivia and was a completely fluent speaker of Mapuzungún who advised on all aspects of translation during the shoot and post-production. When the project was completed, terms of economic compensation were discussed in the event there was any income as a result of the film, but, for the most part, the shoot in the community, and the filming of the clip in general, was a labor of love and collaboration with no real budget to speak of. The music video was uploaded to JAAS' MySpace page and YouTube channel, and the song appears on her first self-produced album, *En este mundo* (2004).[16]

The song "Newen" kicks off with the trill of a *trutruka*, a long horn made with bamboo and bullhorn traditionally used by the Mapuche to call community members together. In the fourth measure, this acoustic sound is joined by a synthetic drum machine loop, creating the instantly recognizable syncopated beat of rap music. JAAS opens by calling out in Mapuzungún: "Newentun! Nawuntun! Mapu! Mapu, Mapu, Mapu! Mapu, Mapu, Mapu!" (Invoking life-force! Power of the Land, the Land, the Land!) Her call to the power of "the Land" cannot be merely understood as the earth or a given territory; it is an appeal to origin itself: to Mother Earth and the inherent power of being connected to the earth, to being a part of that vital original force. Her singing then shifts into Spanish, asking her audience, "How many years of oppression? More than five hundred. The Mapuche people shall be resurrected, persistent in the struggle . . . lethargy doesn't calm the warrior . . . the wind drags away all that is asleep."[17]

JAAS performs multiple identities in a short music video. The video opens with a sunrise in the countryside, layered with silhouettes of Mapuche warriors on horseback and footage of peaceful marches for Mapuche rights. JAAS first appears kneeling at the side of a river, dressed in the traditional clothing of Mapuche women: wearing a black wool robe, *trariwe* (loom-woven colored waistband), and silver *chaway*, or earrings, and crowned with a jingling silver headband. Abruptly, we see her in an urban setting, in sweatshirt and baggy pants, rapping and gesturing straight into the camera in full urban hip-hop mode. She raps in Spanish over a montage of images of Mapuche ceremonies, protests, and confrontations with police. JAAS crouches in the riverbed of the Mapocho, the main fluvial artery of Santiago, where she raps in front of a graffiti mural in her sweats. A lull in the lyrics shows the countryside of southern Chile, virtually all of which is originally Mapuche territory, where JAAS is seen swimming in a shallow stream under a dense canopy of trees, emerging from the chilly waters in her regalia, pressing her bare feet firmly into a muddy embankment, gripping a long thick branch of a tree and sticking it into the earth. Halfway through the song, she shifts to rapping in Mapuzungún. Various scenes of daily life follow: we see elders and children together; short clips of ceremony and dance; scenes of planting, harvesting, and horseback riding. JAAS climbs a tree, wields a lump of untreated lamb's wool, sits at a loom, and, in a modest kitchen lit only by a blazing hearth, she helps slaughter, bleed, and skin a sheep. Next she performs live in a concert in front of a large group of youths, rapping in Mapuzungún while the chorus repeats: "Mapu Mapu Mapu!" Her closing words conjugate both languages, indexing her fluency in both: "Mapu—pisando fuerte la Tierra" ("Mapu—stepping firmly on the land"). Ultimately, her plea is not just to connect to the land but to opt into self-recognition as Indigenous people who honor and defend that special connection to the land.

Newen was selected to screen at the 2006 Smithsonian Institution's Native American Film + Video Festival (NAFVF), presented by the Smithsonian National Museum of the American Indian (NMAI), and subtitled into English and Spanish by co-director Katherine Ross for the purpose of screening at the festival. This was decided so all festival attendees, including JAAS's own counterparts from other regions of Latin America, could fully understand the content of the song. As occurs with many other works from Latin America, English subtitling has been one of the most concrete outcomes of being screened at a festival. The work not only gains a home (a copy remains in the NMAI Study Collection, and the Festival drafts a director biography and film description for its catalog and its online platform), but also becomes available to Anglophone audiences and international festivals, programmers, viewers, and scholars. *Newen* has screened to audiences in Brazil, Canada, Chile, Mexico, and Spain through contacts made via the NMAI. In fact, the video screened in Chile only after screening in New York, as part of a showcase from the 2006 NAFVF held in Santiago in June 2005. This speaks to the enduring impact of an international agency such as an Indigenous film festival in bringing works to light in places where they are otherwise invisible and considered irrelevant.

Mapuche Media's 2.0 Generation

While there is no dedicated archive of Indigenous-produced work in Chile, the Museo Chileno de Arte Precolombino (MCHAP), a private collection located in downtown Santiago, houses an ethnographic video archive that includes over three hundred works from across the continent, of which twenty-eight are about the Mapuche Nation (Carreño González 2014). The works represent 61 percent of the documentaries in the Museum's national video collection, making the Mapuche the most represented Indigenous people of Chile in the collection (Carreño 2014). This archive has been a magnet for scholars, filmmakers, anthropologists, teachers, and students, but it was not a priority for the museum's leadership. Free film programs from the archive were regular, well-attended events at MCHAP beginning in the late nineties, garnering a modest but faithful lunchtime audience for Indigenous-themed videos. Anthropologist, musician, and filmmaker Claudio Mercado, the archive's founder, maintains the collection, along with his other duties as the audiovisual coordinator for the museum. Anthropology student Gaston Carreño was recruited to organize the collection, producing an updated catalog for public use. The collection is open to the public and several videos are currently online (in Spanish or with Spanish subtitles) through the museum's website, *chileprecolombino.cl/archivo-audiovisual*.

Mapuche media now also has dedicated international scholarship. Australian-based media scholar and anthropologist Juan Francisco Salazar directed *De la tierra a la pantalla / From Land to Screen* (2004), a documentary that contrasts Chile's media depictions of the Mapuche struggle with the activism of three Mapuche-run media projects: the Center for Mapuche Communication Jvken Mapu, which hosts the oldest running Mapuche radio program in Chile, *Wixage anai*;[18] Lulul Mawidha, run by filmmaker Jeannette Paillán; and the online news service Mapuexpress. All three collectives are self-generated, long-standing efforts that remain active in media production.

Bilingual radio programs are bridging cultural differences between Mapuche and non-Mapuche. By 2005 at least six different Mapuche radio programs aired regularly, two weekly programs in the southern city of Nueva Imperial (*Nutram Kawün* and *Aim Mapu* on Radio La Granja), the rest in different parts of Santiago, including *La voz del viento*, produced by Agrupación Antu Liwen, and *Iñchiñ Mapuche tati*, both weekly conversational programs aired by Radio El Encuentro of Peñalolén (Ortega Fuentes 2005). Weekly bilingual shows such as *Identidad Mapuche* (on Radio Florecer in La Florida) and *Wixage anai* (produced by Jvfken Mapu and broadcast by Radio Tierra in downtown Santiago) feature Mapuzungún, cover wellness issues, and track current Mapuche political and cultural issues.

The political nature of their work exposes the producers of these radio programs to persecution. In Santiago, Chile, in February 2010, Investigations Police seized computer equipment, audiovisual records, and written material from both the workplace and home of Jvfken Mapu member Richard Curinao, claiming that the program *Wixage anai* had broadcast public statements of CAM. In April 2010, the Red de Comunicadores Mapuche (Mapuche Communication Network) presented Curinao's case to the newly elected govern-ment of Sebastián Piñera, stating that, along with the arrest of Mapuche *lonko* Pascual Pichún, the cases "constitute serious violations to freedom of expression while at the same time are a blow to the communication and information rights of the Mapuche Nation."[19] To date, Curinao has not recovered his equipment and is still being pressured to reveal his sources.[20]

Many new Mapuche media initiatives have emerged on digital platforms. From the news agency Mapuexpress, founded in 2000, to the binational (Argentina and Chile) print and online journal *Azkintuwe* (The lookout), news from Wallmapu is now accessible in Spanish, English, and Mapuzungún. The internet hosts a wealth of Mapuche-run blogs and several sites in Mapuzungún, and Mapuche music vid-eos stream over YouTube, along with documentaries and independently produced videos. Facebook is also populated by individuals, artists, collectives, and groups that self-identify as Mapuche and use the social network to denounce mistreat-ment, educate viewers on Mapuche culture, and issue calls to action.

Support for these initiatives is far-reaching and transnational; Mapuexpress pioneered as an autonomous site supported by the Mapuche FOLIL Founda-tion in the Netherlands and sends out weekly electronic newsletters worldwide from all Wallmapu, linking remote locations and allowing anyone to replicate and amplify their news. It also acts as a news agency for other free and indepen-dent media agencies. A small team of editors works with a wide spectrum of Mapuche organizations and efforts, aspiring "to remain an open, independent, and pluralistic forum from and for Mapuche concerns, consciously avoiding divisiveness or rivalry between different Mapuche tendencies, as a contribution to maintaining unity in action."[21]

For a decade, *Azkintuwe* was a widely-circulated Mapuche newspaper and news agency reporting from Wallmapu with a multicultural perspective through a bimonthly printed newspaper, special supplements, and an online news portal updated daily. A nonprofit media organization headquartered in Temuco, *Azkintuwe*'s network of journalists critically addressed social, cultural, economic, and political developments of the Mapuche Nation in particular and of Indigenous peoples in general. Launched in 2003, *Azkintuwe* was the first Mapuche media outlet with coverage beyond borders, with correspondents in Chile and Argentina. The Azkintuwe News Agency began operating in June 2008, to encourage "media pluralism, tolerance of ideas and solidarity among peoples, considering that communication, facilitated by new information tech-nologies, should play a social role."[22]

In 2009, Pedro Cayuqueo, journalist and founding director of Azkintuwe, was invited to cover a European tour of Indigenous film from Latin America.[23] Seeing the potential of transnational circulation of Indigenous media, in 2010 he added a cultural supplement in the printed edition and online of *Azkintuwe* called "Yekintún," one of the first Indigenous-produced critical spaces for Indigenous media in Latin America, covering both Indigenous media and productions by non-Indigenous filmmakers. Efforts to consistently cover Indigenous-made media have since taken root, as seen with the launch of the government-funded independent website Yepán (*www.yepan.cl*), which offers news, calls for entries, trailers, and reviews of Indigenous film and video (in Spanish), driven by a collective including Mapuche journalist Elías Paillán of Jvken Mapu.

In a joint effort with the human rights and civic advocacy organization Observatorio Ciudadano, Azkintuwe launched the first Mapuche youth media training initiative, Taiñ Azkintun / Nuestra Mirada (Our view). Funded by the Embassy of Canada and the Catholic University of Temuco, the first workshop gathered Mapuche youth from the regions of Araucanía and Los Ríos to create short videos about their communities. The response was enthusiastic, surprising even the organizers; roughly an equal number of men and women, representing a range of localities, participated (Vargas 2010a). Cayuqueo said that he sees a new generation of Mapuche youth who are using and consuming new forms of mass media—Facebook, Fotolog, Vimeo, and YouTube—and interested in more than just denouncing the abuses toward the Mapuche, "not because it's not still relevant, but because it has stigmatized what we are."[24] The workshop's first phase trained youth on location in May of 2010, drawing on committed communicators such as Guido Brevis, a film and television director, and Elías Paillán to train twenty youths. Cayuqueo refers to the next phase as "version 2.0," which will offer a greater degree of specialization by sending some of the youth abroad for further training.[25]

What the Mapuche face daily is what so many Indigenous peoples across the world face: a discriminatory state policy of repression that seeks to protect the interests of powerful extractive industries. The Mapuche activists and supporters of the Mapuche cause—including media makers—have also been caught in the crossfire. In such a landscape, a self-determined, Indigenous-controlled media becomes a critical tool to save lives and seek justice. Edgardo Collinao (Mapuche), a Taiñ Azkintun workshop participant, says this is just the beginning of a process that must continue:

> I hope we're able to get there, since personally I'm training to become a communicator not to profit off my people but to contribute to them in any capacity I have. . . . This should be the beginning of a greater project of our own Mapuche Nation, so that, for example, we can control our own media communications—radio, television, journals—so that when the time comes we have the right people trained to work. (Vargas 2010b)

Conclusion

Aesthetically original works such as Paillán's *Punalka* and Mapuche hip-hop videos such as *Newen* attest to the creative possibilities unleashed through Indigenous audiovisual resistance. Through diverse channels and formats, Mapuche media are being used to rethink history, critically and creatively countering foundational narratives on indigeneity that have emerged from the official historical record. Produced since first contact and captured in footage, photos, and written accounts produced with Western technologies and usually from a European or Eurocentric point of view, these narratives persist and are replicated in fictional renderings emanating from Hollywood and beyond, and are present in the day-to-day reportage of political and social movements in Chile.

Through each of their works, Indigenous filmmakers and communicators in Wallmapu are exploring how video-making can serve as a tool for advocacy, cultural affirmation, and creative expression; to document alternate histories and project their concerns and visions toward future generations; to strengthen contemporary community identity, traditions and language; and to help dispel the myths of the "noble savage" and "disappearing native." In producing innovative experimental and hybrid works, including music video clips, Mapuche media practitioners adapt new and evolving media technologies to give voice to multiple expressions of contemporary identities.

Notes

1. Durán was released ten months later, on August 5, 2016, with all charges dismissed due to insufficient evidence. When arrested, he faced charges that could have resulted in an eleven-year prison sentence (Medrano and Fuentes, 2016).
2. According to the 2002 national census, 4.6 percent of Chile's population self-identifies as belonging to an Indigenous group, of which 87.3 percent is Mapuche (INE 2003).
3. *Wallmapu* is the most widely-used and culturally accepted name for the entire Mapuche territory. In the Mapuche language, Mapuzungún, it translates as "surrounding land" (surrounding—*wall*, land—*mapu*). Different geographical Mapuche sub-regions receive geographically specific denominations, such as Ngulumapu for the territory west of the Andes mountains (central and southern Chile), and Puelmapu, for the territory east of the Andes (southern Argentina). All translations by the author except as noted.
4. For an excellent overview on this process see Juan Francisco Salazar (2004) and his documentary *De la tierra a la pantalla / From Land to Screen* (2004).
5. Such has been the case of the longstanding documentary festival of Belo Horizonte, forumdocBH, that not only screens Indigenous works fairly regularly but also presented Indigenous documentary retrospectives in 2011 and 2015.
6. "Misión Institucional," CONADI, *www.conadi.gob.cl/mision-institucional.*
7. Temucuicui's website can be found at *comunidadtemucuicui.blogspot.com.*

8. The earliest Chilean documentary on the *Mapuche, Nutuayin mapu: Recuperaremos nuestra tierra* (1971), collectively created by Antonio Campi, Luis Ararneda, Samuel Carvajal, Guillermo Cahn, and Carlos Flores, with participation of the Mapuche community of Lautaro, is also an experimental work on the struggle for land recovery. See "El indígena en el documental chileno," Memoria Chilena, *www.memoriachilena.cl/602/w3-article-3389.html* for a chronology of the ethnic documentary in Chile.

9. Original text in Spanish: "la difusión de culturas indígenas en diversas instancias internacionales, permitiendo que los pueblos originarios expongan su propia visión del mundo, especialmente a la hora de proteger la Madre Tierra y reivindicar los derechos y libertades de los indígenas." "Jeannette Paillán: 'Los jóvenes comunicadores serán el futuro de CLACPI,'" *clacpi.org/observatorio/?p=4045*, accessed July 7, 2014.

10. The festival was called FICWallmapu 2015. The festival's website is *www.ficwallmapu.cl*.

11. A classic example is the daily *La Tercera*, a major media outlet that as recently as 2015 called for further investigation into the alleged links between Mapuche organizations and terrorist organizations. For example, see Paula Comandari, "Los correos que muestran el vínculo entre las FARC y el PC," *La Tercera*, July 31, 2015, *www.latercera.com/noticia/los-correos-que-muestran-el-vinculo-entre-las-farc-y-el-pc*.

12. In August 2009, Jaime Mendoza Collío (24) was shot in the back during the police intervention of a peaceful land occupation in Angol, adding to a string of Mapuche young men killed by state military police: Matías Catrileo (22) and Johnny Cariqueo (23), shot in 2008 while taking part in a land occupation, Rodrigo Cisternas (26) shot in 2007, and Alex Lemún (17), shot during a land occupation in Malleco in 2002.

13. More than thirty-seven Mapuche leaders have been imprisoned under these laws, suffering excessive use of force by the police, particularly at land occupations (Dean 2009).

14. Varela's case is not unique. Mapuexpress reported the arrest of two French journalists, Christopher Cyril Harrison and Joffrey Paul Rossj, on March 17, 2008, in Collipulli, while they were interviewing a *werkén* (a traditional Mapuche authority). The police confiscated their camera, equipment, and tapes. Two days later, along with the werkén, they were attacked in the street by a group of twelve people. On May 3, 2008, Italian documentarians Giuseppe Gabriele and Dario Ioseffi suffered similar treatment while shooting a demonstration taking place on a plot owned by lumber company Mininco, claimed for almost two decades by a Mapuche community.

15. I first learned of JAAS in Brooklyn in 2005, where I met a film producer who was assisting in the development of a Chilean hip-hop documentary, *4 Ramas, 4 Armas*, a project directed by Katherine Ross, originally from Chicago and living in Santiago. I was curious if any women were in the documentary, and if there was any Indigenous content in the artists' work, and learned of JAAS. Katherine and JAAS co-directed *Newen* with Freddy Treuquil, producer of the collective Kerruf Newetwaiñ.

16. The video clip is available online at *www.youtube.com/watch?v=MzmdiOCsg_c*, accessed 4/31/2016.

17. Translation by author. Original text in Spanish: "Cuántos años en agresión? Más de quinientos de opresión. . . . El pueblo mapuche sera resucitado, persistentes en la lucha . . . el letargo no calma al guerero . . . el viento arrastra todo lo dormido."

18. *Wixage anaị* is the subject of the documentary *Wixage anai: Despierta y levanta* (2005), directed by anthropologist Anthony Rauld.
19. Jose Luis Vargas, "Comunicadores mapuches entregan al Gobierno antecedentes sobre persecución a periodista" *Azkintuwe* online edition, April 9, 2010, *www.azkintuwe.org/abri1091.htm*. Azkintuwe emerged from the Lientur Counter-Information Collective, a web portal created in 2000 in Temuco by journalists covering abuses suffered by Mapuche communities and organizations in Chile. The journal *Azkintuwe* ceased publication in 2013 but maintains an active social media presence on Facebook and Twitter. Back issues can be read at *issuu.com/azkintuwe*.
20. Richard Curinao, personal communication, October 4, 2016.
21. Quote is from *www.mapuexpress.net/?act=presentation*, accessed August 28, 2012. The current URL for Mapuexpress is *www.mapuexpress.org*.
22. "Quienesomos," *Azkintuwe*, *www.azkintuwe.org/quienesomos.htm*, accessed August 28, 2012.
23. Cayuqueo is an active social media networker: his Twitter account has 138,000 followers, and he regularly publishes columns in the press in Chile, has authored four books and since 2014, and hosts *Kulmapu*, the first show on Mapuche culture, for the private television network VTR. *Kulmapu* is rebroadcast by eleven regional channels and CNN's Chilean affiliate, CCNChile (*www.cnnchile.com/noticia/2014/12/04/kulmapu-la-serie-documental-sobre-la-cultura-mapuche*). Episodes also stream on the VTRChile channel on YouTube.
24. Pedro Cayuqueo, personal communication, June 7, 2010, Santiago, Chile.
25. Pedro Cayuqueo, personal communication, June 7, 2010, Santiago, Chile.

References

Carreño González, G. 2002. "Entre el ojo y el espejo. La imagen mapuche en cine y video." Master's thesis, Universidad de Chile.

_____. 2014. "Entre flechas y rituales: Aproximaciones a la representación del indígena latinoamericano en algunas producciones audiovisuales (1960–2000)." PhD diss., Universidad de Chile. *tesis.uchile.cl/handle/2250/117476*.

Dean, N. 2009. "Mapuche Warriors Sacrifice Life for Redemption of Mapuche Nation." *Mapuche International Link* (August 27). *www.mapuche-nation.org/english/html/news/n-149.htm*.

Ginsburg, F. 1994. "Embedded Aesthetics: Creating a Discursive Space for Indigenous Media." *Cultural Anthropology* 9 (3): 365–82.

INE (Instituto Nacional de Estadísticas). 2003. *CENSO 2002: Síntesis de resultados.* Santiago, Chile: Empresa Periodística La Nación S.A. *www.ine.cl/docs/default-source/FAQ/s%C3%ADntesis-de-resultados-censo-2002.pdf*.

Medrano, C., and R. Fuentes. 2016. "Cristián Levinao y Felipe Durán quedan en libertad por falta de pruebas." diarioUchile (August 5). *radio.uchile.cl/2016/08/05/cristian-levinao-y-felipe-duran-quedan-en-libertad-por-falta-de-pruebas*.

Ortega Fuentes, J. 2005. "Generos radiales y radio comunitaria: Una mirada a las parrillas y la presencia temática." *Programa de Comunicación Social de Base*. Santiago, Chile: Educacion y Comunicaciones (ECO).

Salazar, J. F. 2004. "Imperfect Media: The Poetics of Indigenous Media in Chile." PhD diss., University of Western Sydney.

Vargas, J. L. 2010a. "Comunicadores mapuches entregan al gobierno antecedentes sobre persecución a periodista" *Azkintuwe* online edition (April 9), *www.alainet.org/es/active/37269.*

———. 2010b. "En sector costa culmina etapa de filmación para alumnos de Curso Audiovisual Taiñ Azkintun" (press release). *Tain Azkintun* (August 17), *tainazkintun. wordpress.com.*

Films

Apaga y vámonos (Switch off). 2005. Written and directed by Manel Mayol. 35mm film, 82 min. Spain.

De la tierra a la pantalla / From Land to Screen. 2004. Written and directed by Juan Francisco Salazar. 38 min. Australia/Chile. Available online at *vimeo.com/5285777.*

El velo de Berta (Berta's veil). 2004. Esteban Larraín, director, with Jeannette Paillán. 73 min. Chile.

El juicio de Pascual Pichún / Besieged Land. 2007. Directed by Maria Teresa Larraín. 65 min. Chile.

Newen/Life-Force. 2004. Directed by Jennifer Aguilera Silva/JAAS. 4 min. Chile.

Newen Mapuche: La fuerza de la gente de la tierra (Newen Mapuche: The strength of the people of the earth) 2011. Written and directed by Elena Varela. 120 min. Chile.

Perimontún. 2008. Written and directed by Jeannette Paillán. 7 min. Spain.

Punalka: El alto Biobio (Punalka: The upper Bío-Bío). 1995. Directed by Jeannette Paillán. 26 min. Chile: Grupo de Estudios y Comunicación Mapuche Lulul Mawidha.

Ralco, un mal negocio / Ralco, a Bad Business. 2008. Directed by Nicolás García and Xavier Vaqué. 50 min. Chile/Spain.

Üxüf xipay (The plunder). 2004. Directed by Dauno Tótoro. 73 min. Chile: Ceibo Producciones

Wallmapu. 2003. Directed by Jeannette Paillán. 65 min. Chile.

Wixage anai: Despierta y levanta (Wixage Anai: Wake up and rise). 2005. Directed by Anthony Rauld. 27 min. Chile.

4

Transformations of Indigenous Media

The Life and Work of David Hernández Palmar

By Laura R. Graham

Scholars of Indigenous (and other subaltern) media emphasize the many positive impacts that locally controlled new media—especially radio and video—have within communities and the ways that Indigenous peoples productively use media to advance their cultural and political agendas. Numerous studies, in communities stretching from Canada, the US, Australia, and New Zealand, to Mexico, Brazil, and Bolivia, that follow in the wake of Sol Worth and John Adair's ([1972] 1997) first experiments in "subject-produced film" repeatedly demonstrate that audio-visual media are powerful instruments for the creative expression of identity, self-reflection, political empowerment, cultural transmission, and the preservation of traditional knowledge (see, for example, Ginsburg 1991, 1994, 1999, 2002, 2011; Michaels 1986; Prins 2002; Turner 1991a, 1992, 2002; Wilson and Stewart 2008). They also show that new media technologies give Indigenous peoples powerful means to destabilize hegemonic stereotypes that circulate in the mass media and achieve greater representational sovereignty (Graham 2016; see also Raheja 2010).[1]

Scholars have paid less attention to individuals and ways that involvement in Indigenous media projects affects specific lives and subjectivities.[2] As a step toward redressing this imbalance, this chapter traces the path of David Hernández Palmar, a Wayuu member of the Iipuana clan, from the arid Guajira Peninsula to the international arena and Indigenous film festival scene. It tracks Hernández Palmar's transformation from a young man who, for reasons that will become clear, eschewed politics and political activity to an outspoken advocate for Indigenous film and video and a leading figure in the Latin American Indigenous media movement. I show that David combined his unique talents and abilities with opportunities afforded through his participation in projects that immersed him in discussions of the politics of representation and Indigenous media, and provided critical networking possibilities that helped him launch into the international Indigenous media world. David's story offers an example of the life-changing experiences that participation in media projects may afford Indigenous media makers. The stories of many other unique and inspiring individuals have yet to be told.

The period from 2006 to 2008 was critical to David's exposure to global Indigenous struggles and his developing awareness of and insertion into continental and transnational Indigenous media movements. Projects that David was involved in during this period—especially working on the documentary film *Owners of the Water* (2009), founding the Venezuelan International Indigenous Media Showcase, and partnering with the Venezuelan Ministry of Culture's National Cinema Foundation (Fundación Cinemateca Nacional, usually just called Cinemateca)—afforded exposure to new arenas and discourses, networks and connections, and they opened up possibilities that were critical to David's developing sense of himself as an Indigenous media advocate and activist.[3] As he embraced new opportunities, participated in new forums including film festivals, and expanded his social and professional networks, David became increasingly fluent in the discourses that circulate in these arenas. He became ever more articulate in the language of media politics and more effective as a media advocate. Hernández Palmars's case thus serves as an illustrative example of what Faye Ginsburg (1994) calls the "embedded aesthetics" of Indigenous media. Hernández Palmars's trajectory exemplifies the cultural mediations, social relationships, possibilities, and connections with others that Indigenous media opens up at various levels of scale, from within and across local communities to global partnerships and collaborations.

David's example is also important because, as an educated, urban Indian, David represents an important sector of contemporary Indigenous reality and one that, in discussions of Indigenous media particularly in the Latin American context, is generally overlooked. Faye Ginsburg (1994), in her discussion of embedded aesthetics, draws attention to the diversity of backgrounds and locales among Aboriginal media makers—remote, urban, and rural—noting that these constitute distinct social bases for media makers' understanding of Aboriginality and its representation, especially as it crosses cultural and national borders (369). As a Native person with post-secondary education who has lived most of his live in Maracaibo, Venezuela's second largest city, David complicates the profile of Latin American Indigenous media makers as generally located in remote or rural contexts; his position simultaneously underscores the complexity of contemporary Indigenous and Wayuu realities.[4] He and members of his family, like most of Maracaibo's numerous Wayuu inhabitants, frequently move between the city and the family's home community in the Guajira. While David is firmly grounded in an urban reality, he is also deeply rooted in Wayuu worlds.

This chapter shows that through his work in Indigenous media, David has expanded his connections with other Indigenous peoples, media makers, and communities, as well as their allies, in Venezuela, across Latin America, and beyond. Today David is truly an Indigenous cosmopolitan (see Forte 2010; Oakdale n.d.). He moves fluidly within and across various social, linguistic, geographical, and ontological arenas and divides. David's ability to fluently move between different domains aligns him with other lowland South American Indigenous leaders whose autobiographical narratives, as Suzanne Oakdale and Magnus Course (2014, 4) observe, similarly "seem to be linked to the display of fluency between different domains, both social and ontological." This essay thus contributes to a growing corpus of work within the tradition of scholarship on Native American biography that centers on lowland South America (for example, Hendricks 1993; Kopenawa and Albert 2013; Oakdale and Course 2014; Bacigualupo 2016).

This chapter also extends ethnographic and collaborative work that I have carried out with David since we first met in Maracaibo in December 2005. I partnered with David and others in the making of the documentary film *Owners of the Water* and the conceptualization of the Venezuelan International Indigenous Media Showcase (MICIV), and accompanied him in laying the groundwork for his work with Cinemateca. As an ethnographer, collaborator, ally, and friend, I have followed David's transition from a locally based photographer to his debut into the international Indigenous media scene and witnessed his metamorphosis into a media advocate working actively at continental and global levels.

The material presented in this essay is based primarily on collaborative work, ethnographic observations, interviews, and autobiographical narratives that I have elicited from David over the years.[5] It is rooted in the shared experiences of our joint projects and also in the journey of our friendship. By asking questions, sharing drafts, and incorporating David's comments and suggestions, I have involved David in the process of writing this essay. While we have engaged in a process of "dialogic editing" (Feld 1990), and I incorporate David's voice extensively, I have retained the author's role and voice. I have endeavored to be faithful to David's interpretation of his experiences while conveying my own understanding of the process and evolution of his work and identity. My ongoing ethnographic journey with David has been neither one of me "studying up" (Nader 1972) nor "down," but rather "studying alongside," for David and I have long traveled together as intellectual equals, each learning from the other and mutually benefitting from the others' questions, differentially positioned insights, and critiques. While we are both cognizant of the inherent power differentials of my being a US-based academic and he a South America–based Indigenous intellectual without permanent formal institutional affiliation, we try to work against these positionings.[6]

Photographer Rising

When David Hernández Palmar recalls his first experiments with a camera, his memories date to his early childhood in the Guajira, the arid peninsula that reaches into the Caribbean Sea from South America's northernmost edge, and his life in the heart of the Wayuu homeland.

> When I was little I often went to my grandparents' house to look at books, picture magazines like *Geomundo* (National Geographic), and mail order catalogs. I liked to look at the ones that sold camera equipment. My *abuelos* had a camera, the kind with tiny 110 mm film, for taking pictures of my aunts' and uncles' graduations and other academic events. Sometimes, when no one was paying attention I snuck the camera and secretly took pictures. They always found out though because, when they had the film developed, they discovered my photos. "And these here, who took these pictures?"

If he was not accompanying his mother to the one-room school where she taught elementary children, tagging along behind his uncles as they tended their goat herds, or visiting the town's resident Baptist missionary family to absorb the sounds of their foreign English speech, chances are little David could be found tucked in a corner of his grandparents' house leafing through the picture magazines or photography catalogues that occasionally arrived in the post. He dreamed of the day when he could have a camera of his own, something more sophisticated than the instamatic he took to summer camp when he was six or seven (which was stolen); one with "dials for opening and closing the aperture and controlling shutter speed."

David was born on April 21, 1980, in the Guajira and lived in the town of Paraguaipoa, seat of the Guajira municipality, until he was five or six years old. When he was just beginning primary school, his parents moved their young family to Maracaibo so that David's mother, Flor Angéla Palmar, could become part of an exciting all-Wayuu teaching team that was pioneering innovative methods in what has come to be known as "bilingual intercultural education" (see Graham and Palmar 2014). The family's move to Maracaibo made life easier for David's father, David Júlio Hernández, who no longer had to make the daily commute from Paraguaipoa to Maracaibo for his job repairing electronic equipment. It also gave "Davidcito," as he was affectionately known, more opportunities to look in the windows of camera stores on outings with his father, a pastime he remembers fondly.

In Maracaibo, the Hernández Palmars joined thousands of other Wayuu who, since the 1930s, have moved to the city for the economic, educational, and other opportunities and social services it offers. Approximately 438,000

Wayuu live in a broad region that extends from the area around Lake Maracaibo in Venezuela up through the Guajira Peninsula. This region is now politically divided between the nation states of Venezuela and Colombia, and Wayuu may claim dual citizenship. Many frequently traverse the international border (which they do not recognize) to visit relatives, engage in commerce, or access services. Wayuu are the largest Indigenous group in both Venezuela and Colombia. In Venezuela, Wayuu represent 57.5 percent of the nation's total Amerindian population. Wayuu make up more than 10 percent of the total population in Zulia state and half of these, some sixty thousand, reside in the state's capital city of Maracaibo.[7] Wayuu residences are sprinkled throughout the city, but the population is mostly concentrated in several neighborhoods, the barrios of El Mamon, Las Delicias, and Ziruma, where David and his family now live.

David's parents pooled their modest resources so that David could attend a private primary school. Although he remembers going to classes in the afternoon instead of in the morning as the most challenging part of his transition to Maracaibo, David also recalls the teasing and bullying he suffered from peers. "They called me *Timotea Cuica, Azteca, Maya*."[8] From his mother he learned a valuable lesson that helped him through these taunts: "When a person discriminates against you it is because they are misinformed and unaware." This lesson, which provides a compassionate backdrop for intercultural education and communication, has stayed with David ever since.

In Maracaibo, David picked up Spanish quickly and this also helped him fit in at school. The family slipped into speaking Spanish at home and Wayuunaiki, the native language, receded. As he got older, David sought opportunities to speak English, his third language, which he had absorbed during his early childhood in the Guajira by hanging around the Sellers, the missionary family that lived nearby. Maracaibo has many English-speaking residents and visitors, in large part because its economy centers around the petroleum industry, and David found numerous opportunities to hone his English-speaking skills. His agreeable demeanor, intelligence, articulate manner, and proficiency in Spanish as well as English enabled David to comfortably move cross Maracaibo's geographic, social, and linguistic boundaries. These same characteristics, especially his English proficiency, facilitated David's movement into the international Indigenous media arena.

Purchasing a camera, however, remained out of David's reach through his high school years, which included one year of study at the *Escuela de Artes Plásticas Julio Aragga*. He longed to work in the school's photography lab and experiment with chemicals in the dark room. But, because he did not own a camera, David was not allowed access. To get some experience David began to assist friends who were studying photography. Several of his closest friends at the Universidad Rafael Belloso Cachín (URBE), where he enrolled after high school to pursue a degree in Social Communications, noticed his talent and encouraged him. "Wow David! You are really good at this! You should take a photography course." Hearing this praise David resolved to buy a high quality camera of his own. He identified the camera he wanted, a Canon SLR, and began to save. But before he was able to make his purchase, he had the unexpected good fortune to receive the very camera he wanted as a gift. David recalls that he was nineteen or twenty years old at the time.

> I was counting my *Bolivares* (local currency), saving until I had enough to make the purchase. One day in December, my best friend Emilpe accompanied me to a camera store to look at the prices. Ten days later, I received a gift from my friends Emilpe and José. They got together and gave me my first camera, a Canon that I have to this day. It came with ten rolls of black and white film. I was so surprised and full of emotion that I couldn't even express myself. It took me three days to adequately thank them. This is how I began to take photos.

Shortly after receiving his camera, David enrolled in photography school. He also continued to study at URBE, which, he was pleased to discover and take full advantage of, has one of the best and most well-equipped photography laboratories in Venezuela. David began to assemble portfolios and exhibit his work as part of the requirements for receiving his professional certificate from the Julio Vengoechea Photography School. "The Wayuu Taya Foundation exhibited some of my first photos [at fund raising events] in Miami and New York. Another of my early photos, an image of the *lemna* [algae] on Lake Maracaibo, was exhibited in Japan as part of the United Nations Ecology Program."

In December 2005, when I met David, he was a twenty-five-year-old student at URBE, aspiring to a career (and hopefully a living) as a professional photographer. He worked freelance taking photos for *Wayuunaiki*, a monthly bilingual newspaper printed in Wayuunaiki (Wayuu language) and Spanish that is widely read by Wayuu people in both Venezuela and Colombia, and cobbling together earnings from various freelance gigs.[9] He photographed food for restaurant menus and did *quincenario* photography (girls' fifteenth-birthday celebrations), photo shoots for fashion companies (including Tommy Hilfiger), and some photojournalism. He also helped friends who were aspiring fashion models in need of professional images for their portfolios. David enjoyed opportunities to accompany his mother to various Indigenous communities throughout Zulia state for her work in bilingual, intercultural education. On these trips he photographed activities at Indigenous schools and his mother's workshops, as well as capturing images of the landscapes and peoples they visited.[10]

At the time David was enchanted with the fashion industry and loved to shoot the runway. Part of his passion stemmed from the tremendous reception he and his cousin Luis Cambar received for their idea to launch a fashion venture that merged stunning Wayuu textile arts with high fashion. The South American Art Company (SAAC) featured handbags, dresses, jackets, and more in sophisticated designs that incorporated Wayuu "ethnic chique." For their innovative project, the two were honored along with thirty other young adults from Zulia as recipients of the Panorama IDEAS award, which annually recognizes the state's most outstanding socially responsible business proposals. David was also honored in another competition as one of Zulia's prominent young achievers.[11]

Benefitting from the IDEAS award and associated publicity, in October 2005 SAAC earned a place at the first Caracas International Tourism Fair, FiT-CaR (Feria Internacional de Turismo de Caracas), sponsored by the Venezuelan Ministry of Tourism.[12] To David and Luis's surprise, FiTCaR's organizers situated SAAC's booth not in the Indigenous Pavilion as they had expected, but in the High Fashion Pavilion. In this milieu, David and Luis associated with celebrities from the international high fashion scene, including representatives from Spain's Pasarela Gaudí and other luminaries from Paris, Milan, and elsewhere. David thus gained entrée into the international world of haute couture, a very exciting place for an emerging photographer. Through FiTCar contacts, David gained backstage access to a number of high profile fashion shows and was able to photograph celebrity models. While in Caracas David also encountered the editor of the highly visible national magazine *PaX*, which, in a subsequent short feature, labeled him "Chamán de la Imagen" (The image shaman, Villamizar 2006).

By early 2006, having possessed his own camera for five or six years, David was firmly assuming an identity as a professional photographer. "My name first became recognized within the Venezuelan fashion industry when *El Nacional* [a widely read Caracas-based daily newspaper] published some of my photos, but," he continued, "I really became known in the fashion industry after SAAC." Despite his then-passion for high fashion and the runway, David's favorite photographic subjects were people and landscapes, "especially Indigenous people in landscapes: faces, children, and textures, like skin." Thus, at the same time that David was establishing a name in the fashion world, he was also forming an identity as an "ethnographic photographer."

David points to the work he did work managing photographs for *Wayuunaiki*'s fifth anniversary edition, "Poblados y Pobladores" (Communities and settlements, 2005) as establishing his reputation for photographs of Wayuu people, as well as other Indigenous peoples who live in Zulia state (Añu, Bari, Japreria, and Yukpa). "*Wayuunaiki* made its entire photographic archive available to me for the special anniversary issue." To gather additional material, David traveled extensively with other *Wayuniaki* staff "to photograph and collect oral statements." Photographs he took on these trips significantly expanded his collection. "I became known as the person who had a photo archive of Wayuu images."

In conversations we had in the first months after our initial meeting, David was interested in what I had observed in some of my research among the Xavante people of central Brazil. I told him about the video project in the community of Pimentel Barbosa, peoples' growing awareness of representational politics, and their various projects to manage Xavante's image in public arenas (see, for example, Graham 2005, 2014b, 2016). David was impressed that, in Brazil, Indigenous (and other) peoples have legal rights in relation to their photographed images, including rights regarding permission to publish or circulate, as well as rights to a percentage of royalties generated from publication, exhibit, or sale. David marveled at how advanced discussions about Indigenous representational politics appeared to be in Brazil in comparison to Venezuela at the time (see Baptista and Telles do Valle 2004).[13] While he was very familiar with contracts concerning photographers' rights to image and copyright in the fashion industry, he had not had occasion to give the issue much thought in other contexts. David welcomed opportunities to think about and discuss Indigenous self-representation and media, as these issues were becoming increasingly important in his life and work.

Political Transformations: Encountering Xavante

One afternoon at a café in Maracaibo, David pulled out his laptop and powered up. "I want to show you something," he said as he opened a class project on his screen. We watched *La salida de Yosuu,* a short fictional documentary about a Wayuu girl's dream and oneiric cultural practices; this was one of three short film projects that David had worked on with other URBE students and the most ethnographic. After seeing the film I imagined that, given their shared interest in film and Indigenous representation, a meeting between David and Xavante filmmaker Caimi Waiassé, with whom I had worked, would be fascinating and mutually productive.

The opportunity presented itself a month or so later when I received an invitation from Hiparidi Top'tiro, a Xavante leader and activist (see Top'tiro 2014, 2015; Graham 2014a, 2014b). Hiparidi wanted me to come to Mato Grosso to "tell the story" of events associated with an environmental campaign that the Xavante Warã Association was launching. According to Hiparidi, Waiassé would also be there, doing video documentation. I asked if David could come to photograph, meet Waiassé, and learn about the Association's work. In May 2006, David and I departed for central Brazil on a journey that would be, for David, eye opening and transformative.

Whereas up to this point David's ethnographic focus had been primarily on Wayuu and incidentally on other Indigenous peoples in Zulia state, through his experiences on this trip and with the Xavante, he learned first-hand about other Indigenous struggles. Reflecting on the trip, David stated, "When we arrived there, well, I realized Indigenous struggles have many similarities." The experience opened him up to direct political engagement, and the collaborative film that ultimately resulted (of which I will say more below) provided a platform from which David was able to launch himself into the international Indigenous media scene.

When we arrived in Brazil, we found that Hiparidi and a group from the Xavante Warã Association were planning to stop traffic over the BR-158 highway bridge that crosses the Rio das Mortes at a town called Nova Xavantina. The objective of this protest was to bring attention to the damaging effects the region's burgeoning and unregulated soy industry is having on the river that runs through the heart of the Xavante homeland. The explicitly political nature of this activity, however, made David nervous and uncomfortable. "I was very afraid because some people were violent and [violence] is something that I have always avoided . . . I had never participated in a protest, never been involved in something openly political in public.[14] I was especially nervous when the police came and asked to see my passport." Explaining his discomfort, he continued:

> I went through very stressful situation in Venezuela. My parents are sympathetic to the government, to President Chavez's revolutionary process. On April 11, 2004, there was a coup and that day the police, the opposition, came to our house. . . . They were armed . . . [and] looking for [incriminating] documents. . . . Quickly my sister and I hid any documents that might be used against us. . . . We were very frightened, . . . I was really afraid.
>
> After that I decided that I would definitely not participate in any openly political activity. Not in any way whatsoever! I wanted to avoid repeating that kind of experience, that invasion into my house, into my privacy, my life, my things. So I remembered all this when I was in Brazil. I thought, "I am not going to participate." Then, the Xavante asked me if I wanted to paint myself, and right then, without even thinking, I took off my shirt and they painted my body. At that moment I became one of them, another Wayuu-Xavante. I realized that it was fine for me to participate. I was also good with it. It was positive. I am happy about it to this day. Going to Brazil, the events on the bridge, ruptured my whole paradigm.

The Xavante protest and our participation documenting events on the bridge were life-changing for David. They "ruptured [his] whole paradigm." The moment the Xavante painted him, transforming David into "one of them," David stepped out of his role as a detached documentarian. This unlocked something within, opening him to take an explicitly political stance. Ever since, David has been openly political, about Chavez, Venezuela's revolutionary politics, Indigenous oppression, and the politics of media and image.

Salas Comunitarias and MICIV: Becoming an Indigenous Communicator

Not long after his return to Venezuela David became actively involved in two other projects that also played significant roles in his advancement as an Indigenous media activist, or "Indigenous communicator," as this work is often labeled in Spanish, especially in the Latin American context. One was Cinemateca's endeavor to implement *salas comunitarias* (community screening rooms) in Venezuela's underserved and remote communities. This Ministry of Culture–sponsored project enables community members to designate which films screen in their communities, control scheduling, and arrange other media-related activities, such as workshops, according to locally determined needs and desires.

David organized the implementation of *salas communitarias* in two Wayuu communities in the Guajira, in El Mojan and Yaguasirú. I accompanied David in his negotiations with Cinemateca staff in 2006 as he laid the groundwork for these projects, and I witnessed his outstanding networking and negotiating skills. I also noted his awareness of an "embedded aesthetic" of my presence, for my status as a North American professor studying Indigenous media (and his work) in Venezuela conferred legitimacy and some status, as did the fact that David had registered himself as a professional photographer and film director with the Venezuelan National Center for Cinematography (Centro Nacional Autónomo de Cinematografía de Venezuela, CENAC).[15] David's involvement with Cinemateca also led to his participation in other activities including inaugurating *salas communitarias* in other Indigenous and non-Indigenous communities and eventually giving media workshops.

During this period, David was also becoming familiar with the Latin American Coordinator of Indigenous Peoples' Film and Communication (Coordinadora Latinoamericana de Cine e Comunicación de los Pueblos Indígenas, CLACPI) through internet exploration and also in conversations with Beatriz Bermudez, a Venezuelan anthropologist and leading figure in CLACPI (Bermúdez 2013). In an interview, David indicated that Burmudez had been supportive of his trip to Brazil and the opportunity it would provide him to meet Indigenous media makers there.

The other major project that was instrumental to David's debut into the Indigenous media world was his work inaugurating Venezuela's International Indigenous Film Showcase (Muestra de Cine Indígena de Venezuela, MICIV).

The idea for this festival grew out of a collaboration between David, Armando Zambrano of Cinemateca, and myself after attending the 2006 Venezuelan Short Film Festival in Mérida. The three of us wrote the initial proposal for an Indigenous film festival in Venezuela. David took the proposal and ran with it; he secured funding, sponsorship, and venues. The first MICIV consisted entirely of material from Cinemateca's archive, much of it produced by non-Indigenous filmmakers, and was held in October 2008. It featured screenings in Maracaibo and other towns in Zulia state. Eventually the festival took on a mobile character as some content was screened in Indigenous communities in other Venezuelan states.

After the first MICIV, which was a tremendous success, David teamed up with two colleagues in Maracaibo, Wayuu filmmaker Leiqui Uriana and Yanilú Ojeda, a non-Indigenous filmmaker who has made several films centering on Wayuu. The three founded the nonprofit Wayaakua Indigenous Audiovisual Foundation to support Indigenous media work. Through Wayaakua and in partnership with the National Cinema Center (Centro Nacional Autónomo de Cinematografía, CNAC) and Cinemateca, they organized the second MICIV in 2014. MICIV 2014 screened over one hundred films representing more than 132 Indigenous peoples from across the globe in six municipalities in Zulia and in the cities of Maracaibo, Mérida, and Caracas. The organizers dedicated the festival to the memory of Yukpa leader Sabino Romero who was assassinated in March 2013 (see, for example, *Sabino Romero*). At the time I am writing, David, Leiqui, and Yanilu were organizing the third MICIV, to be held September 29–October 1, 2016. Ultimately David acknowledges that his work in the *salas communitarias* and MICIV have succeeded because of the Venezuelan government's tremendous support for grass roots media.

Gateway to the International Media Scene: *Owners of the Water*

In February 2007, two months after I left Venezuela and intensive collaboration and research with David, I met him and Xavante filmmaker Caimi Waiassé in Gainesville, Florida. This was David's first trip to the US and also his first trip outside of Latin America. The three of us attended and presented our respective work at "In-digenous People, In-digital Cultures: Communication Technologies and the Impacts on Indigenous Languages and Cultural Identities in the Americas," hosted by the University of Florida's Center for Latin American Studies. David was energized by meeting many Indigenous media makers from across Latin America as well as scholars and activists such as Alexandra Halkin, founding director of the Chiapas Media Project (see Halkin 2008).

After the conference—and, because of our shared interest in cultural representation, a trip to Disney World's Epcot Center—we headed to Iowa City, Iowa, for a film-editing workshop. The goal of this workshop was to gain first hand editing experience and to, hopefully, produce something brief, perhaps a five to ten minute short, using footage from the 2006 Brazil trip. The eventual outcome of our collaboration and this workshop was the film *Owners of the Water: Conflict and Collaboration over Rivers* (2009). This film proved to be a gateway through which David entered the international arena of Indigenous media and made his debut on the international Indigenous media scene.

In 2008 I submitted a rough-cut version of the film to Terres en Vues / Land Insights, a major international Indigenous film festival associated with the Montreal First People's Festival (Présence Autochtone).[16] We were thrilled that, even though the film was not yet in its final form, it would be screened in this prominent international venue, seen by a large audience and in association with other outstanding work.

Terres en Vues and other international film festivals that soon-after screened *Owners*, such as the Smithsonian Film + Video Festival (2009), Barcelona Indigenous Film Festival (2009) and Göttingen International Ethnographic Film Festival in Germany (2010), provided a gateway through which David entered into the international arena of Indigenous film, expanding the scope of his knowledge, discourse, and work. These were the first festivals that David attended outside of Venezuela, and his participation immersed him in "the discourse" of international Indigenous film. Reflecting on his experience at Terres en Vue, he commented, "I liked the festival because one learns from the questions, and it provided the opportunity for me to improve my own discourse."

Terres en Vues, the first Indigenous film festival that David attended, also opened up a whole new world of Indigenous storytelling through film; it broadened his awareness of the international scope of Indigenous film and media activism. Elaborating on his experience at Terres en Vue, David commented, "*Owners of the Water* was actually the film that opened the gate for me to be at other venues and understand that there are other cinemas out there from other countries, especially from Latin America. I knew that there was a whole world of storytelling through film out there in Latin America, but I hadn't really seen it." The quality and diversity of the films, the range of perspectives, and the high quality of the curating made an especially strong impression on him. "Terres en Vues was the first film festival out of Venezuela that I ever went to. And, wow, you know, we saw really good work, really good! . . . The programing, the curatorial work at the Montreal First Peoples Film Festival was great! A lot of the films blew my mind at that moment. I still keep them in my memory."

Film festivals and other similar venues such as conferences and workshops provided exceptional networking opportunities, enabling David to further expand his circle and increase the scope of his work. At Terres en Vues, for example, David met prominent figures in the international arena of Indigenous film such as festival founder and organizer André Dudemaine and Jason Ryle, who directs the Toronto-based ImagineNative film festival. David's connections to Jason Ryle and to Amalia Cordova, who curated the Latin American portion of the Smithsonian Museum of the American Indian Film + Video Festival from 2001 to 2012, have been particularly productive and mutually beneficial. Since 2008, David has collaborated with ImagineNative, advising and helping to supply Latin American films. Cordova invited him to participate in the symposium "Mother Earth in Crisis: Protecting our Rivers," at the Smithsonian National Museum of the American Indian's 2011 Native American Film + Video Festival and other events. Both Cordova and Ryle serve as important advisors to MICIV, providing concrete advice and content. David also collaborates with Isuma TV and the Prince Claus Fund in the Netherlands.

David connects with other Indigenous filmmakers, Indigenous media activists, and their supporters at each event he attends, including those in Latin America. For example, the Primer Encuentro Continental de Documentalistas Latinoamericano y Caribeño held in Caracas in October 2008 was a watershed event for his Latin American networking, for he met pioneering Latin American Indigenous filmmakers and founders of the Latin American Indigenous media movement, such as Iván Sanjinés (Bolivia) and Marta Rodriguez (Colombia), as well as Beatriz Bermúdez (Venezuela) whom he already knew. As he has become increasingly more knowledgeable and sensitive to the political dimensions of Indigenous media, he has refined his already eloquent discourse. He moved to thinking of himself not only as a photographer, filmmaker, and producer, but also as a media activist and an "Indigenous communicator" in the Abya Yala discourse of continental Indigenous leaders.

Now firm in his identity and continentally and internationally recognized as a media activist and an Indigenous communicator, David regularly receives invitations to speak at conferences, participate in workshops, and serve on festival juries not only in Latin America but also internationally. Since 2008 he has traveled extensively for his work. To name but a few examples, he has been to New Zealand to learn about and participate in an inspiring project of Maori film repatriation; to Greenland for an Indigenous leadership workshop; to London for "EcoCentrix: Indigenous Arts, Sustainable Acts," a 2013 International Exhibition of Indigenous Art and Performance; he has also made multiple trips to the US. "[A]fter the experience we had with Laura [and with *Owners*], . . . it has been nonstop. I've been travelling to other places in the world because they were really interested in *Duenos del agua, Owners of the Water*, and also because of possibilities of doing collaborative work" (Grant 2014).

At the same time David was becoming increasingly involved in the international Indigenous media world, he was also more and more immersed in

Indigenous media networks in Latin America where he has emerged as one of the movement's leading international representatives and spokespersons. He has curated film festivals in Mexico, collaborated with Ojo de Agua, and attended and juried numerous film festivals and Latin American Indigenous media summits. In early 2016, David was appointed political advisor to CLACPI, and in May 2016 he traveled with a CLACPI delegation to New York. He and other CLACPI representatives spoke at the UN Permanent Forum on Indigenous Issues regarding the importance of Indigenous rights to and control of media communication. According to David, they announced the III Abya Yala Indigenous Communication Summit which would be held November 14–19, 2016, in Tiquipaya, Bolivia. David's ability to speak English has facilitated his movement in the international arena, and his progressively improving Portuguese enables him to move fluidly within both Spanish- and Portuguese-speaking arenas of Latin America.

In February 2015, in a role that David considers one of his highest honors to date, he served as one of four Latin American Indigenous media experts advising the organizers of NATIVe at Berlinale, a film festival in the category of Cannes and the Venice Bianale.[17] Expressing his thanks to NATIVe staff, David eloquently wrote:

> Berlinale is my favorite place for the poetics of resistance. I am so honored to have done such a beautiful work with you and with my colleagues, as the family we are. . . . Berlinale made history with the NATIVe Special Section by becoming Indigenous, native, aboriginal, Wayuu, since it gathered stories to tell and to reaffirm that in order to build a fully diverse and inclusive society, it must be intercultural. NATIVe offers through its curatorial team the chance to learn, listen, feel, live Indigenous languages, narratives, and recognize the contributions that such knowledge brings.
>
> I thank Berlinale and the NATIVe team for the opportunity given to me to suggest films that have made contributions to the narrative that is so needed by mankind right now, but especially for making me feel in those 6 days in Berlin that I was not that far away from home.[18]

Conclusion

As ethnographically informed analyses of Indigenous use of audio-visual media, especially video, during the late 1980s and 1990s shifted attention away from media products, or media texts, to the social processes entailed in their use (for example, Ginsburg 1994, 1995; Michaels 1994; Turner 1991a, 1991b; Dowell 2013), scholars emphasized uniquely Indigenous aspects of production, reception, and engagement with media technologies. Ginsburg's (1994) notion of "embedded aesthetics" directed attention to the cultural mediations, social relationships, possibilities, and connections with others that Indigenous media opens up from within and across local communities to global partnerships and collaborations.

Through hard work and use of his talents, keen observational skills, articulate manner in multiple languages, and sharp intellect, David succeeded in transforming himself from a local ethnographic photographer into a leading Indigenous communicator at national, continental, and international levels. His involvement during the mid-2000s in various collaborative projects helped him to move into the center of the Venezuelan, Latin American, and international Indigenous film and media movements. A series of converging experiences and associated embedded aesthetics helped David to move further along this path. During his trip to Brazil, he identified with the Xavante and broadened his awareness of the broader scope of Indigenous political struggles. Becoming a "Wayuu Xavante" through the body paint and immersion in their environmental protest shattered his commitment to avoid openly political activities. He has been openly political and explicitly committed to media activism ever since.

If David initially drew inspiration and strength from the Xavante, he has been further inspired and nourished through his immersion in a career of media activism. His experiences working with Cinemateca and its *salas comumunitarias*, MICIV, the *Owners of the Water* project, and CLACPI exemplify the importance of process and not simply "product" in the work of Indigenous media (Ginsburg 1994; Salazar and Cordova 2008). The ways the *Owners of the Water* project provided an entrée into the international Indigenous film world are but one example of the embedded aesthetics of Indigenous media; from travel to product, from festivals to networking, it offered opportunities for David to expand his network, shape and refine his vision and discourse, and solidify his sense of himself and his ability to act within and indeed influence a broader context.

If a series of converging opportunities helped facilitate David's movement into the Indigenous media world, another dimension of this convergence was the historical moment in Venezuela. The Venezuelan government and its commitment to advancing Indigenous and community media provided support for David and his work. At a 2014 screening of *People's Media Venezuela* (2012) at the Venezuelan embassy in the US, David expressed his awareness of and gratitude for this support. "In the past decade, Indigenous peoples and new social movements have achieved a profound and democratic transformation in Latin American history. Venezuela, in particular, has been at the forefront of enabling our communities to create their own media and work toward the development of our society. Thanks to the support of President Chávez, our peoples have been made more visible. Chávez is responsible for this new political direction."[19] This statement exemplifies David's political astuteness, and the eloquence he mobilizes as a leading international Indigenous communicator. In looking toward the future, he encourages Indigenous people to use various media modalities to increasingly control processes of self-representation and assert their rights.

Notes

1. Using the term "representational sovereignty, I expand Michelle Raheja's (2010) powerful notion of "visual sovereignty" to underscore the importance of sensory modalities beyond the visual, especially sound and also text, that play important roles in representations of Indigenous peoples and in Indigenous moves to disrupt hegemonic semiotic stereotypes (see Graham 2016, also Arndt 2010, 2015).
2. Turner (2002, 79) mentions the importance of video documentation as path to leadership for some Kayapó.
3. Cinemateca is one of four branches of the Ministry of Culture's national cinema platform.
4. For discussion of audio visual projects involving media makers from remote and rural communities in Latin America, see, for example, Turner 1991; Gallois and Carelli 1995; Halkin 2008; Smith 2010; Wortham 2013. For discussion of urban Indigenous experiences in various national contexts, see, for example, Lobo and Peters 2001; Lawrence 2004; Watson 2014a, 2014b. For an historical account of Indigenous experience in colonial municipalities, see Murillo 2016.
5. Unless otherwise noted, quotes from Hernández Palmar that appear in this chapter are from interviews, conversations, and email communications with the author that took place between 2006 and 2016.
6. I used my institutional position and institutional structures to, for example, get David a US Social Security number, his first US bank account, and a Visiting Scholar visa, which greatly facilitated his ability to travel and receive payment in the US.
7. The most recent national censuses identify the Wayuu population at 413,437 in Venezuela (Instituto Nacional de Estadística 2015, 31) and 270,413 in Colombia (Censo DANE 2005 cited in Ministério de Cultura n.d., 2). Exact population figures for the number of Wayuu in Maracaibo are difficult to obtain because Wayuu move frequently between the Guajira and the city.
8. *Timotea Cuica* is a common Venezuelan racist slur that points to misconceptions and misunderstanding of the pre-Colombians known variously as Timote, Cuica, or Timote-Cuica, an Andean people who lived in the region of the contemporary Venezuelan city of Mérida. Timote-Cuica lived in complex communities and practiced terraced agriculture, irrigated fields, and stored water (see Mahoney 2010).
9. See the Wayuunaiki website at *wayuunaikiperiodicoindigena.blogspot.com*.
10. Speaking of his work for Wayuu Taya Foundation, a nonprofit organization whose mission is to improve the conditions of Latin American Indigenous peoples (*www .wayuutaya.org*), David said, "I managed the area of Indigenous images because I had many photos, primarily photographs that I had taken on trips with my mother and her

work supervising Indigenous schools. I took photos of children from different ethnic groups throughout the state in class, eating, doing their assignments. I had so many images. People began to ask me for my material."

11. Among the recipients of the 2005 Panorama IDEAS award was the young symphonic director Gustavo Dudamel, who has since gone on to receive world renown as the music and artistic director of the Los Angeles Philharmonic and music director of the Simón Bolívar Symphony Orchestra of Venezuela.

12. See "Latest News: Caracas International Tourism Fair—October 2005" on the Consulate General of the Bolivarian Republic of Venezuala website, *www.embavenez-us.org/ _boston/news.php?nid=1729.*

13. In 2009, Venezuela's National Assembly passed the Ley de Patrimonio Cultural de los Pueblos y Comunidades Indígenas (Law on the cultural heritage of Indigenous peoples and communities) which recognizes the nation's Indigenous peoples' right to cultural patrimony.

14. In fact, this was a peaceful protest and there was no violence. There were, however, some expressions of hostility that David must have perceived as violence.

15. David reported in an interview that, in listing his qualifications to Cinemateca, he had cited his work with me and that he would be accompanying me to a conference in the US.

16. I do not have time in this brief essay to elaborate on production and editing processes and the division of labor associated with this film. While I am aware of the critique that Indigenous peoples lack control over copyright and administrative dimensions of this, and other Indigenous films (see Arisi 2015), I assumed the tasks of securing copyright, submitting to film festivals and seeking avenues for distribution because, as a US-based university professor, I had greater institutional support and access to communication infrastructure such as post, internet, and telephone. The three co-directors conferred about these and other aspects of the film via email, Skype, and telephone. Because our objective was to make the film available so others could see and hear its message, and it was most expedient for me to take on these tasks, David and Caimi delegated them to me.

17. Along with David, other advisors from Latin America were José Miguel Álvarez (México), Amalia Córdova (Chile), and Vincent Carelli (France/Brazil). Advisors from North America included Bird Runningwater (Sundance) and Jason Ryle (ImagineNative-Canada).

18. Email from Hernández Palmar to Maryanne Redpath, curator and head of Berlinale's NATIVe section, and Anna Kalbhenn, NATIVe project manager, March 19, 2015.

19. Embajada de la República Bolivariana de Venezuela en Estados Unidos, "David Hernández-Palmar: 'No vea TV, hágala,'" press release, Oct. 16, 2014. *eeuu.embajada. gob.ve/index.php?option=com_content&view=article&id=160%3Adavid-hernandez-palmar-chavez-nos-dio-su-cara-para-proyectar-a-nuestra-sociedad&catid=4%3Aactividades-y-eventos-embajada.*

References

Arisi, B. 2015. Review of *Dueños del agua: Conflicto y colaboracion sobre los rios*, directed by Laura Graham, David Hernández Palmar, and Caimi Waiassé. *Tipití: Journal of the*

Society for the Anthropology of Lowland South America 13 (2): 181–83. *digitalcommons. trinity.edu/tipiti/vol13/iss2/14.*

Arndt, G. 2010. "The Making and Muting of an Indigenous Media Activist: Imagination and Ideology in Charles Low Cloud's *Indian News.*" *American Ethnologist* 37 (3): 499–510.

———. 2015. "Voices and Votes in the Fields of Settler Society: American Indian Media and Electoral Politics in 1930s Wisconsin." *Comparative Studies in Society and History* 57 (3): 780–805.

Bacigualupo, A. 2016. *Thunder Shaman: Making History with Mapuche Spirits in Chile and Patagonia.* Austin: University of Texas Press.

Baptista, F., and R. Telles do Valle. 2004. *Os povos indígenas frente ao direito autoral e de imagem.* São Paulo: Instituto Socioambiental.

Bermúdez, B. 2013. "CLACPI: Una história que está pronta a cumplir 30 años de vida." *Revista chilena de antropología visual* 21: 20–31.

Dowell, K. 2013. *Sovereign Screens: Aboriginal Media on the Canadian West Coast.* Lincoln: University of Nebraska Press.

Feld, S. 1990. "Postscript, 1989." In *Sound and Sentiment: Birds, Weeping, Poetics and Song in Kaluli Expression,* 2nd ed., 239–68. Philadelphia: University of Pennsylvania Press.

Forte, M., ed. 2010. *Indigenous Cosmopolitans: Transnational and Transcultural Indigeneity in the Twenty-First Century.* New York: Peter Lang Publishing.

Gallois, D., and V. Carelli. 1995. "Video in the Villages: The Waiãpi Experience." In *Advocacy and Indigenous Film-Making,* edited by Henrik Philipsend and B. Markussen, 23–37. Højbjerg, Denmark: Intervention Press.

Gilbert, C. 2015. "Sabino Romero: An Indigenous Leader Who Kept His Eye on the Prize." *Counterpunch,* March 14. *www.counterpunch.org/2015/03/04/sabino-romero-an-Indigenous-leader-who-kept-his-eyes-on-the-prize.*

Ginsburg, F. 1991. "Indigenous Media: Faustian Contract or Global Village?" *Cultural Anthropology* 6 (1): 92–112.

———. 1994. "Embedded Aesthetics: Creating a Discursive Space for Indigenous Media." *Cultural Anthropology* 9 (3): 365–82.

———. 1995. "Mediating Culture: Indigenous Media, Ethnographic Film and the Production of Identity." In *Fields of Vision: Essays in Film Studies, Visual Anthropology, and Photography,* edited by L. Devereaux and R. Hillman, 256–90. Berkeley: University of California Press.

———. 1999. "Shooting Back: From Ethnographic Film to the Ethnography of Media." In *A Companion to Film Theory,* edited by T. Miller and R. Stam, 295–322. London: Blackwell.

———. 2002. "Screen Memories: Resignifying the Traditional in Indigenous Media." In *Media Worlds: Anthropology on New Terrain,* edited by F. Ginsburg, L. Abu-Lughod, and B. Larkin, 39–57. Berkeley: University of California Press.

———. 2011. "Native Intelligence: A Short History of Debates on Indigenous Media and Ethnographic Film." In *Made to Be Seen: Perspectives on the History of Visual Anthropology,* edited by M. Banks and J. Ruby, 234–55. Chicago: University of Chicago Press.

Ginsburg, F., L. Abu-Lughod, and B. Larkin, eds. 2002. *Media Worlds: Anthropology on New Terrain.* Berkeley: University of California Press.

Graham, L. 2005. "Image and Instrumentality in a Xavante Politics of Existential Recognition: The Public Outreach Work of Eténhiritipa Pimentel Barbosa." *American Ethnologist* 32 (4): 622–41.

―――. 2014a. "Fluid Subjectivity: Reflections on Self and Alternative Futures in the Autobiographical Narrative of Hiparidi Top'tiro, a Xavante Transcultural Leader." In *Fluent Selves: Autobiographical Narratives in Lowland South America*, edited by S. Oakdale and M. Course, 235–70. Lincoln: University of Nebraska Press.

―――. 2014b. "Genders of Xavante Ethnographic Spectacle: Cultural Politics of Inclusion and Exclusion in Brazil." In *Performing Indigeneity*, edited by L. Graham and H. Penny, 305–50. Lincoln: University of Nebraska Press.

―――. 2016. "Toward Representational Sovereignty: Rewards and Challenges of Indigenous Media in the A'uwẽ-Xavante Communities of Eténhiritipa-Pimentel Barbosa." *Media and Communication* 4 (2): 13–32. *cogitatiopress.com/ojs/index.php/Mediaandcommunication/article/view/438*.

Graham, L., and F. Hernández Palmar. 2014. "*Yaletüsü Saaschin Woumain* (Glory to the Brave People): Flor Ángela Palmar's Creative Strategies to Indigenize Education in Venezuela" (with Flor A. Palmar). In *Indian Subjects: New Directions in the History of Indigenous Education*, edited by B. Klopotek and B. Child, 229–66. Santa Fe, NM: School of Advanced Research Press.

Grant, Jenna. 2014. "Screening Room: *Owners of the Water*." Review. *Cultural Anthropology Online*. (Oct. 6). *www.culanth.org/fieldsights/563-screening-room-owners-of-the-water*.

Halkin, A. 2008. "Outside the Indigenous Lens: Zapatistas and Autonomous Videomaking." In *Global Indigenous Media: Cultures, Poetics, and Politics*, edited by P. Wilson and M. Stewart, 160–80. Durham, NC: Duke University Press.

Hendricks, J. 1993. *To Drink of Death: The Narrative of a Shuar Warrior*. Tucson: University of Arizona Press.

Instituto Nacional de Estadística. 2015. *Censo nacional de población y vivienda 2011: Empadronamiento de la población indígena*. Caracas: Instituto Nacional de Estadística. *www.ine.gob.ve/documentos/Demografia/Censo2011/pdf/EmpadronamientoIndigena.pdf*.

Kopenawa, D., and B. Albert. 2013. *The Falling Sky: Words of a Yamomani Shaman*. Cambridge: Belknap Press of Harvard University Press.

Lawrence, B., ed. 2004. *"Real" Indians and Others: Mixed-Blood Urban Native Peoples and Indigenous Nationhood*. Vancouver: University of British Colombia Press.

Lobo, S. and K. Peters, eds. 2001. *American Indians and the Urban Experience*. Walnut Creek, CA: AltaMira Press.

Mahoney, J. 2010. *Colonialism and Postcolonial Development: Spanish America in Comparative Perspective*. New York: Cambridge University Press.

Michaels, E. 1986. *The Aboriginal Invention of Television in Central Australia, 1982–1985*. Institute Report. Canberra: Australian Institute of Aboriginal Studies.

―――. 1994. *Bad Aboriginal Art: Tradition, Media and Technological Horizons*. Minneapolis: University of Minnesota Press.

Ministério de Cultura. n.d. "Wayuu: Gente de arena, sol e viento." Caracterizaciones de los pueblos indígenas de Colombia. Bogotá: Ministério de Cultura. *www.mincultura.gov.co/prensa/noticias/Documentos/Poblaciones/PUEBLO%20WAY%C3%9AU.pdf*. Accessed Dec. 27, 2017.

Murillo, D. 2016. *Urban Indians in a Silver City: Zacatecas, Mexico, 1546–1810.* Redwood City, CA: Stanford University Press.

Nader, L. 1972. "Up the Anthropologist: Perspectives Gained from Studying Up." In *Reinventing Anthropology*, edited by D. Hymes, 284–311. New York, Pantheon Books.

Oakdale, S. n.d. "Indigenous Cosmopolitans." Unpublished manuscript.

Oakdale, S., and M. Course. 2014. "Introduction." In *Fluent Selves: Autobiography, Person, and History in Lowland South America*, edited by S. Oakdale and M. Course, 1–32. Lincoln: University of Nebraska Press.

Prins, H. 2002. "Visual Media and the Primitivist Perplex: Colonial Fantasies, Indigenous Imagination, and Advocacy in North America." In *Media Worlds: Anthropology on New Terrain*, edited by F. Ginsburg, L. Abu-Lughod, and B. Larkin, 58–74. Berkeley: University of California Press.

———. 2004. "Visual Anthropology." In *A Companion to the Anthropology of American Indians*, edited by T. Biolsi, 506–25. Malden, MA: Blackwell.

Raheja, M. H. 2010. *Reservation Reelism: Redfacing, Visual Sovereignty, and Representations of Native Americans in Film.* Lincoln: University of Nebraska Press.

Salazar, J., and A. Cordova. 2008. "Imperfect Media and the Poetics of Indigenous Video in Latin America." In *Global Indigenous Media: Cultures, Poetics, and Politics*, edited by P. Wilson and M. Steward, 39–57. Durham, NC: Duke University Press.

Smith, L. 2010. "Locating Post-Colonial Technoscience: Through the Lens of Indigenous Vídeo." *History and Technology*, 26 (3): 251–80.

Top'tiro, H. 2014 "Protecting the Amazon Includes Defending Indiginous Rights," interview with Paul Jay, therealnews.com (Aug. 25). *therealnews.com/t2/index.php?option=com_content&task=view&id=767&Itemid=74&jumival=12281.*

———. 2015. "Self Determination and Conservation Challenges for Grassroots Movements. Speakers: Hiparidi Tor'Tiro" In *Chico Vive: The Legacy of Chico Mendes and the Global Grassroots Environmental Movement*, edited by L. Rabben, 98–100. Cambridge, MA: Cambridge Institutes Press, Forest Peoples Programe and Rainforest Foundation. *cambridgebrazil.org/wp-content/uploads/CHICO-VIVE-FINAL070715.pdf.*

Turner, T. 1991a. "Representing, Resisting, Rethinking: Historical Transformations of Kayapo Culture and Anthropological Consciousness." In *Colonial Situations: Essays on the Contextualization of Ethnographic Knowledge*, edited by G. Stocking, 285–313. Madison: University of Wisconsin Press.

———. 1991b. "The Social Dynamics of Video Media in an Indigenous Society: The Cultural Meanings and Personal Politics of Video-Making in Kayapo Communities." *Visual Anthropology Review* 7 (2): 68–76.

———. 1992. "Defiant Images: The Kayapó Appropriation of Video." *Anthropology Today* 8 (6): 5–16.

———. 2002. "Representation, Politics, and Cultural Imagination in Indigenous Video: General Points and Kayapo Examples." In *Media Worlds: Anthropology on New Terrain*, edited by F. Ginsburg, L. Abu-Lughod, and B. Larkin, 75–89. Berkeley: University of California Press.

Villamizar, Pablo. 2006. "Chamán de la imagem." *PaX: Política, actualidad, expedientes* 1 (4): 60–61.

Watson, M. 2014a. "Cities, Indigeneity and Belonging." In *Performing Indigeneity*, edited by R. Graham and H. Penny, 390–414. Lincoln: University of Nebraska Press.

———. 2014b. *Japan's Ainu Minority in Tokyo: Diasporic Indigeneity and Urban Politics*. London and New York: Routledge.

Wilson, P., and M. Stewart. 2008. "Introduction: Indigeneity and Indigenous Media on the Global Stage." In *Global Indigenous Media: Cultures, Poetics, and Politics*, edited by P. Wilson and M. Stewart, 1–35. Durham, NC: Duke University Press.

Worth, S., and J. Adair. (1972) 1997. *Through Navajo Eyes: An Exploration in Film Communication and Anthropology*. Albuquerque: University of New Mexico Press.

Wortham, E. 2013. *Indigenous Media in Mexico: Culture, Community, and the State*. Durham, NC: Duke University Press.

Film

Owners of the Water: Conflict and Collaborations over Rivers (Spanish: *Dueños del agua;* Portuguese: *Donos da agua)*. 2009. L. R. Graham, D. Hernández Palmar, C. Waiassé, directors. DVD. Watertown, MA: Documentary Educational Resources.

People's Media Venezuela. 2012. Produced by Kathryn Lehman and Geraldene Peters. 30 min. Available from Ngā Pae o te Māramatanga Media Centre, *mediacentre.maramatanga. ac.nz/content/peoples-media-venezuela*.

5

Value and Ephemeral Materiality

Media Archiving in Tamazulapam, Oaxaca

By Erica Cusi Wortham

In August of 2014, media professionals from Oaxaca, New York, and Mexico City gathered for the first Encuentro Internacional de Archivitas Audiovisuales de Oaxaca (Meeting of audiovisual archivists of Oaxaca), a two-day event organized by OaxacaCine, an activist-oriented programming group that has revived cinema in the colonial Mexican city (*oaxacacine.com*). The Encuentro combined talks by media makers, academics, archivists, and museum professionals with an extended workshop on community archiving led by Mona Jimenez of the Moving Image Archiving and Preservation (MIAP) program at NYU's Tisch School. Media makers from across Oaxaca came to participate in the initial re-cataloguing of the vast audiovisual collection held by Ojo de Agua A. C., one of the most successful and long-standing Indigenous media collectives in Mexico. Boxes upon boxes of (mostly) VHS tapes were pulled from closets and cabinets to be assessed and entered into database forms created specifically for the workshop.

Preliminary assessments revealed a tip-of-the-iceberg dilemma that repeats itself across Latin American Indigenous communities. As media making, often funded by outside sources, proliferated in many Indigenous communities in the 1990s, few resources were devoted to sustainability within local social contexts, let alone digital preservation of aging media. Two and a half decades later, many media-making communities are losing their analog material. Oaxaca-Cine and the participants gathered at the Encuentro represent one of the few organized initiatives to safeguard the invaluable visual cultural heritage known as Indigenous media by fostering dialogue and skill-building at the community level, in a bottom-up fashion that is the only way to ensure sustainability. My current engagement with the emergence of archiving practices focuses on how the move to preservation poses new but familiar dilemmas about the role of local media as discourses of materiality confront visual ephemerality.

In my early work on Indigenous media, I framed a discussion about the Indigenous community media collective Radio y Video Tamix in terms of a related dilemma that has to do with a media collective that set out to represent its community through media production, found itself forced to prove its own legitimacy (Wortham 2013). While this dilemma seems to contradict one of the principal ways Indigenous media has been characterized by scholars as embedded (Ginsburg 1994; Córdova and Salazar 2008), what it really does is attune us to the fact that embeddedness, in some cases, must be achieved. This point continues to be salient in work I am currently undertaking to understand and support local media-archiving initiatives in media-producing Indigenous communities in Latin America.

In the specific context of Indigenous media making in the highland Oaxacan village of Tamazulapam, home to Radio y Video Tamix, local discourses about value—what is worth saving and restoring—insert media within a regime of materiality that challenges the value of media as cultural heritage. In the face of this I argue that it is precisely media's ephemeral value, a notion best captured by conjuring what happens when you press PLAY, that matters most. I also venture to suggest that the dilemma of achieving embeddedness can be potentially mitigated by resituating media practices within the community through archiving, creating a second chance to reposition media as a participatory, collective endeavor. Exploring questions of value and ownership in the archiving process can engender dialogue and transparency about media making that was not made visible to community members in the 1990s. In so doing, I make the broader argument that community regimes of value and politics of return in Tamazulapam, or Tama for short, reinforce the imperative that the management digital visual cultural heritage must be community driven.

In thinking both practically and theoretically about supporting the creation of a consultable, living archive of Indigenous media whose primary audiences are the media-producing communities themselves, I have been drawn to several key concepts that have to do with value, materiality, and ephemeral value. Notions of value have been a long-running undercurrent in my engagement with Indigenous media. Attuned as we are to its circulation, Indigenous media as objects and stories have social lives just like the people that make them do (Appadurai 1986). As such, they enter and exit a variety of contradictory regimes of value as they circulate in diverse contexts, from villages and local movie houses to universities, museums, and international festivals. Indigenous knowledges maybe somewhat decontextualized in the process, but as Fred Myers (2002, 352, 361) has asserted in the context of Australian Aboriginal oil painting, they have also "reorganized the contexts—the regimes of value—into which they have entered" and "made a kind of Aboriginality knowable to those who view them." Their makers compete for awards and grants—"tournaments of value"—and they are occasionally bought and sold, though their market value is not representative of their sociocultural or political value. I worked for nearly a decade as a media programmer at the Smithsonian Institution's National Museum of the American Indian in New York City, and I often mused about how video, the ugly duckling of the arts anyway, would never command the value of a Navajo rug or a Santa Clara ceramic vessel. Video's low status may be attributed to its reproducibility, its lack of an "aura" of authenticity, but, on the other hand, I would conclude, media do not sit quietly on a shelf. As they play, Indigenous voices and images, stories and histories, are claiming their presence in a contemporaneous reality, whatever the genre, asking audiences to rethink and cast off the way Native people have been constantly portrayed as part of a historical, past imaginary by powerful memory institutions like the Smithsonian.[1] For Indigenous audiences, these media open doors to reflection, dialogue, and solidarity; for non-Indigenous audiences they implicate us in a narrative of disenfranchisement and demand change. Indeed, these media represent an opportunity to "decolonize the screen," as Maori filmmaker Merata Mita (1996) suggests. Indigenous media constitute "screen memories" (Ginsburg 2002) where none existed and mediate grave omissions and misrepresentations in the historical record. They answer Yesef Hayim Yerushalmi's (1982) question in the affirmative: "Is it possible that the antonym of 'forgetting' is not 'remembering,' but *justice*?" (emphasis in original; quoted in Derrida 1995, 50).

If the principal sources of Indigenous media's value are derived from their particular indigeneities, or a connectedness to place-based cultures and situated bases of knowledge and practice, the political, social, and cultural work they accomplish is through their very making and exhibition. I am unquestionably comfortable with my belief that Indigenous media are invaluable cultural products and practices of a special kind. Others agree; Indigenous media fit comfortably within the category of cultural products protected by the UNESCO 2003 Convention for the Safeguarding of Intangible Cultural Heritage (Graham 2009). I am equally uncomfortable with the sense of urgency I feel as I come to terms with how precariously many of these media works have been stored since the 1990s. Under beds, in closets, and in open boxes in villages that experience harsh weather extremes and high humidity, many of these works are literally being lost. Physical degradation is a crucial aspect of Indigenous media's materiality—to be precise, its ephemeral materiality—they do not last. But the fact the media don't play is perhaps the most serious threat to the value of Indigenous media. What I call the ephemeral value of Indigenous media is wrapped up less in their precarity as it is enacted when they play. Like a performance, they transmit social knowledge; they are "acts of transfer," to use Diana Taylor's (2003) language, and highly tooled or deliberate ones at that, because they "reinterpret as they transfer."

In the face of this dynamic of precarity and loss, a politics of return emerges as media makers in Tama, Oaxaca, begin digitizing their collection. In the process, through returning practices, a particular kind of ephemeral materiality is constituted in order to safeguard these media within the community's strong preference for things material, their regime of materiality.

Many of the media makers with whom I have worked for nearly two decades also share the urgency to preserve their media collections. The problem, or dilemma (because it is the same dilemma really), is that, at least in the case of Tama, community members do not necessarily share this priority. As Laura Graham (2009, 187) pointed out several years ago, "the degree to which peoples view their intangible culture practices (or some of these practices) as 'objects' to be documented, recorded, archived or managed as tangible forms, particularly by outsiders, is open to ethnographic investigation." The fact that the media I discuss were "born" intangible does not completely eliminate the problematics Graham engages; indeed, they are imbricated in complex social relations that in turn index long histories of coloniality and inequality. A brief engagement with discourses of materiality helps uncover what is at stake for local communities: collectivity.

When members of Radio y Video Tamix were recording an important *tequio* in 1998, a communal labor event that took place on land at the heart of a heated inter-community conflict, they were told to put their video camera down and pick up a tilling instrument—in short, to do real work. Real work leaves physical evidence: a new field prepared for seeding, a mountainside carved out for a road, a new building made of block and mortar. A year later accusations had mounted and the media makers were accused of individually profiting from images that belonged to the community. At the annual New Year village-wide assembly in 2000, Radio y Video Tamix was shut down and taken off the air (for a more detailed discussion of these events see Wortham 2013). Fifteen years later, members of the collective are still in personal possession of all the footage and programs they recorded and edited. Genaro Rojas, a founding member of the collective and key participant in the 2014 archiving Encuentro, keeps the collective's audiovisual collection in a room in his mother's house that is lined with special cabinets built for the tapes. They have digitized many hours of tape from their collection. In footage captured for the production of a commemorative documentary / visual memoir (still in progress), Genaro reads from a document the collective composed in their search for funds to support the digitization of their material: "The digitalization of our archive has the same meaning as restoring the church or municipal palace. . . . That's why I wanted to project it on the stone wall; to say, you guys want to restore or remodel of the church—because the church was restored, right? And so was the municipal building. It has the same importance. Restore. That's why I wanted to put it up on the wall."[2] Genaro sought to project video programs onto the exterior walls of the municipal building, right onto the *cantera*, or stone, in order to borrow some of wall's materiality. This appeal to the community's preference for materiality was foreshadowed by earlier attempts to weave media production, almost literally, into the community by appealing to one of the village's most iconic material symbols, Tama women's distinctive *reboso*, or shawl. Radio y Video Tamix video programs often ran "Ayuuk color bars" before the opening title sequence instead of the standard NTSC colors bars, a technical requirement for color adjustment purposes during playback or transmission.

While attempts at such Ayuuk-ization of media production were ultimately unsuccessful in establishing the place of both media production and the collective within the community, they illustrate a point Genaro often includes in his discourse about Indigenous media that has to do with media being perceived as coming *de afuera*, from the outside. This inside/outside border—a border of coloniality, really—goes far in explaining why media and media making as a practice are not naturally embedded in Tama, and, oddly enough, the reification of this border puts the collective in the unexpected position of repatriating material that belongs to the authoring community itself. The process of repatriation plays out as a politics of return that resonates with the illness Jacques Derrida (1995) describes as "archive fever," if in rather idiopathic ways.

For Hermenegildo Rojas, also a key member of the collective (and Genaro's brother), returning weighs heavily on his consciousness. The imperative to return that Derrida (1995, 57) describe as an "irrepressible desire to return to the origin, a homesickness" is palpable in Genaro and Hermenegildo's sentiment. But for Tama's media makers, *regresarlo* (to return it) is less about returning to origin than it is about returning to original owner. Indeed, the collection sits in Genaro's mother's house like so much buried treasure, almost as if it had been stolen in the first place. Questions of ownership sit uncomfortably at the juncture between single auteur and collective authorship, an issue of decided complexity and familiarity in critical Indigenous media studies. In Tama, enmeshed within a local politics of return, repatriating video footage and programs feels more like an obligation to reciprocate, to close or complete the circle of giving (Mauss 1990).

Hermenegildo refers to *regresarlo*, and he means this quite literally: to return audiovisual material directly to the people of his community. *Regresarlo* takes shape in at least two ways for Hermenegildo. He would like to burn DVDs of the material for each community member. A DVD in hand may earn video a place within the local regime of materiality, but even in a relatively small village of roughly three thousand residents, that is no easy task, especially when there are thousands of hours of footage to choose from. *Regresarlo* also takes shape as a practice. Hermenegildo and other members of the collective occasionally screen material from their collection in peoples' homes, in town halls, and on the outdoor patios of the smaller *ranchos* (villages) surrounding Tama. *Regresarlo* as a screening practice taps into media's ephemeral value, and residents seem to delight in revisiting past moments.[3] The notion of ephemeral materiality that I am proposing responds exactly to the returning work that Hermenegildo has been undertaking in the community, combining material (DVD) and screening approaches that might satisfy residents' preference for things material while also engaging in dialogue and memory work.

Taken together, these concerns with materiality, value, and ownership bring into view a deeper concern with collectivity. Is it the *cantera*, the stone wall, from which Genero sought to borrow materiality in a strategy to reposition media as a valuable endeavor and cultural product, or the collectivity embedded in the making of the stone wall that challenges media making's legitimacy? Is it the physical evidence of a once-forested field cleared for planting that denies media materiality by comparison, or the collectivity embedded in *tequio* work that confronts media making as a less than collective undertaking? These questions help identify what is of concern to the local community and find ways to reposition media through emerging archive practices. As members of Radio y Video Tamix continue to experiment with returning, they bring members of their community into direct dialogue with the collection, fostering a collective approach and understanding of media making that was not present in the 1990s. Seeing their younger selves, their families and leaders from twenty or more years prior holds the potential to reposition media as *nuestro* (ours) or *de adentro* (from the inside) while facilitating new engagements with visual cultural heritage.

Reviewing tapes from Radio y Video Tamix's collection to prioritize material for digitization has also fostered a return to production. Carlos Efraín Rojas, also a former member of the collective and Hermenegildo's cousin, now operates his own film company, Mecapal Films, in Lyon, France. Rojas came upon a series of takes authored by Genaro in 2003 and post-produced the material into one of the only experimental videos to have come from the group. *Estado de animo / Mood* (2015), an eight minute film, has already had impressive play in film festivals, including at the celebrated Morelia International Film Festival (FICM), in art venues in Oaxaca City, and in Tama, too.

Estado de animo opens on a sparse concrete frame on an outdoor patio. Inside the bare concrete columns, most likely the unfinished dreams of a homebuilder, sits a rusted oil drum. Objects appear on the drum, a series of still-lifes of discarded objects, obviously composed with care by an artist: a bottle inside a can, a broken coffee mug, a Corona bottle. Genaro enters the frame and addresses the camera directly after a long ten seconds of silence, to explain the "exhibition" we are about to see. With village sounds in the background, hammering, and the occasional rooster's crow, he explains that the exhibition is an example of what you can do with video, with your time in the afternoons. He has rescued a series of objects from oblivion, things he has noticed for quite a while, things he shares his life with, but that had gone unnoticed by everyone else.

Through video Genaro can express his loneliness and own feeling of abandonment. He is tired and alone; no cameraman, just him. And he is stressed; he has to get the video done before he loses daylight. The sense of obligation to produce art weighs on him. He exits the frame, and the series of stills, the exhibition, continues: empty, dirty bottles of alcohol; a rusted out frying pan, its plastic handle still intact; a large, bottomless metal wash bucket, resting on its side. Genaro suddenly appears behind the wash bucket, inside a circle inside the rectangle framed by the concrete columns, his mouth agape at first. With an open palm, he smooths the space where the bucket's bottom had been, using circular motions as if he's washing it. He makes one last sweep and brings his hand to his heart. A final object appears in his place: a duck-shaped planter filled with living flora sits inside the rocking wash bucket as the church bells finish their song with one, then two last beats.

This lovely short, made from found footage in their own collection, shows an entirely different aspect of what has mostly been a strict documentary repertoire. The languishing abandonment expressed by Genaro's discourse and the careful arrangement of discarded objects resonates perfectly with the state of their media collection and the collective's idiopathic brand of archive fever. In lifting the ordinary, the forgotten, to the extraordinary by framing it with the camera and the concrete structure, he saves these objects, remembers them, if briefly, in another engagement with ephemeral materiality.

My continuing research with Indigenous media is focused on understanding the possibilities of archiving in terms of the changing digital environment. Tama has an internet café now, smart phones have proliferated, and Facebook has become a place to discuss community affairs and to organize before assembly meetings.[4] Whether the internet is a viable means for making digitized portions of Radio y Video Tamix's collection accessible is a practical consideration of my research. Digital platforms and willing partners that can serve as digital repositories exist. One such is ISUMA TV, a collaborative multimedia platform for Indigenous filmmakers and media organizations established in 2008 in Igloolik, Nunavuut, Canada, by award-winning Inuit filmmaker Zacharias Kunuk and his partner Norm Cohen (*isuma.tv*). Isuma TV offers communities like Tama the opportunity to upload material on to Isuma's servers in the context of a community- or peoples-specific "channel." Isuma compresses video uploads into five different versions (high HD, low HD, high SD, etc.) to accommodate different internet capacities and safeguards original uncompressed files on their servers. For remote Arctic communities with insufficient internet bandwidth for streaming, Isuma offers mediaplayers that store material on local hard drives that connect to the internet only at designated times to refresh material. Closer to home, an international organization, Rhizomatica, is helping communities in the Oaxacan sierra set up independent cellular networks using microwave technology that promote a reterritorialization of airspace (*rhizomatica.org*). As cellular and digital environments are retooled to reflect local concerns and ways of doing things, community sensibilities to ephemeral material can find more comfortable footing.

Rick Prelinger (2009, 170), an archivist best known for his collection of ephemeral films (industrial, corporate, educational films), has written about the "accessible archive" as user-centered and proactive, a living archive where "use augments value . . . because you learn about an archive's holding by witnessing how others use them." That usage often generates valuable metadata. He advocates "an access oriented regime" and proposes that "we measure the success of an archive by how much new work and study it facilitates" (174). Radio y Video Tamix's archive has already been successful on these terms, evidenced by the success of *Estado de animo*. I have proposed experimenting with an online archive or channel of Radio y Video Tamix's collection that the community and its schools can access via the internet or through a local kiosk connected to a mediaplayer. Radio y Video Tamix members are on board with experimenting in this direction and have agreed to participate in archiving partnerships toward building a platform.[5] Access by people outside the community is something that needs careful attention, as Indigenous cultural heritage often confronts the "information wants to be free" ethos of the West with specific protocols that limit access to certain material. Several broad-based initiatives on this front are already in place to mediate the complex and potentially damaging terrain of digital access. Two important projects are Mukurtu and Local Contexts. Mukurtu CMS (*mukurtu.org*), a "safe keeping place" managed by Washington State University, is a "free, mobile, open source platform built with Indigenous communities to manage and share digital cultural heritage."[6] Local Contexts (*localcontexts.org*) works with communities to build a "new paradigm of rights and responsibilities that recognizes the inherent sovereignty that Indigenous communities have over their cultural heritage."[7] Using traditional knowledge (TK) labels, Local Contexts offers education about and ways to navigate copyright and public domain law to the benefit of Indigenous communities.

Ethically minded and culturally sensitive technical "solutions" exist and can be adapted to address the numerous hurdles facing media makers in Tama and across Latin America as they shift from tape to digital file–based media. Preservation and access must be discussed and determined with local interests and politics in mind. With a deeply participatory and collaborative archive, built and maintained collectively from the bottom-up with institutional partners, an opportunity exists to embed or bring digital visual cultural heritage *adentro* (inside). By taking advantage of the broad, more gender-balanced usage of the internet and Facebook among the younger generations while dialoging with older generations for whom remembering may be more poignant, a more collective politics of return can open discursive spaces for Indigenous media locally.

Notes

1.   I recently had the opportunity to return to NMAI's Film and Video Center as a contractor, this time to help dismantle the ad hoc collection of audiovisual material from Latin America. Handling collections notes I had made over a decade prior was not as unsettling as NMAI's decision to disaggregate their collection and end the hemisphere's most prominent Indigenous film and video festival. Ironically, what I considered to be the most valuable video programs in NMAI's possession were not considered "published," a regime of value upheld by Smithsonian Library that assigned much of the community-produced material to a liminal position. Much of this material was transferred as a special collection to New York University's Bobst Library where, with inspired leadership and co-stewardship from the Center for Media Culture and History, the material should enjoy an active, healthy, and long shelf life. Supporting local, community-based archiving is all the more imperative when institutions of such stature as NMAI choose not to step up.
2.   Genaro Rojas, 2014. Footage for memoir documentary, shared with the author.
3.   Hermenegildo Rojas, 2014. Footage for memoir documentary, shared with the author.
4.   Ingrid Kummels, August 2014. Personal communication.
5.   My colleague Carol Kalafatic and I sought to secure funding for the creation of an Indigenous Latin American Digital Media Archive (ILADMA). More recently, this initiative has begun to take shape through NYU Libraries' Special Collection of Indigenous Media.
6.   Homepage, *murkutu.org*, accessed Dec. 12, 2017.
7.   Homepage, *localcontexts.org*, accessed Dec. 12, 2017.

References

Appadurai, A. 1986. "Introduction: Commodities and the Politics of Value." In *The Social Life of Things: Commodities in Cultural Perspective*, edited by A. Appadurai, 3–63. Cambridge: Cambridge University Press.

Córdova, A., and J. Salazar. 2008. "Imperfect Media and the Poetics of Indigenous Video in Latin America." In *Global Indigenous Media: Cultures, Poetics and Politics*, edited by P. Wilson and M. Stewart, 39–57. Durham, NC: Duke University Press.

Derrida, J. 1995. "Archive Fever: A Freudian Impression." Translated by Eric Prenowitz. *Diacritics* 25 (2): 9–63.

Ginsburg, F. 1994. "Embedded Aesthetics: Creating Discursive Space for Indigenous Media." *Cultural Anthropology* 9 (3): 365–82.

_____. 2002. "Screen Memories: Resignifying the Traditional in Indigenous Media." In *Media Worlds: Anthropology On New Terrain*, edited by F. Ginsburg, L. Abu-Lughod, and B. Larkin, 39–57. Berkeley: University of California Press.

Graham, L. 2009. "Problematizing Technologies for Documenting Intangible Culture: Some Positive and Negative Consequences." In *Intangible Heritage Embodied*, edited by D. Ruggles and H. Silverman, 185–200. New York: Springer.

Mauss, M. (1950) 1990. *The Gift: The Form of Gift Exchange and Reason for Exchange in Archaic Societies.* London: W.W. Norton

Mita, M. 1996. "The Soul and the Image." In *Film in Aotearoa New Zealand*, 2nd edition, edited by J. Dennis and J. Bieringa, 36–56. Wellington: Victoria University Press.

Myers, F. 2002. *Painting Culture: The Making of an Aboriginal High Art.* Durham, NC: Duke University Press.

Prelinger, R. 2009. "Points of Origins: Discovering Ourselves through Access." *Moving Image* 9 (2):164–74.

Taylor, D. 2003. *The Archive and the Repertoire: Performing Cultural Memory in the Americas.* Durham, NC: Duke University Press.

Wortham, E. C. 2013. *Indigenous Media in Mexico: Culture, Community and the State.* Durham, NC: Duke University Press.

Yerushalmi, Y. 1982. *Zakhor: Jewish History and Jewish Memory.* Seattle: University of Washington Press.

Film

Estado de animo / Mood. 2015. Directed by Genaro Rojas, produced by Carlos Efrain Perez. 5 min. Tamazulapam, Oaxaca: Radio y Video Tamix / Mecapal Films.

6

Making Media

Collaborative Ethnography and Kayapó Digital Worlds

By Ingrid Carolina Ramón Parra, Laura Zanotti,
and Diego Soares da Silveira

In *The Chicago Guide to Collaborative Ethnography*, Lassiter (2005, 15) comments, "While collaboration is central to the practice of ethnography, realizing a more deliberate and explicitly collaborative ethnography implies resituating collaborative practice at every stage of the ethnographic process, from fieldwork to writing and back again." This chapter conceptually and empirically extends the notion of collaborative ethnography by tracing the co-creation of a research partnership with one Kayapó-Mebêngôkre community, A'Ukre, in the central Brazilian Amazon. The goal of the research and partnership is to support a media-making project and media center, the latter being envisioned as a site for archiving images and films produced both locally and by outsiders, a resource for film production, a space for addressing the digital divide, and a borderland that can support current and future goals of sovereignty, sustained livelihoods, and well-being. Taking a cue from Lassiter (2005) to "resituate collaborative practice," we illustrate how science and technology studies (STS) and feminist political ecology (FPE) frameworks are supportive of collaborative research designs that align with Indigenous self-determination efforts and visual sovereignty. We describe the collaborative process as one based on building and sustaining relationships with a series of actors (Indigenous communities, nongovernmental organizations [NGOs], and public universities) who are creating new networks of solidarity. In doing so, we examine the challenges and limitations of "engaged," "collaborative," and "symmetrical" ethnography, and propose that the iterative rhythms of collaboration are not limited to fieldwork and writing but extend to other forms of production and practice.

Three goals are folded within the fabric of the project. First, we argue that media making and media worlds are embedded in larger projects of sovereignty, especially a growing interest in visual sovereignty (Ginsburg, Abu-Lughod, and Larken, 2002). Recent work within Indigenous media studies has increasingly drawn upon Raheja's (2010) concept of "visual sovereignty" to describe media-making efforts by and for Indigenous peoples. As described by Smith (2012, 330), "Visual sovereignty is one of many Indigenous methodologies designed to decolonize knowledge production." We extend this concept further to not only represent different decolonizing processes of knowledge production, but as Raheja (2010) conceptualized the concept, as a space where vitality and richness can be a part of media making efforts. We further emphasize, as Raheja does (2010, 22), the discursive agency that media makers employ to create new subjects of filmmaking.

In this project, which we named "Self-Determination in a Digital Age," visual sovereignty has methodological, epistemological, and ontological implications. Leaders and filmmakers in A'Ukre find film, the internet, and other digital worlds sites for knowledge acquisition, production, and expression, as well as a productive space to fight for self-determination. Visual sovereignty for community members in A'Ukre extends beyond film itself to the entire media-making assemblage, which includes:

1. on-site capacity to train community members in all aspects of film production,
2. the ability to determine and choose and maintain equipment and infrastructure used to produce film,
3. a low barrier to entry software and affordable maintenance costs,
4. data management platforms and storage capacity for lengthy films and extended raw footage,
5. the production of films for and by community members that do not have to conform to outsider aesthetics and where Kayapó filmmakers have control over the aesthetics they wish to deploy (e.g. length of film, sequencing of shots, presentation of community members, etc.), and
6. the ability to distribute and circulate films in forms that are portable, secure, and easily shared.

Thus, Kayapó communities creatively operate within multiple media worlds as they engage with internet and communication technologies (ICTs) as part of both individual expression and sovereignty efforts. From the sharing of songs on cell phones to home-grown documentarians in Kayapó villages, the Kayapó peoples have been at the front lines of expanding the possibilities of digital forms of expression, and communities like A'Ukre have seen a blossoming of digital media over the past decade (Wilson and Stewart 2008). Within this context and as a response to community interest, we acknowledge and honor individual expressive forms, community desires, and intergenerational shifts in this work. Moreover, given transitional shifts in Indigenous livelihoods in Brazil from a post-authoritarian rule marked by the struggle of territorial control to neo-development political economic realities of the commodification of landscapes and livelihoods, intergenerational use of and engagement with digital media worlds offer political possibilities to advance the Kayapó peoples' concerns in different ways (Ebenau 2014; Zanotti 2016).[1]

Secondly, from a methodological standpoint, honoring community desires for visual sovereignty has been borne out in this project through a collaborative design that interweaves STS with FPE. In doing so, we reconsider "collaborative" work to extend its reach beyond the researcher-community dyad. In accordance with the community principles of visual sovereignty, we instead consider researcher-student-community-NGO-village-institution networks as a productive space for transdisciplinary work that has the capacity to support Kayapó livelihoods in a time of acute and rapid change. Thus, this project is composed of alliances that include the village of A'Ukre, Purdue University, Universidade Federal de Uberlândia, the Associação Floresta Protegida (the Protected Forest Association), and the National Indian Foundation (FUNAI). We acknowledge our indebtedness to relationships with the University of Maryland, especially with Dr. Janet Chernela, as well as collaborations with Phil Nash and Emi Ireland. These collaborations, and their complex scaffoldings point to one vibrant aspect of this project: the intersections between participation, collaboration, power, and visual sovereignty.

Furthermore, as non-Indigenous academics working at the interface of Indigenous and non-Indigenous knowledges, we consider the different divides that may be ruptured at personal, professional, and other levels as we work alongside Indigenous communities (see Zanotti and Palomino-Schalscha 2016). Diane Rocheleau notes that doing FPE demands a "critical informed" perspective that allows one to be "open in living in a networked world."[2] In this way, FPE is well-suited for this type of work as a research framework that examines Indigenous projects in a multiscalar context, drawing attention to asymmetrical power relationships while valuing diverse knowledge systems for managing and governing the world (Elmhirst 2011). We also draw upon STS as a site to engage with decolonizing methodologies, symmetrical practice, and the rhizomatic networks inherent in Indigenous media making efforts. When combined, they offer space for an anthropology that is at once multiscalar, political, and deeply committed to collaborative ethnographic practice and research partnerships. Thus, in the third arm of this work, we further outline how these frameworks have expanded the notion of a "deliberate" practice through theoretically grounding the research design from the beginning as a shared endeavor with common goals of navigating the "tricky ground" of research (Tuhiwai Smith 2008, 113).

As a final note, while the multiple registers in which media making takes place in the community vary, much is at stake and the political implications for

Indigenous politics cannot be overlooked. We concede, as leaders in the community have told us, that media is a powerful venue in which to act out justice concerns (Sikor 2013).[3] Kayapó peoples are marshaling media technologies to solidify efforts that support activist campaigns, self-reflexive heritage-building activities, individual aesthetic expression (for instance, training youth in digital technologies), creating new mediascapes (see Appadurai 1996; Joyce and Gillespie 2015), and forging multicultural educational programs. Moreover, drawing from the rich histories of media-making efforts in the village, elder and youth generations in A'Ukre are re-imagining the possible ways in which storytelling takes place, identifying new forms of knowledge and expressions of indigeneity, and advancing the political possibilities of media efforts.

Graham and Penny (2014) remind us that Indigenous peoples' relationships with the visual have always been political, and Indigenous strategic use of media has mediated Indigenous/outsider relationships while at the same time provided a venue for Indigenous expression of identity and cosmology that is ontologically distinct. Coleman (2010, 488) also suggests, "Whenever and wherever individuals and groups deploy and communicate with digital media, there will be circulations, reimaginings, magnifications, deletions, translations, revisionings, and remakings of a range of cultural representations, experiences, and identities, but the precise ways that these dynamics unfold can never be fully anticipated in advance." These ideas are echoed in the comments we have heard from community members, who emphasize the different positions that filmmakers take, and ultimately the way media making is at once an individual and a collective project that serves many goals at once.

We proceed by offering a brief history of the research project, demonstrating how deliberate choices were made along the way in order to co-craft a project that aligned with the desires of the community. We then provide the conceptual grounding to the research design, which we hope will serve as a flexible framework that other researchers interested in collaborative work can draw from in co-generating collaborative practice. We conclude by providing some preliminary findings from one phase of this project, especially as they relate to gender in media making, and close by pointing to possible futures.

Project Background

This project was forged out of long-term ties that Soares, Zanotti, and Ramón Parra have to the Kayapó-Mebêngôkre community of A'Ukre in the Brazilian Amazon. A'Ukre is a village of more than three hundred people in the Central Brazilian Amazon, one of the forty villages that comprise the federally demarcated Kayapó Indigenous Lands. When Soares and Zanotti started working together with the peoples of A'Ukre (in 2008), we noticed the weight given to digital media worlds by our Kayapó partners. What was and has been a topic of conversation since then is the growing prominence of film, photography, and other media and digital forms as part of the fabric of the quotidian and activist efforts in the community. For example, home videos and family portraits, events and ceremonies (e.g., soccer tournaments; A'Ukre's thirty-fifth anniversary), pedagogical tools, cultural heritage archives, and news-making efforts were all much talked about and practiced or desired sites of media production. Moreover, individual expressions of, familiarity with, access to, and use of digital media varied greatly within the community, signaling early on the importance of generational and gendered shifts in engagement with different media worlds. Initial observations made by Soares and Zanotti through conversations with community members indicated that gender, status, age, and participation in research or educational projects influenced familiarity with digital media use.

In addition to these conversations, we also knew of the long history that the Kayapó peoples have had with digital media worlds. Vincent Carelli, the founder of Video nas Aldeias, began some of his pioneering work with the Kayapó as he was starting off. Kayapó efforts were later made popular by the work of anthropologist Terence Turner. Turner became a frequently seen figure in media projects and theoretical inquiries that examined Indigenous use of media and resistance over the course of the 1980s and beyond (Boyer 2006; Turner and Fajans-Turner 2006). Turner's research and collaborative efforts reflect the enduring engagement Kayapó communities have had with media and its impact on anthropological engagements with this subject matter (Turner 1990a, 1990b, 1991, 1992, 1995, 2002a, 2002b; but also note that Turner's work with the Kayapó in general began in the 1960s). While "the Kayapó" had gained renown within anthropological circles based on their engagements with film, especially through Terence Turner's work, the effects of this project were uneven throughout the Kayapó Lands.

Vanessa Lea (2012, 26) reflects that, in 1976, film and television were already important to Kayapó communities. More recently, Glenn Shepard and Richard Pace, working with the villagers from Turedjam and other communities, have become involved with Kayapó digital media productions. Shepard and Pace's work reflects what our project also throws into relief, particularly the growing use of different material objects, including new (digital media) technologies among multiple generations of Kayapó women and men. While certainly there were one or two individuals in A'Ukre who had known or participated in Turner's project, there was limited active media making that took place in the community, due to lack of access to resources or means to travel, from 2004 to 2009.

While only a few men had seen or been exposed to digital cameras in 2004, which was Zanotti's first visit to A'Ukre, by 2013 several men in the community across a variety of ages owned compact point-and-shoot digital cameras that had been either purchased with their own money or donated during research projects in the area.[4] From informal conversations, it seems that only two or three of the men had had experience with editing films, which were primarily used to record naming ceremonies and other events and were meant to circulate within the community and beyond.

Also during this time period, cell phones and point-and-shoot cameras with video options also were used to make short films, which could be images from visits to town, Kayapó soccer games, ceremonies, or political events that the Kayapó were involved with. For example, Luis,[5] a twenty-year-old father in the village, noted the changes within the community by commenting on his cell phone usage versus other types of communicative forms that had been stronger in the past: "We used to have powerful shamans that could travel long distances overnight and send messages to communities. Now we have radio and cell phones." Luis discussed the difficulties of making choices about what to keep on his storage card. He had photos of his oldest daughter from a Brazilian holiday festival she had participated in. Browsing the images on his camera, he talked about how he wanted to keep the photos. However, he also wanted to record parts of an upcoming naming ceremony. As a budding filmmaker, he was torn between his desire to archive his daughter's photos and the need to make room for footage to give back to the community. In the end, he said, he would probably have to delete the photos of his daughter if he could not find a way to get a new memory card before the ceremony began.

On the other hand, Cláudio, one of the elders in the community, was not interested in generating content of his own but was keen on assembling old photographs and films so they could be returned to the community. "Please contact João in São Paulo," Cláudio once said to Zanotti on her departure. "He knows where several old Kayapó films are, and I would like to be able to see them here." Cláudio noted this after a lengthy conversation with Zanotti about creating a cultural center or media center in the village, and discussing his desire to not only access new media content but to have old footage and film repatriated to the community. These informal conversations point to the varied space-making arenas digital media is creating in Kayapó lives, from awareness of new possibilities of access to constraints regarding storage. The opportunities for sharing stories and developing new expressions in familiar communicative forms seem to be percolating along with different generational interests in the use, circulation, viewing, and storage of films. Moreover, where men of differing ages had had varied experiences with film cameras in the past, point-and-shoot digital cameras and video-capable cell phones are now much more commonplace in the village, and more and more women are accessing them for personal and family use.

When this project started in 2013, there was a marked difference between men and women in the community regarding digital media use. Whereas women in the community were frequent users of the radio that they fondly called Bira after a Kayapó myth, they were noticeably absent as participants in camera work and other digital forms of communication. Most of the women in the community had limited access to cameras, many of which were owned by husbands, spouses, sons, and brothers. Even so, several young women (ages eighteen to thirty) expressed interest in knowledge of photography and film to Zanotti over the course of her work there beginning in 2004. Zanotti gave her camera to different individuals to experiment with while she was working in A'Ukre. For example, during preparation of fish in wrapped with manioc flour in banana leaves for an award ceremony to culminate the village Olympics, Zanotti asked if she could photograph the food-making process. Keila, a young Kayapó woman who was working on the food, asked if she could take the photos instead. After Zanotti showed her the basics of the point-and-shoot Sony Cybershot camera, Keila took several pictures of one of the team members (also her boyfriend) finished off preparing the last of the fish cake bundles. Afterward, Keila and Zanotti browsed through the photos, which contained careful close-up sequences. Also at this time Zanotti was also frequently asked by women of the community to archive different moments, taking portraits of families and young children or recording ceremonial sequences that featured the women or their kids. In these cases, the women requested hard copies of the photos as well as digital versions of the films.

While the women desired formal portraits, at the same time many of them were hesitant of candid portraits or images that showed them without their ceremonial regalia on, or, at minimum, without being freshly bathed. These preferences point to general Kayapó sensibilities that we have seen in many photographs of individuals in the community, where it is customary to have some ceremonial adornments on, gaze directly at the camera, and avoid smiling. These types of photographs are layered and evocative of many things—the personal biographies of the individual's present, the ongoing fight of Kayapó communities to retain their lifeways in the face of unpredictable changes, and the visual politics that dominate Indigenous efforts to gain recognition, respect, and dignity (Ramos 1994; Conklin 1997; Vargas-Cetina 2013). Moreover, these gendered practices have changed in recent years, in some ways, as a result of the dialogues and practices that have emerged from this project. Interactions and conversations Zanotti had with the women in the community, and that Zanotti and Soares had with the men, led to discussions within the community of A'Ukre about the gendered dimensions of filmmaking practice. As the media-making project became underway, Zanotti and Soares sought to extend these conversations further and recruited graduate students and other non-Indigenous participants to work on various segments of the project. In a later section, we elaborate on Ramón Parra's research to showcase one arm of the project developed to work specifically with women in the community.

Thus, the project does not have a clear start date, as it emerged through ongoing conversations between various community leaders, within community forums, and with researchers since 2004. With growing interest in media in the community, upon the village's request Soares and Zanotti officially started to apply for funding in 2012 and 2013; they also began to build the joint non-Kayapó and Kayapó team. Also at that time, community leaders identified strong interests in cultural heritage activities as a venue for engagement work and in building an on-site media center. Working with community leaders and partners at three community meetings, we outlined the following collaborative program: (1) train youth in digital film production; (2) create local capacity for on-site film production; (3) create on-site capacity for media archiving and storage; and (4) create a dedicated viewing space for community-produced films. Over the years, these project goals have also extended to include providing sustainable, long-term solutions to maintaining the media center, including addressing data management and software, energy, and storage needs and coming up with strategies for dealing with barriers to its longevity. Zanotti and Soares have made visits to A'Ukre for this project and for a joint field course they co-lead with the community every year beginning in 2008, with the exception of 2009. Ramón Parra joined the team in 2013 and made her first visit to the community in 2014.

Speaking for, Speaking about, Speaking with: STS Meets Feminist Political Ecology

Bringing researcher-community-institution relationships into focus in this project is not just about media but also about the process of ethnography and the collaborative co-construction of shared projects. In this work, we critically consider relationality, especially its connection to the position of researchers in the collaborative work and their ability to create a "symmetrical dialogue" within research programs and across all phases of the research (Bishop 1994, 179; Latour 2014; Lassiter 2005). As such, we have relied upon several intellectual and participatory trends in crafting this project, and in this section we outline the conceptual frameworks that have made these methodological choices possible and which also have provided a structure for ongoing critical and reflexive feedback among all project partners. We suggest that this type of collaborative work requires theoretical dispositions that flexibly respond to community desires, demand accountability across all phases of the research design, and are suited to collaborative practice. Moreover, we suggest that these frameworks extend the notion of collaboration beyond a "field-to-writing" spectrum by incorporating other collaborative outputs, such as supporting local film production and media making.

What has been called "shared anthropology" by Rouch (1991:56),[6] collaborative research (Lassiter 2005), engaged anthropology (Low and Merry 2010), and symmetrical anthropology (Latour 2014) have all served as foundational frameworks for us. Moreover, we align this work with Gubrium and Harper's (2009, 2) acknowledgment that "new visual technologies are changing the ways that anthropologists do research and opening up new possibilities for participatory approaches appealing to diverse audiences." We also envision digital technologies as possibilities to get at what Hollbraad, Pedersen, and Viveiros de Castro (2014) have posited, which is the joining of the politics of ontology with the political. They clarify: "it means giving the ontological back to 'the people,' not the people back to 'the ontology,'" and furthering the mission is a process of striving for "permanent decolonization of thought" (Viveiros de Castro 2009, qtd. in Hollbraad, Pedersen, and Viveiros de Castro 2014).

In this way, we approach collaboration from a FPE perspective, which is an actor-oriented framework that draws attention to asymmetrical power relationships (gender, class, race, ethnicity, and other markers of difference) in complex socio-ecological and political economic landscapes (Cruz-Torres and McElwee 2012; Rocheleau 2008; Rocheleau, Thomas-Slayter and Wangari 1996). Similar to other scholars, within FPE we find a homogenous notion of "community" troubling (Agrawal and Gibson 1999). This is what Andrew Matthews (2011, 211) has described as the "mythological freight carried by the term 'community' which presupposes that communities are homogenous entities when in reality they are often bitterly contested." We agree that the heterogeneous and historically situated composition of communities is often not recognized or acknowledged so that the inequitable and uneven partnerships based on neoliberal agendas and historical trajectories continue to marginalize and devalue Indigenous peoples—and their knowledges (Radcliffe 2007). Elmhirst (2011, 131) adds that with FPE, researchers are asked to give an attentiveness to "the 'material and emotional dimensions' of subjectivities . . . through spatial practice." These sensibilities, along with a focus on politics, media-making efforts, and the intersectional sites of production and reception, all guide our practice.

We have especially found FPE to be a responsive framework that is attentive to both individual and community desires throughout this project. As outlined above, our emphasis on gender and generational shifts emerged out of many conversations we had with different community members over several years, all whom expressed interest in a media project and who had shared goals but different preferences on how goals would be met in practice. Informed by FPE, we co-crafted the partnership with multivocality in mind, making sure the project was broad enough to encompass the variety of individual needs and desires while staying attentive to the goals that ultimately aligned with the community's notions of visual sovereignty. FPE also invites critical reflexivity across networks of practice, and thus has served as a generative space for collaborative work as we have undergone multiple iterations of this project through ongoing dialogues and meetings. Relatedly, scholars that champion Indigenous methodologies highlight that research should develop meaningful reciprocal relationships based on trust and respect between researchers and communities and should honor the "diverse interests" of Indigenous peoples (Tuhiwai Smith 2008, 113, 129). Thus, we also suggest FPE provides a framework from which to forge respectful relationships while remaining open to producing different academic and community outputs.

Moreover, taking an interactionist approach, we find the combination of FPE and STS amplifies the goals of this collaborative project and provides an important epistemological grounding to the research design. As the emphasis of this project is to support Kayapó peoples' visual sovereignty and cultural-heritage-building activities, STS provides several concepts that are formative to guiding the collaborative sensibilities of this work: symmetrical anthropology, networks, translation, and economy of otherness (Callon 1986, 1990; Latour 1993, 2005; Law 2002; Viveiros de Castro 2015).

First, taking a decolonial stance, STS work breaks down the divide between "we" ("moderns," who have "science" in our side) and "others" (with their "subjective beliefs"). This requires the suspension of any ethnocentric judgment about the existence of an epistemological hierarchy between Western science (and technology) and others. Second, STS demands a focus on the relationship between human and nonhuman, which requires a recognition and analysis of the agency of both (Viveiros de Castro 1996). Third, STS is attentive to how individuals, in this case Kayapó community members, translate technology within their own political interests and interface with technology in daily life. As a collection, folding these concepts into our research design better enables us to identify and analyze the sociotechnical network established around this project. We ask: What is the dynamic of this network? Who are the actors directly involved in this project? What conceptual perspective are they putting into action? How do they build associations and relations among themselves? What is their perspective about digital media, and how does this perspective converge or diverge with the perspectives of other actors?

We argue that this network is pierced by multiplicity and complexity, and that, to co-create a collaborative research design, non-Indigenous scholars have to discard any kind of ontological and topological determinism: in fact, networks can take many forms, in different moments, going from hierarchical to rhizomatic formats (Law 2002; Soares da Silveira 2012). Part of creating a collaborative project, then, entails a conceptual embracement of the principles of ethnomethodology. These principles are founded within engaged, collaborative, and symmetrical anthropology, which necessitates taking seriously what Kayapó interlocutors have to say about the world they live in (ontology) and about their positions on the controversial issues with which they are involved (topology).

Scholars working within the field of Amazonian ethnology have shown very clearly the centrality of difference and otherness for Indigenous cultural identity and well-being (Gordon 2006; Viveiros de Castro 2002, 2015; Lea 2012). For example, difference in Western philosophy and science demonize otherness as a threat or risk to the continuity of the cultural identity; however, difference and innovation for many South America Indigenous peoples, including Kayapó peoples, is always a process of appropriation and transformation of cultural and cosmological elements that come from other societies, human or nonhuman. To meaningfully engage with and co-create a project with Kayapó perspectives in mind, we examine their work within the broader processes of appropriation of other elements that come from the Western world and in multiscalar contexts in order to avoid the pitfalls ascribing to a dominant narrative that considers any kind of change as erasing Indigenous identities and ways of life (Gordon 2006; Lea 2012).

While we hope this conceptual framing serves as a structure from which to build collaborative work, we also want to emphasize that, by responding to community desires or supporting community efforts, we are not referring to a top-down understanding of local capacity-building, where Indigenous peoples "learn" how to use the camera, learn how to make movies (as Westerners do); rather we are considering a long term cultural process of transformation for visual sovereignty and expression. Thus, translation also serves as a key locus of analysis. There is no way the project can translate without transforming (in linguistic terms but also in ontological terms) different knowledge systems, and this translation process is always at the fore of dialogical interaction and shared outputs. Our research shows that collaborative projects can support Indigenous cinema that not only aligns with Kayapó worlds but also produces projects that support visual sovereignty. In this way, the project challenges Western ways of thinking about image, representation, and Indigenous peoples to revolutionize Western modes of history telling by supporting new forms of storytelling that open new doors to the human imagination.

In the next section of the chapter, we move away from the conceptual frames that guide the project to a more in-depth empirical analysis of one piece of the project as it unfolds. A team of filmmakers currently works closely with Ramón Parra, Soares, and Zanotti to carry out initial portions of the project. We highlight a segment of this project by turning to Ramón Parra's recent work with women filmmakers in A'Ukre. This next section demonstrates how gendered norms and generational tensions (as exhibited in age grades) in the community are salient in understanding emerging media-making practices in the community. Responding to these concerns through ongoing interpersonal and intersubjective reflections, Ramón Parra describes how community-based participatory filmmaking adheres to overall project goals of collaborative practice. Moreover, she highlights the ways in which collaborative ethnography demands respectful and responsive changes to the project and showcases the preliminary spaces in which visual sovereignty is exerted and supported.

Menire Making Movies

At the end of the film *The Kayapó: Out of the Forest* (1987), anthropologist Terence Turner narrates the closing scene as the camera pans to Kayapó dancers engaged in a ceremony. His narration finds a delicate balance between hope and caution as he claims that the Kayapó from the village of Gorotire are dancing with much fervor and pride as they continue to face challenges surrounding self-determination, land management, and control of the natural resources from their territories. Turner asks the viewer, "What does the future hold for the Kayapó peoples?" This scene is striking for a few reasons, the biggest being one particular *menire* in the scene.[7] She is not dancing although she is in full ceremonial dress with accompanying black body paint and the vibrant red designs of the urucum seeds; she is holding a large video camera and filming the ceremony. Revisiting this scene from time to time, Ramón Parra has gained a deep appreciation for it. It captures the village of Gorotire at a height of economic prosperity and, perhaps unintentionally, foreshadows Turner's involvement with the Kayapó through his video projects (Turner 1990a) and the Kayapó's appropriation of media technologies. But what do we make of the Kayapó woman filmmaker?

Within the Self-Determination in a Digital Age project, one central concern that emerged early on was regarding the gendered dynamics of media-making practice. As such, one leg of this project, which began in July 2015 and is ongoing at the time of this writing, centers on gender and inquires into the gendered contexts of media production. Specifically, this portion of the project aims to investigate Kayapó women's use of and engagement with audiovisual media and its production. Past media projects among the Kayapó have tended to focus exclusively on men's media appropriation; however, this project attempts to broaden media scholarship by questioning the gendered aspects and general composition of Kayapó "media worlds" (Ginsburg, Abu-Lughod, and Larken 2002). Additionally, working primarily but not exclusively with Kayapó women provides rich opportunities to examine gendered practices and analyze gendered conceptualizations of media and the audiovisual process.

This section presents preliminary findings that have emerged during the first stages of the work, with a focus on the case studies and participant-created images and videos. Using ethnographic and visual methods, Ramón Parra's project started technical media training of an all-women cohort at A'Ukre. Along with case studies, this project makes use of interviews with Kayapó women to hone in on women's conceptualizations of media and its practice. Developed out of conversations that were part of the Self-Determination in a Digital Age project in 2015, the community of A'Ukre chose four young women to learn to operate handheld camcorders and to learn preproduction, editing, and media sharing.

These young women were all teenagers, and one of the four participants was married with no children, although all were within the same age grade (women without kids). Ramón Parra has been told more than once that the reason the participants are all young women without children is because women with children have a lot of responsibilities and cannot dedicate themselves fully to the project. Although older women are interested in learning media making and may even have the time to learn, their responsibilities in the community may be preventative to the ongoing close collaboration asked of the filmmakers as they work with the community and researchers, which is possibly why community leaders and elders identified four young women as the initial participants.

The participants did have difficulties finding time for the project. For example, Luisa, the married participant, was very busy working at home; when Ramón Parra asked her if her interest in the media project was waning, she said it was not, but the amount of work she had to do at home left her exhausted and with little time to dedicate to the project. It was later shared that she was pregnant, and about five months into the project she left for the city to obtain prenatal care. Another young woman who is married but does not have children was later formally accepted into the media project. Collaborative and participatory work can be time-consuming for both researchers and project participants. An attentiveness to "resituating collaborative practice at every stage of the ethnographic process" (Lassiter 2005, 15) means adjusting to community norms and desires regarding the type and degree of project engagement and having a flexible timeline that accommodates for and honors other activities that participants value.

The young women have previously experimented with image and video making. This includes learning to operate an HP laptop, to manage media files, and to work with video editing applications. The subjects of their photographs and videos vary widely; they make use of a variety of shots include long, medium, close, and extreme close-up ranges. There were times when the participants were given cameras for a few hours, and other times when participants were given cameras to use for days uninterrupted. Participants were not given instructions on what subjects to capture, what angles to use, or other elements of photographic composition such as lighting, perspective, depth of field, etc. Part of this work relies on participants to experiment and explore media making at their own pace. This experimentation resulted in a series of diverse photographs and videos that capture many quotidian and ceremonial activities. In addition, their media practice reflects other elements like social relationships, age-grade specific activities, and notions of space.

In this way, space has emerged as a preliminary theme while working with women. Because the Kayapó peoples have gender divisions of practice and tend to socialize with their own age grades, the emergence of space as a salient theme may not come as a surprise. Space here refers mostly to the physical spaces that are occupied, traveled through, labored in, and created in the village. Although the women participants in this project have prior experience engaging in image making, that experience was mostly limited to taking and viewing pictures on standard-quality cellular devices. In the beginning of the project, participants were given a point-and-shoot camera with built-in still-image and video capabilities. During technical workshops the young women were asked to take images and videos of whatever they wished and were given uninterrupted access to a point-and-shoot camera for three hours; the river was chosen as the initial location for these workshops. Participants took still and moving images of river activities while women and children were bathing, washing clothes, playing, and socializing.

Once, Ramón Parra suggested that the group practice shooting video during the daily soccer matches that take place in the evenings. The subsequent refusal of the young women participants to go to that space signaled to her not that they were not interested in soccer, but that the activity was a male activity and perhaps they did not feel comfortable being in that space at that time. Capturing images of young men could possibly be interpreted as flirting or interest. Additionally, women do not frequent these soccer matches even as spectators, so their presence would have been out of the norm and the visibility caused by the cameras would have added another layer to their presence. The soccer field is a fluid space; during certain times of the day young children play around in it, and at other times young women practice playing soccer. Nearly every evening, young men have soccer matches. During exciting soccer matches with other villages, men, women, and children all occupy the soccer field together.

Although many in the community are aware that these young women are part of the video project, there is still a level of visibility that taking pictures yields. While Ramón Parra was away from the village for a short time period, the community held a large naming ceremony that had taken months to prepare. Some of the young women decided to take images and video of the ceremony. Upon Ramón Parra's return, a male filmmaker told her that one of the young women, Flor, had been capturing the ceremony from the inside of her home, and he had heard other community members making negative remarks about her media practice. Flor's pictures and videos from this particular event show many but not all of the images had been taken from one particular fixed location: the young women's home. It is unclear why this participant chose to take the pictures from the inside of her house, but what is evident is that she was able to negotiate her visibility and have control of the space she inhabited while still engaging in image making. There is a series of pictures that Flor took that illuminates on the negotiation of space, spectatorship, and visibility. During a portion of the ceremony, Flor took images and videos of the dance as she stood in the veranda space of her family home. As with the other images of the ceremony, she was enjoying the ceremony as a spectator but was also documenting the dance with her small camera. Although physically she remained in the same location, Flor used the zoom feature to "move closer" and capture the dance from a variety of angles, using the zoom to full capacity, recording not only the movement of the dancers across the village plaza but also highlighting individuals in the group.

Although Flor had many images and videos taken from the veranda of her home, there are other images that also suggest that she is becoming more comfortable with image making in relation to space. In the beginning of the technical workshops, as already noted, young women were reluctant to take pictures of a soccer match where mostly men were playing soccer. A few months later, Flor took a small number of images of a soccer match and zoomed in on the players in the field. Other images and videos also show a change in Flor's comfort and movement through the village space, including images and videos from later parts of the naming ceremony that were taken from the plaza periphery, and not from the veranda of her home. Use of the camera zoom employed not just by Flor, but by other project participants, afforded the possibility of movement during these initial stages of their media practice development. The zoom was used not only to cut distance and bring subjects closer in ceremonial dances or in scenes of everyday life, it was also used to capture detail and to bring nonhuman subjects closer. Some examples include using the zoom to show a close-up of unripe coconuts on the tree, salted fish drying on a clothing line, beadwork details, and even astronomical phenomena: a close-up of the October blood moon.

These preliminary findings highlight space as an emerging theme in the initial stages of working with the women. Young women negotiated their image-making endeavors as they experimented with learning in different village spaces and within different events. These negotiations play out variably depending on the participant, the activity, and the village space, pointing to overall heterogeneity of media-making practice. Although selected by the community for the project, the young women emplaced filmmaking as part of the daily routine, prioritizing other livelihood practices over the project when needed. Moreover, for the most part, young women's preferences for filmmaking aligned with norms associated with customary gendered roles and activities; they were more hesitant initially to film in spaces that otherwise would not be appropriate for someone in their age grade. Further, men filmmakers, women filmmakers, and community members all expressed different desires for the outcomes of the women's work, but, overall, all were interested in a final product that would align with community interests. As frameworks for collaborative work, FPE and STS accommodate the kind of critical reflexivity required to make real-time adjustments to the project as well as providing a trusting space for responsive feedback that continues to resituate collaborative practice. Finally, while not all filmmakers might have an explicit political focus, the production of film and photography with Kayapó sensibilities links to broader questions of the ontological politics and the recognition of difference within sociocultural understandings of space, place, and identity—all critical to visual sovereignties.

Conclusion

The goals of this chapter have been threefold. The first was to map out the project design, which we noted was based on collaborative, symmetrical principles and partnerships forged within a relational network of several entities, including the Kayapó community of A'Ukre, Purdue University, Universidade de Uberlândia, FUNAI, and the Associação Floresta Protegida. We have suggested that in forging this collaborative project, FPE and STS have been especially fruitful frameworks from which to co-create this work. In particular, we argue that media making in general and digital media in particular are providing new terrains for practice. This is reflected not only in community-based desires and concerns about media production in the community but also in broader understandings about supporting Indigenous-driven media-making efforts that formulate new expressive cultures rooted in Kayapó lifeworlds and cosmovisions. We also suggested that this project, while aligning with earlier work such as that of Turner, also diverges from this work in that it explicitly engages with gender and intergenerational shifts, recognizing the broader dynamics of heterogeneous communities and individual artistic expressions while at the same time acknowledging shared sensibilities and goals of visual sovereignty.

As Soares da Silveira (2012) emphasizes, this necessarily emplaces the project into a sociotechnical web where Indigenous media makers, anthropologists, digital media, and other human and nonhuman actants emerge as part of a new generation of practices. Distancing ourselves from "capacity-building" projects, we envision this work as a collaborative endeavor where the community and individuals within it are defining and shaping new subject positions according to local ontologies, rather than appropriating Western technological advancements for Indigenous use. This belies the long history Indigenous peoples have of incorporating the essences, material objects, landscapes, and knowledges of other human and nonhuman beings over time. Certainly with Kayapó communities, it would be too simplistic to simply frame the project in terms of an essential binary of Indigenous versus modern; rather, it is a site of production of creative possibilities for expression, activism, and enactment at an intimate and collective level.

Ramón Parra details the intimacies of media making as a new cohort of young women filmmakers in the community start their craft. Highlighting the design of the project, which relies on experimentation and limited instruction, Ramón Parra describes how Flor and other filmmakers navigated these landscapes and embodied ways of knowing and being. She suggests this necessarily reflects on gendered and sociospatial divisions already in place in the community, but it also outlines how the work of the larger project becomes responsive to the demands of collaborative practice.

What we have shown here is the diverse network that undergirds digital worlds now emerging as commonplace practices in A'Ukre. We also highlight how collaborative ethnography can intervene as a possible generative site of production and exchange in this new digital landscape. It is a terrain in which new worlds can be made and enacted while reinforcing alternative expressive forms that challenge Western conceptualizations of difference, place, and space. We hope that future collaborative work in this area will continue to support local efforts at self-determination and sovereignty, especially as Indigenous rights in Brazil are increasingly tenuous due to new developmental programs in the region and changing rights-based conversations.

Notes

All authors have equally contributed to this piece. Earlier portions of this paper were presented by Ramón Parra with Zanotti and Soares' contributions at the InDigital Conference at Vanderbilt in 2015, Ramón Parra and Zanotti at the American Ethnological Society Meetings in 2014, and Soares and Zanotti at the American Anthropological Association Meetings in 2014.

1. We acknowledge Ginsburg's (2006, 132–33) observation that, "those who are out of power struggle to become producers of media presentations of their lives, a project that has been enabled through work in video documentary over the last two decades. Indigenous media activists have found that in using video to create documentaries about their cultural worlds and histories they were able to take some steps to reverse processes through which aspects of their societies have been objectified, commodified, and appropriated."

2. "Diane Rocheleau Speaks," Public Political Ecology Lab (PPEL) at University of Arizona (Sept. 28, 2015). *ppel.arizona.edu/?p=1033*. Video, 6 minutes 24 seconds.
3. Engagements with digital media work in different ways in communities. From elders wishing to archive cultural heritage events, parents desiring to share photos and songs, mothers and fathers wanting family portraits, and Facebook users sharing life events, to young people making documentaries and leaders creating activist films, digital media has a robust presence in Kayapó villages.
4. Although digital cameras were then emerging, different individuals in the community had owned or used nondigital film cameras or VHS camcorders.
5. All names in this chapter are pseudonyms.
6. For example, Rouch (1991:56) writes, "For a production to be truly collaborative the parties involved must be equal in their competencies or have achieved an equitable division of labor. Involvement in the decision-making process must occur at all significant junctures."
7. *Menire* is the Kayapó term for women.

References

Agrawal, A., and C. Gibson. 1999. "Enchantment and Disenchantment: The Role of Community in Natural Resource Conservation." *World Development* 27 (4): 629–49.

Appadurai, A. 1996. *Modernity at Large: Cultural Dimensions of Globalization*. Minneapolis: University of Minnesota Press.

Bishop, R. 1994. "Initiating Empowering Research?" *New Zealand Journal of Educational Studies* 29 (1): 175–88.

Boyer, D. 2006. "Turner's Anthropology of Media and Its Legacies." *Critique of Anthropology* 26: 47–60.

Callon, M. 1986. "Some Elements of a Sociology of Translation: Domestication of the Scallops and the Fishermen of St. Brieuc Bay." In *Power, Action and Belief: A New Sociology of Knowledge?*, edited by J. Law, 196–223. London: Routledge.

———. 1990. "Techno-economic Networks and Irreversibility." *Sociological Review* 38 (S1): 132–61.

Coleman, E. 2010. "Ethnographic Approaches to Digital Media." *Annual Review of Anthropology* 39: 487–505.

Conklin, B. 1997. "Body Paint, Feathers, and VCRs: Aesthetics and Authenticity in Amazonian Activism." *American Ethnologist* 24 (4): 711–37.

Cruz-Torres, M., and P. McElwee. 2012. *Gender and Sustainability: Lessons from Asia and Latin America*. Tucson: University of Arizona Press.

Ebenau, M. 2014. "Comparative Capitalisms and Latin American Neodevelopmentalism: A Critical Political Economy View." *Capital and Class* 38 (1): 102–14.

Elmhirst, R. 2011. "Introducing New Feminist Political Ecologies." *Geoforum* 42 (2): 129–32.

Ginsburg, F., L. Abu-Lughod, and B. Larken, eds. 2002. *Media Worlds: Anthropology on New Terrain*. Berkeley: University of California Press.

Ginsburg, F. 2006. "Rethinking Documentary in the Digital Age." *Cinema Journal* 46 (1): 128–33.

Graham, L., and G. Penny, eds. 2014. *Performing Indigeneity: Global Histories and Contemporary Experiences*. Lincoln: University of Nebraska Press.

Gordon, C. 2006. *Economia selvagem: Ritual e mercadoria entre os índios Xikrin Mebêngôkre*. São Paulo: Fundação Editora da UNESP (FEU).

Gubrium, A., and K. Harper. 2009. "Visualizing Change: Participatory Digital Technologies in Research and Action." *Practicing Anthropology* 31 (4): 1–3.

Hollbraad, M., M. Pedersen, and E. Viveiros de Castro. 2014. "The Politics of Ontology: Anthropological Positions." Theorizing the Contemporary. *Cultural Anthropology* website (January 13), *culanth.org/fieldsights/462-the-politics-of-ontology-anthropological-positions*.

Joyce, R., and S. Gillespie, eds. 2015. *Things in Motion: Object Itineraries in Anthropological Practice*. Santa Fe, NM: School for Advanced Research Press.

Lassiter, L. 2005. *The Chicago Guide to Collaborative Ethnography*. Chicago: University of Chicago Press.

Latour, B. 1993. *We Have Never Been Modern*. Cambridge: Harvard University Press.

———. 2005. *Reassembling the Social: An Introduction to Actor-Network Theory*. New York: Oxford University Press.

———. 2014. "Anthropology at the Time of the Anthropocene—A Personal View of What Is to Be Studied." Paper presented at the Annual Meeting of the Association of American Anthropology, Washington DC (December 2014).

Law, J. 2002. "Objects and Spaces." *Theory, Culture & Society* 19 (5-6): 91–105.

Lea, V. 2012. *Riquezas intangíveis de pessoas partíveis: Os Mēbēngôkre (Kayapó) do Brasil central*. São Paulo: EDUSP.an

Low, S., and S. Merry. 2010. "Engaged Anthropology: Diversity and Dilemmas." *Current Anthropology* 51 (2): S203–26.

Mathews, A. 2011. *Instituting Nature: Authority, Expertise, and Power in Mexican Forests*. Cambridge, MA: MIT Press.

Radcliffe, S. 2007. "Latin American Indigenous Geographies of Fear: Living in the Shadow of Racism, Lack of Development, and Antiterror Measures." *Annals of the Association of American Geographers* 97 (2): 385–97.

Raheja, M. 2010. *Reservation Reelism: Redfacing, Visual Sovereignty, and Representations of Native Americans in Film*. Lincoln: University of Nebraska Press.

Ramos, A. 1994. "The Hyperreal Indian." *Critique of Anthropology* 14 (2): 153–71.

Rocheleau, D. 2008. "Political Ecology in the Key of Policy: From Chains of Explanation to Webs of Relation." *Geoforum* 39 (2): 716–27.

Rocheleau, D., B. Thomas-Slayter, and E. Wangari. 1996. *Feminist Political Ecology: Global Issues and Local Experiences*. New York: Routledge.

Rouch, J. 1991. "Speaking for, Speaking about, Speaking with, or Speaking alongside: An Anthropological and Documentary Dilemma." *Visual Anthropology Review* 7 (2): 50–67.

Shepard, G., Jr., 2013. "Kaya-Pop: The Brave New World of Indigenous Music in Brazil." *Anthropology News* (June 14). *www.anthropology-news.org/index.php/2013/06/14/kaya-pop*.

Sikor, T., ed. 2013. *The Justices and Injustices of Ecosystem Services*. New York: Routledge.

Smith, Laurel. 2012. "Decolonizing Hybridity: Indigenous Video, Knowledge, and Diffraction." *Cultural Geographies* 19 (3): 329–48.

Soares da Silveira, D. 2012. *Redes sociotécnicas na Amazônia: Tradução de saberes no campo da biodiversidade*. Rio de Janeiro: Multifoco.

Tuhiwai Smith, L. 2008. "On Tricky Ground: Researching the Native in the Age of Uncertainty." In *The Landscape of Qualitative Research*, edited by N. Denzin and Y. Lincoln, 113–44. Thousand Oaks, CA: Sage.

Turner, T., and V. Fajans-Turner. 2006. "Political Innovation and Inter-ethnic Alliance: Kayapó Resistance to the Developmentalist State." *Anthropology Today* 22: 3–10.

Turner, T. 1990a. "The Kayapó Video Project: A Progress Report." *CVA Review* (Fall): 7–10.

———. 1990b. "Visual Media, Cultural Politics, and Anthropological Practice: Some Implications of Recent Uses of Film and Video among the Kayapó of Brazil." *CVA Review* (Spring): 8–13.

———. 1991. "Defiant Images: The Kayapó Appropriation of Video." *Anthropology Today* 86: 5–15.

———. 1992. "The Kayapó on Television." *Visual Anthropology Review* 81: 107–12.

———. 1995. "Representation, Collaboration and Mediation in Contemporary Ethnographic and Indigenous Media." *Visual Anthropology Review* 112: 102–6.

———. 2002a. "Representation, Politics, and Cultural Imagination in Indigenous Video: General Points and Kayapó Examples." In *Media Worlds: Anthropology on New Terrain*, edited by F. Ginsburg, L. Abu-Lughod, and B. Larkin, 75–89. Berkeley: University of California Press.

———. 2002b. "Representation, Polyphony and the Construction of Power in a Kayapó Video." In *Indigenous Self-Representation in South America*, edited by K. Warren and J. Jackson, 229–50. Austin: University of Texas Press.

Vargas-Cetina, G., ed. 2013. *Anthropology and the Politics of Representation*. Tuscaloosa: University of Alabama Press.

Viveiros de Castro, E. 1996. "Images of Nature and Society in Amazonian Ethnology." *Annual Review of Anthropology* 25: 179–200.

———. 2002. "O Nativo Relativo." *Mana* 8 (1): 113–48.

———. 2015. "Who is Afraid of the Ontological Wolf? Some Comments on an Ongoing Anthropological Debate." *Cambridge Journal of Anthropology* 33 (1): 2–17.

Wilson, P., and M. Stewart. 2008. *Global Indigenous Media: Cultures, Poetics, and Politics*. Durham, NC: Duke University Press.

Zanotti, L. 2016. *Radical Territories in the Brazilian Amazon: The Kayapó's Fight for Just Livelihoods*. Tucson: University of Arizona Press.

Zanotti, L., and M. Palomino-Schalscha. 2016. "Taking Different Ways of Knowing Seriously: Implications and Challenges for Non-Indigenous Researchers Working with Indigenous Peoples." *Sustainability Science* 11 (1): 139–52.

PART THREE

Sounds and Images

7

National Culture, Indigenous Voice

Creating a Counternarrative on Colombian Radio

By Mario A. Murillo

In December 1992, the Regional Indigenous Council of Cauca (Consejo Regional Indígena del Cauca, CRIC) organized a massive, day-long procession to mark the anniversary of the brutal massacre of twenty Nasa women, men, and children on the Nilo estate just one year earlier.[1] Thousands of people marched through the winding roads and small towns leading to the historic site located on the Huellas *resguardo* (reserve) in the municipality of Caloto, in the southwestern department of Cauca, Colombia. After marching from the early morning hours until the evening, participants young and old converged on the Nilo compound to commence CRIC's Sixth Regional Congress, a quadrennial gathering designed to set the course of Colombia's oldest Indigenous organization for the next four years. Despite their collective exhaustion, they were now bracing themselves for the several days of intense deliberation and debate still before them—more urgent than ever given the national process that was underway to put into action measures that had been recently ratified by the Constituent Assembly in the 1991 constitution related to Indigenous rights, territorial demarcation of their lands, and political participation in the Colombian congress.

As the warm Cauca sun set slowly behind the rolling Andean foothills, long lines of people started forming around the enormous communal pots simmering with the family-sized servings of *sancocho de gallina*, or chicken stew, prepared by the dozen or so people who had arrived at the site earlier in the day. Throughout the empty colonial-style house and the expansive grounds of the Nilo estate, little children ran around playing while adults kicked back to rest their feet as they listened to a group of young Nasa musicians performing their traditional songs of protest. Under an immense tree that loomed over the center of the yard, a large group of about twenty-five men huddled around in silence, listening intently to a small transistor radio dangling precariously from a nail hammered into the bark.

Intrigued by the focused intensity of this gathering, I drew closer to get a sense of what it was that they were listening to. It turned out to be the championship match of Colombian league *fútbol*, or soccer, broadcasting live from the nearby city of Cali. The game featured two cross-town rivals—América de Cali and Deportivo Cali—competing in what could be described as Colombia's equivalent to baseball's "Subway Series" between New York's Yankees and Mets. As the broadcast progressed, diverging team loyalties began revealing themselves in the circle of enthusiastic listeners, sighs and screams reflecting the allegiances of those gathered around the tree. In the end, América prevailed, capturing its eighth national title and, once again, local bragging rights, proudly celebrated by its assembled partisans at this historic Indigenous mobilization.

This seemingly minor episode—one of my earliest experiences with the Indigenous movement in the country as a radio feature reporter in the early nineties—vividly illustrates how the Indigenous communities of Cauca, and all of Colombia for that matter, regularly participate in the events that captivate the national psyche of the majority population despite their repeated demands for autonomy and self-determination as a people. Notwithstanding the years of dispossession, discrimination, and subjugation that they have experienced (Amnesty International 1992; Laurent 2005; Mondragón 2005; Villa and Houghton 2005), and despite their ongoing resistance to the often-forced imposition of non-Indigenous cultural concepts into their own social spaces (Caldón 2005; Galeano Lozano 2005), Indigenous communities are not immune to the popular, commercial distractions of the "typical" Colombian. As the example above demonstrates, it is often through the medium of radio that Indigenous peoples are enticed into this collective national body that is Colombia today, whether it is through popular music programs, major sporting events, or the breaking national news reports disseminated on the major radio networks.

At the same time the medium interpellates listeners, it and television are also used to deliberately exclude and systematically marginalize Indigenous peoples from the Colombian nation. Given this inherent bias in the national corporate media, the emergence of Colombia's broad network of local and regional Indigenous radio stations is a remarkable achievement. These alternative media platforms have played an important role in strengthening grassroots participation in the communities they serve, while also providing non-Indigenous audiences across the country a counternarrative to that of the mainstream broadcasters.

One of the historical functions of non-Indigenous radio in Colombia was to forge a sense of Colombian "nationhood" that emphasized the commonalities of a very diverse populace. The primarily white European elite in the capital, Bogotá, shared very little in common with the predominantly African-descendant populations of the Caribbean or Pacific coasts, the settler cattle ranchers of the eastern plains, or the traditional Indigenous families living in the Amazonian region or Andean highlands. Therefore, for the dominant economic and political class in Colombia that had its grip on the burgeoning industry of radio, the medium was seen as a unique opportunity to reintroduce this diversified public to a common cultural experience, specifically one constructed and legitimized by their own privileged positions in both the public and private realms. This state-imposed concept of Colombianness was an essential component of nation-building in a neocolonial framework largely informed by the worldview of those in power. It was a Colombianness considered elusive for generations, given the country's complex geographical landscape, its intense regional divisions, and the extremely diverse cultural and racial underpinnings that have characterized Colombia since its independence in the early part of the nineteenth century. The Indigenous communities in particular, reflecting an incredible diversity that included over one hundred different ethnicities spread throughout the national territory and predating the arrival of the Spanish, were clearly seen by the ruling class as an obstacle to achieving that uniform notion of what it meant to be Colombian.

Colombia's early radio broadcasters looked to impose a hegemonic and, in many respects, alien (at best) cultural product on a broad cross section of the population. Programming ranged from highly commercial formats imported from the United States that were designed to attract and maintain large audiences in order to maximize profits, to the highbrow vision of the cultural and political elite, which sought to "educate" the masses to its own supposed supremacy and legitimacy. Whichever their approach, the new broadcasting entrepreneurs emerging in Colombia looked to establish a common Colombian identity through the magic of radio (Silva 2000; Murillo 2003).

Tragically for the country's Indigenous communities, with rare exceptions like the one described above, radio has locked them out rather than brought them into this national dialogue. This has been accomplished by either making Indigenous people invisible, or, worse yet, made to look backward or uncivilized to the majority (i.e., white population), and, in turn, an obstacle to progress and the future economic development of the country (Proyecto Antonio Nariño 2004). The emergence of Indigenous radio over the last twenty-plus years, therefore, is a manifestation of the Indigenous movement's open rejection of the hierarchical, primarily European, individualist, and consumerist conception of the Colombian nation that has dominated broadcast media, first radio and later television, since the 1930s. Their use of radio—and indeed other electronic media forms—as a unifying force in local and regional settings is similar to how the early national broadcasters sought to unleash the power of radio on a national level. But while the elite historically viewed "unity" as a vehicle of social control by the European-dominated state and its counterparts in the private sector, Indigenous radio seeks to create and promote a strong sense of Indigenous unity, identity, and awareness that recognizes, indeed embraces, its rich diversity. This is accomplished through self-determined communication methods rooted in Indigenous traditions and programming content designed to place them within, not apart from, the larger pluricultural, multiethnic context of the Colombian nation.

In this way, many of the communities see their radio projects as more than just an internal communication tool for themselves, notwithstanding the importance of their radio stations in information dissemination, public deliberation, and community mobilization. In this essay, I will attempt to demonstrate how Indigenous radio—especially in places like the department of Cauca where the Indigenous movement is very strong—is directed outward as well, to the non-Indigenous public. The medium as such is employed to establish an ongoing dialogue with the dominant society and articulate a vision about Indigenous people's fundamental concerns, organizing structures, and proposals for the country as a whole that is distinct and more nuanced than what is typically presented in the mainstream media. In this way, Colombian Indigenous radio is emblematic of the generational struggle for communicative democracy and one of the crowning achievements of the media-justice movement in Colombia.

A Brief History of the Colombian Radio Industry

From its earliest days, the evolution of Colombian radio has been shaped by powerful forces representing both public and private interests that have primarily considered the medium an important tool to promote specific economic and political agendas (Waisbord 2002; Fox 1997). Commercially-driven radio stations emerged in the 1930s, following both the advertising and programming model of the large radio companies based in the United States (Fox 1997). These stations were promoted with the tacit support of government institutions that were run, to a large degree, by those members of the bourgeoisie with substantial interests in the private sector: members of the privileged class who not only had access to higher levels of education, but also had the ability to travel often to the United States, where they were exposed to and eventually sold on the commercial model of radio.

Radio got its first real spark when Colombia's most powerful capitalists looked to create and expand a domestic market for its consumer products, a market which, up to that point, was generally nonexistent. To support the urgent need of capitalist industry to create an internal market demand for its products, the dominant classes saw radio and, specifically, the use of commercial advertising on the airwaves, as the perfect tool (Pareja 1984). The constant barrage of commercial messages, directed primarily at a small yet important urban middle class, would ostensibly create public demand for products and services, the prerequisite to a successful market economy. Content on commercial radio, therefore, was shaped to suit those messages, attract those listeners, and, in the process, transform them into consumers. With radio, a market was born along with an emergent and narrowly defined sense of who did (and did not) constitute the nation.

Imagining radio's listening audience primarily as a pool of consumers of commercial goods and services is taken right out of the playbook of the US commercial and corporate media (McChesney 1999; Croteau and Hoynes 2001). The owners of these media, forever threatened by the nefarious hand of state intervention in their lucrative enterprises, serve the public's interests by giving the people exactly what they demand, not what the state tells them they should provide. This is at least theoretically how it is supposed to work. However, given the extraordinary discrepancies in the distribution of wealth in Colombia, the cultural diversity of its population, and the extreme levels of marginalization endured by Indigenous, Afro-Colombian, and poor peasant communities, particularly in the countryside, this market approach to the media systematically excluded a broad cross-section of the population from the target audiences desired by commercial enterprise. In essence, they were not considered to be adequate consumers, rendering them invisible to the radio station programmers, their private commercial underwriters, and the complicit state institutions that embraced the commercial-hybrid model of radio in Colombia.

Radio Networks and the Consolidation of a Commercial Culture

The first national commercial radio networks began to emerge in the 1940s. These networks developed with the support and financing of foreign multinationals, both media-oriented firms like RCA and companies in other areas of industry, such as the German pharmaceutical company Bayer, which played a role in the first radio network in Colombia in 1940. Domestic capital quickly took note of the potential importance of the new networks, and by 1946 the first domestically owned national network began operating in Colombia: CARACOL—Cadena Radial Colombiana (the Colombia radio network).

The CARACOL network was financed by powerful economic interests tied to the Liberal Party, who saw the network as an essential component of its strategy to control information, surpassing even newspapers in terms of importance (Perez Angel 1998). In 1949, the second major network, RCN—Radio Cadena Nacional, the National Radio Network—was established and grew at an equally rapid pace as CARACOL. Both CARACOL and RCN remain the dominant forces of Colombian television and radio today, notwithstanding the increased media competition that was the result of the liberalization of the economy in the 1990s. Today, they continue to wield tremendous influence on the commercial and political culture of Colombia simply due to the massive scale of their media enterprises, which include not only television and radio but a whole collection of other media industries that maintain an extensive reach throughout the country.

The Creation of a National Identity on the Airwaves

Despite the growth of commercial radio in the late 1930s, there was considerable debate at the time within the Colombian legislative and executive branches between those lawmakers and Ministry of Education officials who supported a more educational/cultural function for radio, and those sectors who advocated the more commercially driven system that was being firmly consolidated in the US.[2] Proponents of an educational/culturally driven model frowned upon what they perceived as the crass commercialism of the network programs. They championed radio as a fundamental component of an ambitious cultural campaign to establish for the first time "an authentic popular university whose teachings would reach the entire national population," fomenting a nationalist spirit (Silva 2000). For this camp, a state-run, nationally distributed radio network was seen as the principal vehicle by which to transmit this "educational" mission to the public.

This debate led to the establishment of Radiodifusora Nacional, or the National Radio Distributor, which began operating in 1940. Radiodifusora Nacional is best understood within the framework of a much broader national campaign that was part of the so-called "Liberal Republic," the period between 1930 and 1946 when the Liberal Party controlled the executive branch. The regime had vision of political and social reforms promoted to the public as an antidote to the repressive influence of the Conservative Party's reign of the previous decades. These new leaders, exclusively drawn from Colombia's dominant racial and economic classes, determined that it was their duty to distribute to the broader public what constituted, in their view, Colombian cultural output, from literature to music to cinema, as a basic prerequisite for national integration. A carefully curated and narrow, top-down conception of Colombian culture would be the vehicle by which to create a unified nation while at the same time negating differences that the elite considered threatening to their economic and political control. The National Radio was created by these same interests to serve as an educational tool to impose this elitist cultural vision on all Colombians.

On the surface the cultural intentions of the "Liberal Republic" could be characterized as democratic. Party leaders saw it as a key function of the state to educate the masses and inculcate them with what they believed to be fundamental democratic principles. This would be accomplished by making culture, as defined by the elite, accessible in every region of the country, particularly to those communities most marginalized by Colombia's socioeconomic order. The belief was that this embrace of a dominant national culture—primarily white, European, urban, Catholic—would lead to broader public participation in the daily life of the nation. However, the inclusion of diverse, or even dissenting, perspectives in the construction of a Colombian national identity was not part of their game plan (Silva 2000).

The Liberal vision for radio's role was not a benevolent one designed to open up spaces to the most marginalized sectors of Colombian society. Those in power viewed their cultural program as part and parcel of a larger political strategy that looked to create a uniform vision of nationhood that would lead to "social homogeneity and intellectual conformity" (Silva 2000). In turn, this would ultimately benefit the Liberal Republic's own long-term political objectives. For example, through part of its programming, the Radiodifusora Nacional drew the attention of its listeners to different regions of the country in an effort to provide the audience with a better awareness of the way "fellow Colombians" lived outside of the large cities. However, this programming focus was never intended to give these marginalized communities a voice that could be heard by the broader public, let alone critically inform the national body politic or expand the public sphere. Rather, the carefully constructed representation of marginalized communities was co-opted for an oppositional end: to bring these communities into "the same rhythm" of the state-imagined majority of Colombians and create a mythologized, uniform history of the country, negating the diversity of Indigenous communities, their cultural and linguistic traditions, and, perhaps most importantly, their territorial rights. The dynamic, participatory vision of Indigenous people, for example—at the time still considered minors under Colombia's Constitutional framework—was in direct conflict with Liberal Party leaders and so-called reformers who were actively displacing thousands of Indigenous families from their *resguardos*, or reserves, as part of the state plan to revamp the economy and modernize its agricultural sector (Molano 1991; Sanchez 1992). Proponents of the educational/cultural radio model were by no means attempting to establish an inclusive media system, despite their lofty rhetoric of democratic-institution building and their harsh critique of commercial culture and its undemocratic tendencies.

The Liberal's approach to culture and education reflected an authoritarian streak whose elitist nature has been described by some Colombian observers as fascistic. As Colombian anthropologist Carlos Páramo eloquently observes, this cultural vision was based on the racist mythology that poverty, vulnerability to infectious disease epidemics, and other indices of systematic oppression were not attributable to state policies, institutional racism, and capitalist forces, but supposedly arose from "the Colombian people's inability to grapple with the faulty byproducts of its mestizaje, or mixed race" (Pareja 1984, 124). It was a vision based in white supremacy that cut across political party lines, Liberal and Conservative.

To these thinkers, the crisis in the Colombian cultural environment was symptomatic of a much broader problem, one that threatened the social order and their privileged position within it. The problem was reflected in the decadence manifest in extreme commercialism and, what they viewed with tremendous and historic concern, its direct (and unacceptable) cultural offspring. They were particularly worried about interracial marriage and the threat of overt, uncontrolled sexuality it implied, which were contradictory to the logic of white supremacy, male dominance, and economic exploitation (Pareja 1984; Silva 2000). Ostensibly, those in power viewed the Radiodifusora Nacional as an important medium to rectify this crisis in Colombian culture in a period when they feared their grip on the larger national fabric was threatened. Under their watch, national state-run radio would be promoted as "a living academy" of the airwaves, as historian and researcher Renán Silva described it, "purely and broadly national" in scope, providing a line of "communication between the people and the state" (2000, 14). But in playing this "enlightening" role, the network's initial programming would reflect, on the one hand, the tremendous levels of diversity in Colombia, but on the other, the controlling state interests' need to establish and maintain hierarchies within this diversity. This would be accomplished through the widespread promotion of a homogeneous, vigilantly policed Colombian national identity. In short, state-run radio in the 1940s was integrated into the government's broader campaign to get the population to "tune into one historic moment, a homogenous moment" shared by all as part of the so-called "national unity" (Silva 2000, 14). By its nature, however, the approach was top-down, racist, and paternalistic.

After the National Front, the Consolidation of the Neoliberal Model

Over the next forty years, with the commercial/market and the public/state radio paradigms functioning alongside one another, the internal civil conflict in Colombia provided the state with the legal justification to repress the right to truly independent, free expression and access to unfiltered information (Murillo 2003; Uribe Celis 1991). Alternative and dissenting perspectives have thus been curtailed for many years—a trend that continues today. With very limited exceptions, this censorship held sway in both the commercial and public radio worlds, as well as in the country's newspaper industry. Resistance to the undemo-cratic restrictions that resulted from this media climate became the rallying cry for broadcast reform activists, intellectuals, independent journalists, and social movements. The Indigenous communities were at the forefront of the conflict as they struggled for fundamental social and political change in Colombia from the 1970s into the early 1990s. By 1991, as a result of mass mobilization on the part of many sectors demanding political reforms in the country, Colombia embarked on the cumbersome process of reforming its antiquated constitution. For the first time, Indigenous communities participated in the process.

In the 1990s, Colombian broadcasting assumed a number of characteristics that were the result of increased privatization of the economy and the general effects of globalization (Fox and Waisbord 2002). The country's most power-ful economic families lobbied the Constituent Assembly vigorously to force changes in the regulatory framework of the media industries, opening the way to even further privatization of television and radio.

Today, with the intensified competition between massive domestic and global media conglomerates for new investments, new technologies, and new audiences—fundamental characteristics of the corporate transnationalism of the twenty-first century—the power and interests of private industry have once again taken center stage. Naturally, these conglomerates wield unprecedented influence over the state, not only in relation to media regulatory policies, but also in the overall political and economic direction of the country. In this rapidly changing media and cultural environment, the exclusion of alternative spheres representing marginalized communities and oppositional perspectives remains the guaranteed norm. Nevertheless, thanks to the struggles of a broad cross section of progressive forces a generation ago, the Constitution of 1991 recog-nizes the rights of all citizens to access and disseminate information through mass-mediated communication and has opened up exciting opportunities for new grassroots citizen's media projects throughout the country (Murillo 2003). This mobilizing eventually led to the establishment of a dynamic network of community and Indigenous radio broadcasting experiments that exist today as a counterbalance to the entrenched, culturally homogenous, and exclusionary mainstream corporate commercial media.

Community Media in Indigenous Territories

The complicated regulatory measures that resulted from the new constitution had a positive impact on Colombian community broadcasters (de Greiff and Ramos 2000, 52; Geerts and van Oeyen 2001; Murillo 2003). Even with the relatively slow process of implementing these changes, the regulatory provi-sions represented an important break from a history of repression of pirate and community radio operators throughout the country (RECORRA 1999). Despite some hesitation, if not skepticism, the Indigenous movement eventually reaped the benefits of the progressive changes in communications regulations (Dorado and the Radio Payu'mat staff 2004; Unidad de Radio del Ministerio de Cultura 2000).

Today, many Indigenous communities in Colombia have their own media channels and are using them extensively for both everyday communication and during times of crisis. There are twenty-six Indigenous radio stations around the country licensed as public interest broadcasters. In addition, dozens of smaller low-power community stations broadcast in local Indigenous territories in every region of the country.[3] Their respective programming approach varies considerably from community to community, as does the level of local participation in the production, programming, and management of the stations. As one would expect, those stations linked to strong organizations tend to be more effective at reaching audiences and engaging the community than those that have been set up in places with weaker organizational structures.

On a national level, the National Indigenous Organization of Colombia (Organización Nacional Indígena de Colombia, ONIC) has its own interactive website, which includes a virtual radio station. In addition, dozens of other regional Indigenous organizations are using a variety of digital platforms—web streaming, blogs, social media—to disseminate a diverse range of cultural and social programming content. For over fifteen years, ONIC has been streaming the voices of Indigenous activists from many of the 101 officially recognized Indigenous nations, including full-length programs in the sixty-five existing Indigenous languages of Colombia. Together, these low-power, web-based, and public service licensees of these Indigenous communities have collaborated directly and indirectly in an effort to present an alternative narrative to the rest of the country and the world. In many respects, these independent media have been successful in generating support for the Indigenous movement on an international level, especially getting NGOs, international solidarity organizations, and other human-rights groups to pay attention to events in Indigenous territories. Nowhere is this multifaceted media work more evident than in the Department of Cauca, where the Indigenous movement first emerged in the southwestern region of Colombia in 1971.

The Indigenous communities that have been most successful over the years at confronting the myriad threats to their autonomy are those with the strongest organizational structures, legitimized by being in a constant dialogue with their base communities (Unidad de Radio del Ministerio de Cultura 2000). Not surprisingly, these are the same communities that continue to play the role of interlocutor with other non-Indigenous actors, be they state institutions, different social sectors like the peasant or trade union movements, and international NGOs and solidarity organizations. These Indigenous communities, like the *cabildos*, or councils, that make up CRIC and its regional affiliate, the Association of Indigenous Councils of Northern Cauca, ACIN, see their own independent media channels as essential components of their collective resistance (Murillo 2004). Their communication work springs from a long trajectory of independent grassroots community media projects that have emerged throughout Colombia over the past thirty years, which coalesced with the rewriting of the constitution in 1991 (Rodriguez 2008), as indicated earlier. But perhaps more importantly, these media are part of a continuum of a social process grounded in traditional communication practices that serve as the foundation of Indigenous organizing (Dorado and the Radio Payu'mat staff 2004). In the long run, strong organizational bases make the groups more secure, given the high levels of violence that are directed toward independent voices in Colombia and in particular Indigenous leaders. The Nasa communities of northern Cauca in particular, with their long history of mobilization in the spirit of constructing sustainable, democratic alternatives, are working strategically with these transformative communication practices.

The *Tejido de Comunicación* as a Foundation of Organizing

In this context, the concept of the *tejido*, or fabric, is important to understand. The term *tejido* not only describes ACIN's communication program—*el tejido de comunicación*, "Fabric of communication—but is the rubric that explains the structure of the Indigenous movement and its relationship to other sectors both within and outside of Colombia.[4] The use of the term *tejido* is deliberate in that it reflects a complex fabric that is weaved by many different sources, creating a dynamic, elaborate quilt whose whole can only be as strong as the sum of its many interconnected parts. That social fabric, while strengthened through the autonomous structures that the communities and the movement have erected, can only survive if it is connected to those on the outside, engaged in a broader dialogue that is multidirectional and multicultural (Espinosa Alzáte 2003; Dorado and the Radio Payu'mat staff 2004; Wilches-Chaux 2005). It is the polar opposite of the narrow, homogenous conception of Colombian nationhood that the elitist broadcasters projected during radio's early days.

Constantly expanding and fortifying the tejido is one of the primary goals of the movement. Communication—from the small family group gathered around the fire in the mountainside to the massive, high profile protest mobilizations that can go on for weeks at a time cutting through the entire national geography—facilitates the process of expanding the social fabric and strengthening the overall mission of the traditional authorities, the organization, and the many communities that make it up. The Indigenous assemblies, first on the level of the *vereda*, or neighborhood, then the *resguardo*, or reserve, all the way up to the regional congresses of CRIC, are other concrete manifestations of the tejido that is constantly "being weaved." The annual participation of Indigenous delegates to the UN Permanent Forum on the Rights of Indigenous Peoples takes the tejido onto the international stage, as do other diplomatic and solidarity efforts carried out almost daily by emissaries of the communities. The concept of the tejido is in its essence participatory and is designed to foment civic engagement on every level to promote, protect, and strengthen the life plan of the Indigenous communities (Espinosa Alzáte 2003).

Therefore, the *tejido de comunicación* is the glue that binds the overall organizing structure of ACIN, which is made up of many tejidos in a constant state of dialogue and exchange with one another on many different structural levels. The issues addressed by the different tejidos are each discussed in a multitiered, deliberative dialogue, an exchange of information that they call their "communication-action process." The process starts with information sharing amongst the members of the group and then moves into an intense period of reflection and analysis where everybody can interject their views about the situation or proposal before them. Based on the ideas that come about during the period of reflection and analysis, the members of the group carry out a deliberative decision-making process. Most often, the decision results in taking direct action. This is the basis of what they call "traditional communication," and, again, is executed at every level of the organizational structure, from the bottom up (Espinosa Alzáte 2003). Radio as a technological tool, therefore, has provided the communities with yet another space to carry out this elaborate communicative process. Its video production, website, and social media platforms allow them to expand their tejido even further.

Just as they have tejidos that deal with the environment, economic development, human rights, and justice, the *cabildos*, or councils, joined under ACIN's umbrella felt it was essential that they link all these efforts through a broader, multidimensional communication strategy that facilitates both internal and external communication with traditional as well as newer forms of mass communication. Their objective was to create a more systematic way of bridging all the work accomplished at the individual tejido level (through the traditional communication-action model) to more inclusive levels through the broadcast media now under their control. This greatly facilitates information sharing, along with reflection and analysis, leading to reasoned decision making that is a natural extension of a long tradition of grassroots, Indigenous communication.

The Indigenous movement had already established newsletters and its own newspapers dating back to the earliest stages of their organizing under the banner of CRIC. Furthermore, they had launched two community radio stations, one in the municipality of Toribio and the other in Jambaló in the mid-1990s, just as the government was beginning to regulate and issue licenses to community radio stations.

The origins of these community media projects go back to the 1980s when the local communities began considering ways to expand and promote their work in the midst of an intense wave of confrontations with powerful local landowners and persecutions by both the state security forces and paramilitary militias. When the government began soliciting licenses for community radio stations in 1995, the cabildo of Jambaló put in a proposal, seeing it as a natural extension of their communication strategy. They finally received the license in 1997, along with the hundreds of other community organizations in municipalities throughout the country, and went on the air for the first time a year later (Unidad de Radio del Ministerio de Cultura 2000).[5] Today, Voces de Nuestra Tierra, which means "voices of our land," continues to broadcast important community programming on its 250-watt transmitter from its small studios located in the middle of a steep road on the edge of Jambaló, overlooking the scenic mountainside. Its staff proudly points to its news and information content as its strongest asset. There is a core of highly skilled Indigenous reporters and announcers who produce in-depth newscasts throughout the program day, distributing much of their content to the other stations of ACIN as well as to the rest of the informal radio network broadcasting to Indigenous communities throughout Cauca.

Radio Nasa in Toribio started transmitting even earlier as a community radio station, in 1995. For years, the station broadcast under the mandate of the cabildo as part of the internationally acclaimed Proyecto Nasa, the Nasa Project, but without a license. This made them one of the most visible pirate stations in the country, especially during times of intense conflict when, on several occasions, rebels of the Revolutionary Armed Forces of Colombia, or FARC, and government troops clashed in the center of the municipality. There was some debate within the cabildo whether it was even necessary to solicit a license from the government, based on the principles of autonomy spelled out in the 1991 constitution and the rights of Indigenous communities to access the resources on their territories. Like many other media activists around the world, the leadership perceived the airwaves to be a natural resource that belonged to the people. They felt the cabildo was the most qualified entity to establish a station that would serve the public interest and did not need to get "permission" from government bureaucrats in Bogotá who were completely detached from the needs of the community.[6] Eventually, the cabildo did apply for a license, but was turned down in the first wave of solicitations. During this time the station was shut down repeatedly by the Ministry of Communications, drawing the ire of the community. People saw the clampdown as political in nature, given the community's constant criticism of the presence of government forces on their territories. Radio Nasa had clearly satisfied all the technical and administrative requirements that Colombian regulatory measures called for in community radio licensees, but because they had been rejected in the first round of solicitations, they were considered to be operating illegally. Eventually, the station was granted a license during the second wave of community radio license solicitations that was initiated in 2005 by the Ministry of Communications. By then, ACIN's largest radio project, Radio Payu'mat, had already been on the air for three years as a Public Interest licensee. *Payu'mat* is the Nasa Uwe term meaning "welcome, you're at home." The tejido chose that as their name in order to make everyone in the community feel a sense of ownership for the station. Radio Payu'mat started broadcasting in 2002 from its offices and studios in Santander de Quilichao, the second largest city in Cauca, serving the northern reaches of the department with its large Indigenous and Afro-Colombian population. Unlike the other two low-power stations mentioned, as a public interest licensee, Radio Payu'mat has a much larger signal reach. The station, and twenty-five other Indigenous stations like it established around the country, was part of the Ministry of Culture and the Ministry of Communication's so-called Programa Comunidad Señal de Cultura y Diversidad (Community program for culture and diversity) which was a project carried out in collaboration with the National Development Fund (FONADE) in the late 1990s to provide radio stations to Indigenous and Afro-Colombian communities.

Radio is not the only community media that is being produced by the different cabildos that make up ACIN. There is widespread use of video cameras to document a whole array of developments taking place in the communities. ACIN has produced a number of short- and long-form videos, which, along with CRIC-produced documentaries, serve as the primary content for their so-called *cineforos*, or video forums, organized in veredas all over the region. The film screenings are a great way to bring people together in the most remote areas and open up discussions about everything from violations of the rights of Indigenous people to the construction of mega-projects in Indigenous territories and the resulting displacement they will potentially cause. These video screenings continue to be promoted and announced on the community radio stations in the territory in order to guarantee attendance and mobilize audiences in the very remote areas.

Conclusion

The Indigenous communities of Colombia are using radio, as well as video, the internet, and social media, to promote their own cultural identity and community values, very often in direct contradiction to the centralist, top-down mandates of the dominant political and social classes. In this way, Indigenous radio is a form of resistance to colonization (whether by the government or its transnational partners), and, by extension, the forced imposition of a national consciousness shaped, in the Indigenous movement's view, by rampant materialism, environmental destruction, militarism, greed, and corruption. But Indigenous media channels are not insular nor designed to cut the community off from the rest of Colombian society. This, however, is contrary to views expressed regularly in mainstream media accounts of Indigenous protest mobilizations and direct actions that news reporters—citing public officials and so-called independent experts—are quick to characterize as primarily "indigenist" in scope, meaning the emphasis is on the Indigenous leadership's priorities vis-à-vis the needs and concerns of the rest of the Colombian people (Convenio Unión Europea / Universidad del Valle 2004; Murillo 2009). This characterization of "the other" negates the Indigenous movement's insistence on being a part of a national, broad-based, multicultural alliance for social change. The push for Indigenous autonomy has never been a reflection of the movement's desire to separate itself from the Colombian nation, but rather demonstrates its insistence on mutual respect and recognition in order to be an active partner in the construction of the nation.

Furthermore, the Indigenous movement's alternative view of resistance articulated in their high profile protests, their media channels, and their outspoken leadership is shared by many other segments of the popular movement in Colombia, including the public sector trade unions, displaced peasant farmers, Afro-Colombian sugar cane workers, and vast numbers of the urban and rural poor. In covering the shared experiences of all these sectors from an Indigenous perspective, the programmers of Indigenous radio, such as the staff of Radio Payu'mat and the entire tejido de comunicación, fulfil its two principal objectives designed to reflect and advance the broader Indigenous movement. First, ACIN's media arm provides a viable public sphere that promotes dialogue between the community base, the local Indigenous authorities, and ACIN's leadership regarding the issues affecting people within their territory. Second, Indigenous media offer a genuine alternative for a broad cross-section of Colombians who are also committed to confronting harmful conceptions of nationhood, development, and security embraced by the dominant culture and promoted for years by the mass commercial media.

As I described earlier, radio, like the press, evolved as an instrument of influence and control in the country. Radio remains a steadfast gatekeeper for the dominant public sphere and all its consumer-based, commercial cultural trappings, thereby consistently excluding truly dissenting voices. At the same time, notwithstanding these very closed structures, there is a rich tradition of alternative media in Colombia resisting the top-down nature of the major media institutions. The communication tejido of ACIN, therefore, can be seen as one very important manifestation of a convergence of the dissenting traditions of media democracy and social justice activism. Just as they are organically part of a broad-based social movement, they are also linked to a long line of grassroots communication activists, scholars, and practitioners who see the right to create, impart, and receive information as a necessary precondition to social and political transformation. What makes the development of Colombia's radio institutions relevant within the context of understanding the emergence of contemporary Indigenous radio is that the new Indigenous radio stations represent a complete departure from the early notion of creating a unified national identity. Their existence today is ample recognition that Colombia is a multicultural, pluriethnic society that needs to reject once and for all the faulty notion of Colombia as a homogenous, primarily European entity. Indeed, as Colombia's political and social spaces have opened up over the last twenty-five years, its radio industry has finally come full circle.

Notes

1. For more details about the Nilo massacre and the many protests and arrangements made between the Huellas community and the government, see Corporación Colectivo de Abogados "José Alvear Restrepo" (CCAJAR), "IACHR Meets Privately with the ACIN to Follow Up on the Case of the 'El Nilo' Massacre," Oct. 28, 2008 (*colectivodeabogados.org/IACHR-MEETS-PRIVATELY-WITH-THE*). Also see "Second Report on the Situation of Human Rights in Colombia, Inter-Am. C.H.R., OEA/Ser.L/V/II.84, Doc. 39 rev. (1993)," University of Minnesota Human Rights Library (*hrlibrary.umn.edu/iachr/country-reports/colombia1993.html*).
2. The future direction of radio was also the subject of discussion within the cultural and intellectual elite. One minister referred to the emerging commercial stations as "vehicles of verbal trash" that were being wasted in promoting "endless forms of gibberish, storefront folk music and non-stop rumors" (Silva 2000, 13). A newspaper editorial attacked radio as "the imbecile invention of the devil that fills the house with cheap announcements, old songs, and tasteless jokes" (*El Tiempo*, March 24, 1934).
3. Prior to the establishment of the Indigenous public interest and community radio stations, the National Indigenous Organization of Colombia, ONIC, produced a weekly radio magazine that was broadcast over the Radiodifusora Nacional in the early 1990s. CRIC also produced a radio show that aired on the university station in Popayán. Other Indigenous communities produced similar programs—usually weekly, half-hour magazines—that also aired on local university stations. However, there was never one broadcast station dedicated explicitly to Indigenous concerns and worldviews, programmed and controlled exclusively by the traditional authorities, and licensed officially by the state. Radio Nasa in Toribio began

broadcasting in 1995 as a pirate station, and Voces de Nuestra Tierra in Jambaló a year later.

4. The word tejido is translated as "fabric" or "textile," as well as "weave" and "tissue." To *tejer* is to weave or spin a fabric (*The New World Spanish/English, English/Spanish Dictionary*, 2nd ed. [1996]). The metaphor looks at every member of the community as a *tejedor*, or a weaver, someone willing to work to expand the fabric. The *tejido* is weaved from within the community but also with outside sectors as well, the idea being the social fabric will be stronger, more intricate and dynamic, when it is being weaved from many different sources. It is not exclusionary in nature, because both Indigenous and non-Indigenous people can play a role of weaver, although some communities have been less open to outsiders playing a direct role. An excellent text that addresses the complexities of the intercultural communication and collaboration that goes on daily within the Indigenous movement is Rapaport 2005.

5. The decision to apply for a license came from an assembly of the cabildo of Jambaló, which, after a period of discussion and deliberation about the idea, voted in favor of the project. The station programming is produced and carried out by representatives of the many different working groups that make up the Proyecto Global, including health, education, legal, and human rights issues, and culture. The cabildo maintains regular assemblies of "analysis and discussion" regarding the programming on the station, a process of permanent "evaluation and consultation" with the communities that they represent. (Unidad de Radio del Ministerio de Cultura 2000).

6. From author interviews with Leonardo Jurado, director of Radio Nasa, August 8, 2005, in Toribio, Cauca, and Ezekiel Vitonás, chief counsel of ACIN, May 2005, New York City.

References

Amnesty International. 1992. *The Americas: Human Rights Violations against Indigenous Peoples*. New York: Amnesty International USA.

Bergquist, C., R. Peñaranda, and G. Sánchez, eds. 1992. *Violence in Colombia: The Contemporary Crisis in Historical Perspective*. Wilmington, DE: SR Books.

Caldón, J. 2005. "Los indígenas y el conflicto armado en Colombia: A propósito de las acciones bélicas del as FARC en Toribío, Caldono y Jambaló." *Etnias y política* (1): 26–34.

Convenio Unión Europea / Universidad del Valle. 2004. *En Minga con los pueblos indígenas y por el derecho a su palabra: Monitoreo de medios de comunicación masiva*. Cali, Colombia: Convenio Unión Europea / Universidad del Valle.

Croteau, D., and W. Hoynes. 2001. *The Business of Media: Corporate Media and the Public Interest*. Oakland, CA: Pine Forge Press.

de Greiff, M., and C. Ramos. 2000. *Regimen jurídico de radio y televisión en Colombia*. Bogotá: Legis Editores, S.A.

Dorado, M., and the Radio Payu'mat staff. 2004. "Radio Payu'mat: Una experiencia de comunicacion en la zona norte del Cauca." PhD diss., Universidad Pontificia Bolivariana, Anthropology Institute.

Espinosa Alzáte, R. 2003. *El gobierno comunitario de los territorios indígenas del norte del Cauca Colombiano: Descentralización o autonomía.* Cauca, Colombia: ACIN-CODCOP.

Fox, E. 1997. *Latin American Broadcasting: From Tango to Telenovela.* Bedfordshire, UK: University of Luton Press.

Fox, E., and S. Waisbord, eds. 2002. *Latin Politics, Global Media.* Austin: University of Texas Press.

Galeano Lozano, M. 2005. *Resistencia indígena en el Cauca: Labrando otro mundo.* CRIC-InterTeam, Popayán, Colombia.

Geerts, A., and van Oeyen, V. 2001. *La radio popular frente al nuevo siglo: Estudio de vigencia e incidencia.* Quito, Ecuador: ALER, Associacíon Latinoamericana de Educación Radiofónica.

Gumucio Dagron, A. 2001. *Haciendo olas: Historias de comunicación participativa para el cambio social.* New York: Rockefeller Foundation.

Laurent, V. 2005. *Comunidades indígenas, espacios politicos y movilización electoral en Colombia, 1990–1998.* Bogotá: ICANH/IFEA.

López de la Roche, F. 2001. "Medios de comunicación y movimientos sociales: Incomprensiones y desencuentros." In *Movimientos sociales, estado y democracia en Colombia*, edited by M. Archila and M. Pardo, 475–94. Bogota: Centro de Estudios Sociales, Universidad Nacional de Colombia.

McChesney, R. 1999. *Rich Media, Poor Democracy: Communication Politics in Dubious Times.* Urbana: University of Illinois Press.

Molano, A. 1991. "Violence and Land Colonization." In *Violence in Colombia: The Contemporary Crisis in Historical Perspective*, edited by C. Berquist, R. Peñaranda, and G. Sánchez, 195–216. Wilmington, DE: SR Books.

Mondragón, H. 2005. "Disuasión y corrosion: La política del gobierno de Álvaro Uribe Vélez para los pueblos indígenas." *Etnias y política* 1: 15–26.

Murillo, M. 2003. "Community Radio in Colombia: Civil Conflict, Popular Media and the Construction of a Public Sphere." *Journal of Radio Studies* 10 (1): 120–40.

———. 2004. *Colombia and the United States: War, Unrest, and Destabilization.* New York: Seven Stories Press.

———. 2009. "The 2008 Indigenous and Popular Minga in Colombia: Civil Resistance and Alternative Communication Practices." *Socialism and Democracy* 23 (3): 137–56.

Pareja, R. 1984. *Historia de la radio en Colombia, 1929–1980.* Bogotá: Servicio Colombiano De Comunicación Social.

Pérez Angel, G. 1998. *La radio del tercer milenio: Caracol 50 años.* Bogotá: Editorial Nomos, S.A.

Proyecto Antonio Nariño. 2004. *Calidad informativa y cubrimiento del conflicto: Estándares de calidad periodística en el cubrimiento del conflicto armado en Colombia.* Bogotá: NED

Rappaport, J. 2005. *Intercultural Utopias: Public Intellectuals, Cultural Experimentation, and Ethnic Pluralism in Colombia.* Durham, NC: Duke University Press.

RECORRA [Red Colombiana de Radios Comunitarias]. 1999. *Memorias: IV encuentro nacional de radios comunitarias.* Bogota: Ministro de Cultura.

Rodriguez, C., ed. 2008. *Lo que le vamos quitando a la Guerra: Medios ciudadanos en contextos de conflicto armado en Colombia.* Bogotá: Centro de Competencia en Comunicación para América Latina.

Sanchez, G. 1992. "The Violence: An Interpretive Synthesis." In *Violence in Colombia: The Contemporary Crisis in Historical Perspective*, edited by C. Berquist, R. Peñaranda, and G. Sánchez, 75–123. Wilmington, DE: SR Books.

Silva, R. 2000. "Ondas nacionales: La política cultural de la República Liberal y la Radiodifusora Nacional de Colombia." *Análisis político, Instituto de Estudios Políticos y Relaciones Internacionales, Universidad Nacional de Colombia* 41 (Sept./Dec.): 3–22.

Uribe Celis, C. 1991. *Democracia y medios de comunicación*. Bogotá: Ediciones Foro Nacional.

Unidad de Radio del Ministerio de Cultura. 2000. *Memorias: Radios y pueblos indígenas – Encuentro Internacional de Radios Indígenas de America*. Bogotá: Ministro de Cultura.

Villa, W., and J. Houghton. 2005. *Violencia política contra los pueblos indígenas en Colombia: 1974–2004*. Bogotá, CECOIN.

Waisbord, S. 2002. "Grandes Gigantes: Media Concentration in Latin America." openDemocracy website (February 27), *www.opendemocracy.net/media-globalmediaownership/article_64.jsp*.

Wilches-Chaux, G. 2005. *Proyecto Nasa: La construcción del plan de vida de un pueblo que sueña*. Bogotá: UNDP.

8

The Shaman and the Flash Drive

By Guilherme Orlandini Heurich

One lazy afternoon in Paratatsɨ, the Araweté village where I conducted most of my fieldwork, I was lying in my hammock trying to organize my field notes when Matadzɨ, my next door neighbor, came into the house and asked me if she could listen to some songs on my radio. While we sat there and listened to the words of a deceased woman sung through the voice of a shaman, Jaka, a young man, arrived carrying his baby and joined us. A few minutes later, Matadzɨ's grandmother came in to drink some of the coffee I had prepared, and, when she was about to leave, her granddaughter told her about a part of that song in which the dead woman complained about her husband, who was still alive—the grandmother sat down to wait for it to come round. Soon after, another couple came by to drink some of my coffee and were also convinced by Matadzɨ to wait and listen to the now almost-famous bit of music. The seven of us sat there and waited for over an hour for the part in which a deceased wife complained that her husband was gossiping with other women. It was only one line, which went "Can you see that he is whispering in her ears?" The audience laughed heartily and after a few more sips of coffee, left. Matadzɨ then turned off the radio, smiled at me, and also left.

There were only a couple of small battery-powered radios with USB ports when I arrived at the Araweté for the first time in 2011, and the ones they had usually just played regional Brazilian music styles such as *brega* and *melody*, and other romantic songs. One day a few months after I arrived, while bathing in the river, a young Araweté man named Majoro and I came up with the idea to transfer some of the recordings I had made of shamanic songs to one of my flash drives,[1] which we inserted into one of these radios and listened to a couple of times in the small shed I occupied at the time. He left with the flash drive, which he played on his radio several times over the next few days, attracting a lot of attention from others in the village. A little more than a week later I woke up at dawn with someone banging at my door shouting "Diréme, wake up! Let's put the shaman in the flash drive!" Unfortunately, I had to leave the field that same month due to a serious illness. On my return, four months later, instead of two radios and three flash drives, there were now thirty-one radios and some fifty flash drives in the village, and I spent much of the next few months transferring files from one flash drive to the other in order to meet the Araweté's desire to listen to their songs.[2]

The Araweté are four hundred maize cultivators and hunters who live in eastern Amazonia in seven villages in the Brazilian state of Pará. They have been in contact with Brazilian government representatives since the late 1970s, and most of them currently speak Portuguese even though they only communicate with each other in Araweté, a Tupi-Guarani language.[3] Araweté music is primarily vocal with rare instrumentals, and their songs are divided into two main genres—*opurahẽ me'e* and *oñiñã me'e*—with different poetic forms. While the *opurahẽ me'e* are linked to warfare, "danced" (*opurahẽ*) in a courtyard, and structured by specific formulaic expressions, the *oñiñã me'e* are linked to shamanism, presented (but not danced) in a courtyard, and structured through refrains. The *oñiñã me'e*, which I translate as songs "that sing," present the words of deceased Araweté through the shaman's voice.[4] A shaman travels to the land of the *Mai*—the gods the dead live with and eventually become—and brings back one or more deceased relatives to sing among the living. In these songs, the dead describe their arrival in the *Mai*'s domain and how they were treated by the cannibal-gods, including how they were devoured by them and remade, taking new spouses and forming new families. One of the axioms of Araweté shamanism is that a shaman can only bring back a deceased woman or man to sing whom he knew in life, and because the shamans that knew him or her will themselves die one day, that deceased person will eventually no longer be able to sing. Briefly, the existence of the dead *qua* music is directly related to the living shamans' collective memory. This is an important aspect of Araweté shamanism that I will come back to further ahead.

A song starts with the shaman still in his hammock, at night or at the break of dawn. At the beginning he only sings the chorus or refrain, that is, the bit of music that he repeats after each verse. After a while, his wife hands him his rattle. With the rattle in his hands he slowly moves out of the hammock, crouches on the floor and sings in this position for a few minutes. He then leaves his house and sings in his patio for a long time, sometimes between two to two and half hours. If this happens during a festival or ritual ceremony the singing may last even longer, and if the deceased person who sings through the shaman's voice happens to mention one of the villagers, the shaman, led by his wife, walks slowly toward that person's house. His wife waits for him and brings him back home to his hammock at the end. It is important to note that a shaman will only sing each song once and no other shamans will reproduce a song after its original execution.

When a shaman brings a deceased person to sing, the *Mai*-gods always follow his journey even though their words can only be heard when the dead quote them. The living never hear the gods' words directly, but only through a complex chain of citations that include one or several deceased and are uttered by the shaman. Anyone can record a shaman's song as long as he or she does not cross his path toward the patio or back to the house. Crossing a shaman's path might have deleterious effects because it enrages the gods, who might knock the shaman down to the floor—he might not recover from the fall, remaining with the gods and abandoning his living body. Another precaution that one must take while recording these songs is to avoid overlapping one's shadow with that of the shaman, as it can also knock him down.

The Araweté have recorded their shamans' songs for some time now. Thirty years ago, a small number of Araweté were given tape recorders, at their request, by Eduardo Viveiros de Castro and representatives of the Brazilian National Indian Foundation (FUNAI). At the beginning of the 2000s, a few Araweté leaders also purchased some digital recorders, but they didn't do this to obtain more storage for songs—this is not an issue since the production of songs is constant, with the shamans singing weekly (some of them even daily) and due to the Araweté's great interest in the latest release. Of course, some of them have their favorite songs, but they have no great problem with overwriting old songs with new ones. In the past five years, there has been a significant increase in the number of active shamans among the Araweté, and during the same time there has also been a surge in the number of flash drive radios. The Araweté acknowledge the relationship between the increase in the number of radios playing the shamanic songs and the increase in the number of shamans. However, interestingly enough, they say that it is not enough to listen to other shamans to become a shaman. For that, one needs to smoke a lot of tobacco, and so it is tobacco—not the flash drives—that has led to the sudden increase in the number of shamans, which jumped from five in the middle of 2011 to some twenty-two at the beginning of 2013.

Carriers and Doubles

It seems difficult to talk about verbal art and shamanism without referring to notions such as body or double in Amazonia, where bodies seem to be transitional, provisional, or "unstable," in Aparecida Vilaça's (2005) words, and require a whole lot of work to become more permanent, definitive, and stable. There is usually something attached or related to this body, something most frequently called a soul, spirit, or double. Songs require a medium to circulate, and, among the Araweté, this function is served by the *hiro*, a word that can be used to describe a house, a bottle, a canoe, or a person's body, and can be translated as "container" but also as "carrier," which better communicates the idea of movement that is so important in Amazonian shamanism (Hugh-Jones 1996). By translating *hiro* as "carrier," we broaden our scope and can include other objects and subjects as potential things that move other persons and things around, such as the shaman's rattle and the shamans themselves, but also the *tocaia* (a large palm tree leaf structure used for hunting small animals and birds), body paints, and earrings. The Araweté use the red annatto dye to paint their bodies and put feather earrings shaped like flowers in their ears in order to "become-gods." However, they also advise caution with this practice, for the use of ornamentation can take us to the gods' world, from where it might not be easy to return. As such, feather ornaments and body paints are much more similar to canoes and rattles than one would think: these are all objects that share in the capacity to move subjects and objects. The question that remains is if the "carrier" moves things and persons around, what exactly are they moving?

The relationship that a shaman develops with the *Mai*-gods over the years has a primary objective, which is to bring the dead to sing among the living. In this moment, the shaman "carries" (*-ereka*) the dead just as a mother carries a child, but it is also an action usually marked with a suffix that indicates reciprocity, which is why the deceased singer will describe it as an action that they perform, rather than the shaman. In the morning following a shaman's singing, people will wonder about who the shaman brought to sing the night before by asking "whose music was it?" or "whose double sang yesterday?" There is a strict connection here between someone's "music" (*marakã*) and his or her "double" (*a'owe*), and both can be carried by a shaman and brought to sing.

Moinayoro's double singing in Jakamitoro's voice:

Te ku he pue nerereka'i herajime'i
Didn't I tell you when I carried you, son-in-law?
Te ku he pue Mai depe puku ropy nerereka'i herajime'i
Didn't I tell you while carrying you through Mai's big path, son-in-law?

In this brief passage, a deceased man recollects what he said to his son-in-law, who is also a shaman, when they were travelling in the land of the gods and while they walked the "big path" (*depe puku*) that leads to that world. What is carried is his son-in-law's *a'owe* or "double," a portion of the living person that travelled to the gods after death: a "double" that can no longer have a body or that is no longer defined by its relationship with a body. While a person is still alive, the notion of *a'owe* designates his or her shadow, which reaffirms the relationship between body and spirit or, in the Araweté case, between "carrier" and "double." A deceased person's "double," then, is something that shamans and their rattles carry, and most importantly it is something that reveals itself as music: it is that which shamans can "make sing." From the point of view of the living, the dead have little left to do in their "life" but sing.

Only the Dead Can Sing on the Radio

After the flash drive incident I asked Eduardo Viveiros de Castro for his recordings of Araweté songs from the 1980s and permission to digitalize them.
I transferred the songs onto flash drives and gave these as gifts to the Araweté
—they seemed so interested in listening to recent songs that I thought they
would enjoy listening to old shamans, even though some of them are still singing today. They did enjoy it, but something else also happened. Apart from
the songs themselves, there were also recordings of conversations between the
anthropologist and some Araweté. One of these conversations was with the
late Meñano, the oldest Araweté to make contact with non-Indians, and in
the recording he explains how the world came to be as it is now, how the god
Aranamĩ abandoned the Araweté and left to create the upper layer of the cos-
mos where the gods now live. The Araweté enjoyed listening to Meñano talking
and were also interested in everything else that was going on in the soundscape
that surrounded him, such as dogs barking and people whispering, but there
was another recording of a conversation with Ceará, which the Araweté advised
me not to copy onto anyone's flash drive. I complied, of course, but couldn't
help wondering why. Was it because of what he was saying? Was there, perhaps,
something inappropriate in his words? Or, maybe the people advising me just
didn't like him and didn't want his voice to be reproduced? The answer I received to my queries was quite different. My Araweté interlocutors said that I
should not "put him in the flash drive" because he was not yet dead.

There is a triangulation, here, to be observed between body, radio, and
voice: a person should not have his or her voice reproduced while they are
alive, they should not be put inside a radio because they still have a body. This
means that a dead person's voice is a voice without a body and that a radio is
like a body, which carries the voice of the dead.[5] The issue at hand is the kind
of relationship that enables the reproduction of a voice and how it is produced
between the shaman and the voices that he carries: a relationship that produces
two subjects—the carrier and the carried—both of them dead, though in different ways. Several works have emphasized the deadly aspect of shamanism in
Amazonia, that is, that being a shaman is a way of dying (Viveiros de Castro
1992; Vilaça 2005). A shaman, then, is dead, as are those that he carries with
him and brings to sing, the deceased Araweté. As such, carrying voices necessarily involves carrying the dead's voices. To reproduce a voice, as the shaman
does when he utters a deceased relative's voice or as the radio does with the conversations of deceased relatives, is to be a body that carries a voice. Conversely,
the voice of the living can only be uttered by themselves, or, in other words,
should not be carried by someone or something else.

Some Araweté shamans also commented on their performance to Eduardo

Viveiros de Castro (1992, 224), and a phrase used by one shaman at the time has become quite famous in Amerindian ethnology: "Shamans are like radios," he stated, in order to explain that the words sung by the shamans are not their own. What I have been trying to do here, in a way, is to explore the idea that a radio is like a shaman. I have mentioned how both are carriers of other's voices and that shamanic reproduction and mechanical reproduction are acts of quoting. A radio is a body with a voice other than its own, and in this sense it seems very similar to a shaman's performance. However, it is precisely the performative act that is missing from the mechanical reproduction of Araweté songs.

Radio, Context, Quote: Echoes

I have dealt with the possible connection between radios and shamans as means of carrying voices or doubles, that is, as bodily forms, an approach that does not concern discourse in its strictest sense, even though it hinges on it. However, there is another characteristic of the flash drive radios that resembles certain verbal actions among the Araweté that are pervasive and discursive—namely, their quoting practices. Could it be that a radio quotes people? What sort of mechanism defines the act of quoting? What does it mean to quote someone else's exact words? And could the mechanical reproduction of sounds resemble that mechanism in any way?

The Araweté use direct speech in quotes on a daily basis, in hunting narratives, news from other villages, and reports of what other people have said, as well as in every genre of Araweté verbal art. There is a direct speech marker in the Araweté language, the *iku/*, which is used in a sentence to indicate that the words that came immediately before it are a quotation—one can say that the *iku* marker "closes" a quotation. It is used both in everyday and ritual language and is characteristic of several Amerindian languages. This marker also makes it possible to place a quotation inside another quotation through its simple repetition. For instance, when someone asks about what someone else has said, one can reply: "xxxx iku wĩ" (xxxx he/she/they said), or, when the respondent has heard that piece of information from another person, she may say, "xxxx iku wĩ iku wĩ." In the following example, the person replying is thus creating a chain of quotations by placing "I will go" within another quote.

Me'e pu ku wĩ?[6]
- What did he say?
He aha iku wĩ iku wĩ.[7]
- " 'I will go,' he said," he said.

Context is an important issue in the study of reported speech, or, more precisely, the difference between the context in which a sentence is first uttered and the context in which that particular sentence is quoted is important.[8] There is an underlying premise that the person quoted and the person uttering the quote are not in the same context, or at least that there is a time lapse between the original sentence and the quotation. Context in quoting has been dealt with by Joel Sherzer in his work among the Kuna, particularly in relation to the *arkar* or "interpreter." In that ethnographic setting, whenever there is a speech at the gathering house, the *arkar* is responsible for explaining the speech to the audience since the speaker's discourse frequently draws on specialist language, which that is not shared by everyone and thus requires interpretation and translation (Sherzer 1981). The author thus suggests that the *arkar* interpretations are a form of meta-communication and that quoting is the main example of this metacommunication.[9] Sherzer argues that embedding quotes is a communicative form that has two consequences. The first is to make discourse ambiguous, that is, to make it purposefully harder to identify who is actually speaking. The second effect is to avoid confrontation, thus maintaining the Kuna ideal of nonviolent behavior.

Among the Araweté, the same mechanism that creates a chain of quotes in daily conversations occurs in songs uttered by their shamans. A deceased person quotes another deceased person's quote of what the gods said, and this chain of quotations is uttered by the shaman when he sings. Actually, what the shaman sings is never his own words or the god's words but always what a deceased person is saying. In other words, the shaman is always quoting someone. Some of the Araweté shamans I talked to emphasized how they were not even there during their performances, how they could not remember any of the words they sang and, consequently, could not comment on them. The shamans' interpretations of their own performances inverts the traditional way of posing the time gap question in quoting. Usually, we assume that the absent person in a quoted sentence is the one who said those words, but, if we follow the shamans' interpretations of their own performances, we find a situation in which the absent person is not the one being quoted—for those are the deceased, who have been brought to sing—but the utterer: the shaman, the one whose visible body we can see and whose voice we hear. A shaman's body during a performance, then, is a body with a voice but no presence.

Permanence and Impermanence

An important aspect of Araweté shamanism is that it makes visible the relationship between living and deceased kin. A lot has been written in Amerindian ethnology on the relationship between the living and the dead, particularly since Jules Henry's (1941) work on the Xokleng and Claude Lévi-Strauss's (1955) work on the Bororo, and also since the works of Helene Clastres (1968) and Pierre Clastres and Lucien Sebag (1964). One fundamental work on the subject is Manuela Carneiro da Cunha's (1978) take on Kraho eschatology, in which she argues that there is a fundamental antagonism between the living and the dead: the dead are enemies and there is no room for any sort of ancestor cult. Recent works on the subject insist that the living must sever their relationships with the deceased in many forms: by not pronouncing their names (Conklin 1995) or by "eras[ing] any trace of the dead" (Albert 1988). In other words, every single trace that connects a dead person to its living relatives must be removed, erased, forgotten.

It seems to me that this emphasis on the relationship between the dead and the living appears in the Araweté's verbal arts, and the consequence is that music and death are frequently linked. Mechanical reproduction is not the only means of song reproduction among the Araweté: women sing shamanic songs while weaving their cotton skirts, little girls sing them in groups of five or six while playing and reproduce the shaman's body movements, and grown men sing war songs to put their babies to sleep. One might say that these reproductions are echoes of the shaman's unique utterance of a song. However, this does not mean that these reproductions are any less significant. The creation of an echo is an important aspect of female action during the performance of shamanic songs. When a shaman returns to his house after singing, he lays in his hammock and his wife takes the rattle from his hand. He then utters two or three more verses *a cappella*, verses that his wife repeats without the melodic line that characterizes a shaman's singing. This repetition has a very specific function: it aims to "calm" the dead and make them return with the gods. In other words, it prevents the dead from wanting to stay here and eases them into forgetting the living. The Araweté say that the dead have a hard time forgetting us, which is why they keep asking the shamans to bring them here to sing and visit their living relatives who they miss and want to see one more time.

Forgetting is also of some importance here because of the need to make the dead forget the living and go live among the gods, and the echo of a shaman's song is, precisely, a way of making them go back to the gods' domain, where they will eventually forget about the living. As I stated earlier, the disappearance of a deceased person's voice is directly related to the collective memory of living shamans, since a shaman can only carry the dead that he once knew, and thus one aspect or dimension of forgetting among the Araweté seems to be linked with the shaman's collective memory of those he once knew.

Araweté songs always present the deceased's words, and, thus, these words have always been present among them, but mechanical reproduction poses some interesting questions. What happens when the dead can sing forever?

Unfortunately, I do not have the answer to this question at the moment, but I feel it is important to speculate on some possibilities here. As mentioned earlier, music storage is not a problem for the Araweté, because they are keen on the newest releases and not so much on old classics. It is possible that this desire for the new might reveal the inner workings of a forgetting mechanism, which I hope to have demonstrated in relation to Araweté verbal art, and thus the long-deceased might just fade into their desire for the newest songs. A second possibility is the Araweté's interest in the soundscape surrounding old recordings, which shows that they are not only interested in the songs but also in the other sounds that appear in the recordings.

A shaman will eventually die and with him dies the possibility to "make sing" those relatives he once knew. In other words, a shaman's body cannot vocalize songs forever. Compared to a shaman's body, a radio can last a long time and carries the words of the dead regardless of whether it knew them or not. It is as if the radio has a perfect memory and the capacity to remember a lot more than a shaman, but no capacity to bring the recently deceased to sing, though its echoes of their songs might also help them to forget the living. Since a flash drive radio can carry the voices of dead people long forgotten, what happens when the living hear the words of people their shamans can no longer bring to sing? I hope that future research will elucidate this question.

Notes

1. "Flash drive" is a USB data storage device. It is known by several different names, such as data stick, key drive, pen drive, thumb drive, or USB memory stick.
2. My research colleague Camila de Caux had a similar experience. See Caux (2015).
3. I conducted thirteen months of fieldwork among the Araweté between 2011 and 2014 and returned briefly in March 2015. My research involves the anthropological analysis of their musical genres, focusing mainly on the relationship between music, death, and forgetting.
4. o-ñĩñã-me'e
   3–to sing–NMLZ
   "singer(s) / that sing(s)"
5. Or, maybe, it means that a deceased's double is a body in itself.
6. Me'e pu ku wĩ?
      What INT FOC he/they
      What did he say?
7. He aha iku wĩ iku wĩ.
      I to go RS he/they RS he/they
      "'I will go,' he said," he said.
8. See, for example, Michael's (2001) discussion of the works of Voloshinov, Bakthin, and Tanner, where contextual difference is a core issue, particularly for Tanner.
9. "The retelling way of reporting is characteristic of a range of Kuna contexts, from the

most everyday to the most ritual and ceremonial. Discourse of all kinds is heavily embedded with speech that has previously occurred, typically in the form of first person direct quotations. . . . And direct quotations are often embedded within direct quotations" (Sherzer 1981, 6–7).

References

Albert, B. 1988. "Temps du sang, temps des cendres: Représentation de la maladie, système rituel et espace politique chez les Yanomami du sud-est (Amazonie brésilienne)." PhD diss., Université Paris Nanterre.

Carneiro Da Cunha, M. 1978. *Os mortos e os outros*. São Paulo: Hucitec.

Caux, C. 2015. "O riso indiscreto: Couvade e abertura corporal entre os Araweté." PhD diss., Programa de Pós-Graduação em Antropologia Social do Museu Nacional, Universidade Federal do Rio de Janeiro.

Clastres, H. 1968. "Rites funéraires Guayaki." *Journal de la societé des américanistes* 57: 63–72.

Clastres, P., and L. Sebag. 1964. "Cannibalisme et mort chez les Guayakis (Achén)." *Revista do Museu Paulista* (14): 174–71.

Conklin, B. 1995. "'Thus Are Our Bodies, Thus Was Our Custom': Mortuary Cannibalism in an Amazonian Society." *American Ethnologist* 22 (1): 75–101.

Henry, J. 1941. *Jungle People: A Kaingang Tribe of the Highlands of Brazil*. New York: J. J. Augustin.

Hugh-Jones, S. 1996. "Shamans, Prophets, Priests and Pastors." In *Shamanism, History and the State*, edited by N. Thomas and C. Humphrey, 32–75. Ann Arbor: University of Michigan Press.

Lévi-Strauss, C. 1955. *Tristes tropiques*. Paris: Plon.

Michael, L. 2001. "*Ari ixanti*: Speech Reporting Practices among the Nanti of the Peruvian Amazon." PhD diss., University of Texas, Austin.

Sherzer, J. 1981. "Tellings, Retellings, and Tellings within Tellings: The Structuring and Organization of Narrative in Kuna Indian Discourse." Sociolinguistic Working Paper Number 83. Austin, TX: Southwest Educational Development Laboratory.

Vilaça, A. 2005. "Chronically Unstable Bodies." *Journal of the Royal Anthropological Institute* 11 (3): 445–64.

Viveiros de Castro, E. 1992. *From the Enemy's Point of View*. Chicago: University of Chicago Press.

9

Kawaiwete Perspectives on the Role of Photography in State Projects to Colonize the Brazilian Interior

By Suzanne Oakdale

Kayapó videographers, wearing beaded necklaces, armbands, and earrings, shirtless with shorts and flip flops, rushed in to film Indigenous speakers making impassioned cases for why the Altamira Dam should not be built in the 1989 protest in Altamira, Brazil. They filmed Kayapó dancers with their brilliant feather diadems and black body paint as they entered the arena where the event was held. They filmed the expansive Kayapó dance formations outside in the open air, and they filmed themselves doing all of this (*The Kayapó: Out of the Forest* 1989). Photos of these men, with their video cameras resting on their shoulders, became well-known after this event, almost icons of a new style of indigeneity. Terence Turner (1991) observed that Kayapó interest in video centered as much upon its role in the creation of social reality as upon its documentary potential (see also Boyer 2006, 49). He noted that Kayapó videographers, even after the Altamira protest, have consistently made a point of filming themselves filming Brazilians or their own rituals. According to Turner, "control over the power and technology of representation, even more than over the image per se, became a symbolic benchmark of cultural parity" for Kayapó (1991, 306).

Following this orientation toward media suggested by Turner and Kayapó videographers (among others), I turn here not to Indigenous use of media, but rather to the history of photography and film as it has been used by the Brazilian government in twentieth-century projects to colonize the country's interior. Here too the act of filming was as important as the representations produced. In other words, film and photography have been important for state attempts to produce a kind of social reality as well as to record it, a topic that has been explored particularly well with respect to the British Empire (Ryan 1997) and in postcolonial Africa (Buckley 2010).

My interest in this subject followed from my research on a project focused on the autobiographical accounts of Kawaiwete individuals, men who lived in the Xingu Park, a multiethnic reservation in central Brazil where most Kawaiwete continue to reside, just south of Kayapó areas.[1] Many of the men I interviewed had interacted with government teams sent out to "contact" the Kawaiwete in the early part of the twentieth century or had later worked on government teams to contact other Indigenous peoples. As these men described their experiences of working on and being photographed during these missions, they often stopped to search their memories for the name of one or other of the photographers who accompanied the teams. Rather than starting from the existence of photographs from earlier eras and using these to elicit memories, as much anthropological research involving photography often does (e.g., Buckley 2014; Wright 2013; Young 1998), memories of interacting with photographers and stories about the role of photography in events of "first contact" are my starting point. Many of the photos taken during these government expeditions have likely disappeared, and, if they do exist, they are not in circulation at a local level.[2] Instead, stories about photographers and photography, most often embedded in longer narratives about other topics, are what remains.

Through these men's narratives, I came to the realization that photography has been a significant part of colonization projects in Brazil for a very long time and has been familiar to many Indigenous individuals in that context. In other words, media's impact in the Brazilian interior is surprisingly historically deep (see Tacca 2011). To repeat Faye Ginsberg's (2002, 39) observation, prompted by the 1922 documentary *Nanook of the North*, filmed with Inuit actors and relying on Inuit camera work, media is not simply a phenomenon of the past two decades for many Indigenous peoples. While this chapter does not look at the historical depth of Indigenous use of media, it does focus on how Kawaiwete individuals have been aware of its connection to state projects for a considerable length of time. Two narratives that elderly Kawaiwete men told me in the 1990s show how, for those being photographed, photography was clearly understood as a part of state coercion, as part of the process of how the government teams opened the way for members of the national society to move into Indigenous territories in the first half of the twentieth century. The association between photography and the state, while not one that Kayapó people necessarily emphasize, does deepen understanding of Kayapó uses of this type of media. The production of indigenous film and photography is an activity in which a practice central to colonization has been reworked and revalued.

Photography, the State, and Indigenous Peoples in Brazil

Photography was a part of what in early twentieth–century Brazil was called "pacification." According to the idealized form of this practice, government teams would travel to the interior to peacefully "attract" isolated peoples by offering them industrially produced goods such as axes, knives, pots, and clothing. Once the goods were accepted, these people were then encouraged to settle at posts and eventually join the progress of "civilization," as well as, in the process, relinquishing their territories to settlers. The pacification process was central to the workings of the Commission for the Construction of the Telegraph Lines founded in 1889, then later of the Serviço de Proteção ao Índio (Indian Protection Service, SPI) when it was created in 1910, as well as the Inspetoria Especial de Fronteiras (Inspectorate of the Borders) when the SPI was moved under its jurisdiction in 1934 (Diacon 2004; Guzman 2013, 115). All of these institutions eventually came under the direction of Cândido Rondon, a figure considered to have been the architect of early twentieth-century Brazilian Indigenous policy (Diacon 2004; Lima 1995).[3]

The pacification process carried out under Rondon went hand in hand with photographic documentation. Rondon contracted with professional photographers to accompany expeditions to the interior from as early as 1890 and with filmmakers from as early as 1907 (Maciel 1997). By 1912, the SPI had a Division of Cinematography and Photography under the direction of Thomaz Reis that employed permanent photographers (Tacca 2002, 189). Reis even traveled to Europe for the latest equipment (189). Under Rondon, 1,200 photos and eleven films were produced, as well as many others that were lost in river crossings or eaten by insects (192). As a part of marketing the expensive projects of the SPI, such as stringing telegraph wires into the interior and lengthy pacification expeditions to contact Indigenous peoples, Rondon deliberately disseminated these images in the form of photo albums to politicians and civic leaders and staged exhibitions for the general public, both at home and abroad in Europe and the US (Diacon 2004, 132; Tacca 2002). Rondon had strong support from the Brazilian press, and images were also frequently published in Brazilian newspapers (Tacca 2002, 191). The reception of photos and films linked the interior of Brazil to coastal cities, at least in the minds of more elite urbanites who were able to visualize these regions and their inhabitants after visiting exhibitions, seeing films, or reading newspapers.[4] The drama of pacification portrayed through this media also allowed urban Brazilians to envision the transformative power of the modern Brazilian state, perhaps especially important in the first few decades of its transition from monarchy to republic.

These early images focused largely on control over nature, on the stringing of telegraph lines through forest or swampy terrain. With respect to Indigenous peoples, the images fell into two types: they were either centered on the process of "civilization" of more or less generic Indigenous people and the fruitful occupation of their lands, or, somewhat contradictorily, on distinctive Indigenous customs (Tacca 2002). The first type of images were not so much ethnographic as "a demonstration of the SPI's actions" (Tacca 2002, 192; Lima 1995, 164).

Films and photos featured the dressing of Indians in Western clothing by SPI agents, at times even in the military uniforms of the SPI, and groups of Indigenous people in Western dress standing attentively in front of the Brazilian flag or uncomfortably eating with silverware at a table (Tacca 2002, 194; see images in Rondon 1953, 221). Films featuring posts and schools increased after the SPI was put under the direction of the Inspectorate of the Borders in 1934 (Guzman 2013, 115).

The photos of native people wearing full sets of Western clothing contrasted with the previous nineteenth-century studio portraits of Indigenous individuals, often taken by European photographers living in Brazil, especially in Manaus, that featured semi-dressed individuals—women with the bodices of their dresses hanging down or men in suit coats but no pants (see images in Tacca 2011). Fully clothed people, in contrast to this earlier semi-nudity, represented an "advancement in civilization," "progress" with respect to the reshaping of Indigenous customs.

While the photos themselves depicted the cultural domination of Indigenous peoples, photographic reproduction is also, of course, a kind of domination in and of itself and an index of the power of "modern" society with respect to the "backward" interior. Given the fact that, at this point, the balance of power in many local arenas was still in the hands of Indigenous groups who outnumbered and at times killed members of the government teams, the photographer or filmmaker outfitted with the latest equipment imported from Europe was, perhaps, an important reminder of the "higher" power of modernity and progress with respect to the interior and its inhabitants for the other team members as well as for urban viewers. In fact, each of Rondon's publications of SPI photos, titled *Índios do Brasil*, volumes I, II, III, begins with the same preface by Rondon in which he describes some of the dangerous situations SPI team members encountered with respect to Indigenous peoples (Rondon 1946, 1953, 1956).

The second body of images produced by the SPI, according to Fernando de Tacca, was more ethnographic, featuring distinctive Indigenous material culture and ritual events. While these had the appearance of being less staged than those celebrating the "civilizing" of Indigenous bodies, at last some were, according to Tacca, also very much deliberately arranged. In his discussion of Thomaz Reis's film *Rituais e festas Bororo*, focusing on a Bororo mortuary ritual, he observes that evidence of all the extensive contact with missionaries the Bororo had experienced since 1906 had been carefully avoided by the camera in this 1917 film, with the exception of one sugar cane press (Tacca 2002, 198). In no image nor in any textual part of the film was the extensive Salesian missionary presence explained. Similarly, the fact that the Bororo had, years earlier, worked as laborers with Rondon on the telegraph line was also not mentioned (198). The film, instead, featured this particular Indigenous group as "untouched." These sorts of pictures served as a demonstration of the starting point for the state's actions, a visual measure of how far progress had advanced among other peoples who were now wearing full suits of clothing and eating their meals at tables.

During the early decades of the twentieth century, scientists also were often part of telegraph and SPI teams, including specialists such as biologists, botanists, and anthropologists (Tacca 2002, 189). As anthropologist Edgard Roquette-Pinto wrote in 1912, while a member of one of the Rondon Commission's teams, "the construction of the telegraph line was a pretext, scientific exploration was everything" (quoted in Sá, Sá, and Lima 2008, 784). Anthropologists also often visited SPI posts to do independent field research. Whether a member of an SPI team or traveling independently, these individuals also took photographs, and, while they were at times only tangentially connected to government institutions, they too were likely understood to be part of the state presence from the perspective of the Indigenous visitors and residents at posts. For example, at the Kawaiwete (then known as Kayabi) post Pedro Dantas, in 1927, the German ethnologist, Max Schmidt, took many photos of Indigenous visitors during his two-month stay (Bossert and Villar 2013; Schmidt 1942). These photos have the appearance of being less staged, featuring groups of Kawaiwete people gathered in conversation or interacting with post personnel, though full body portraits were also common in Schmidt's photos (1942). Though unattributed, Max Schmidt's photos of Kawaiwete at Pedro Dantas are also featured in one of the government publications of Indigenous photos from throughout Brazil *Indios do Brasil* (Rondon 1953, 49–51, 53).[5]

In 1942 the SPI created a special department, the Seção de Estudos (SE), or Studies Section, to more formally include scientific study in state indigenist projects (Mattos 2011). Anthropologists working in this division did ethnographic research and worked on practical problems of how best to assist Indigenous groups, debating different policies such as those focused on isolation or assimilation (Mattos 2011, 215). Film and photography became central to the research and documentation of the SE. In the first ten years of its existence, SE photographers took twenty thousand photos, shot twelve films, and made four hundred recordings of Indigenous music (Mendes 2011, 247).[6] Under the first director, Harold Schultz, photos were to be ethnographic as well as give meticulous documentation of Indigenous bodies (Mendes 2011, 234). His work plans for a 1942 expedition to Mato Grosso, for example, read as follows: "The Indians: one by one photographs, showing the front, the back, the profile, full body and just of the head. . . . Typical Indian groups walking, seated, speaking, working, fishing, hunting, dancing fighting. . . . Photographs just of the hands, the feet, the faces, the way of sitting, walking and swimming, etc." (quoted in Mendes 2011, 234, translation by author).

Despite the somewhat clinical sound of such detailed documentation, Marcos de Souza Mendes points out that cinematographers employed by the SE also managed to produce portraits that showed the humanity of the subjects, such as, for example, the pictures by Heinz Förthmann that revealed the tenderness of mothers toward their children (Mendes 2011, 235). Detailed scientific documentation in the case of Förthmann's photos had the potential to emotionally connect the urban viewers of these photos to Indigenous individuals in the hinterland.

The SE's detailed photographic documentation was focused on particular groups, such as the Bororo and the Urubu. The Bororo were the subject matter of extensive photography in 1943 and 1944, when Förthmann took 2,102 photos and made fifty recordings and several films, including one of his major works, *Funeral Bororo* (Mendes 2011, 235). When filming the Urubu for a month in 1949, the previous plan of exhaustive documentation gave way to a new interest in recording the life of an exemplary Urubu couple, footage that Förthmann used to create the mise en scène documentary (Mendes 2011, 240). In 1953, the SE created the Museu do Indió in Rio, headed by anthropologist Darcy Ribeiro. This museum was also dedicated to forms of photographic and film documentation. The Museu do Índio "strove to present to the public various aspects of Indigenous life through showing Indigenous artifacts, cinematographic and sound documentation" (Mattos 2011, 219).

Photography was also important in the Roncador-Xingu Expedition of the Central Brazil Foundation, created in 1943 as a part of Brazil's "March to the West." This government project sought to open up the interior for mineral extraction and agriculture, and later also to create landing strips to connect Rio to Manaus and Miami, and Lima to Dakar, on a straight flight pattern (Menezes 1999). The government rhetoric describing the March emphasized that teams of explorers and scientists were encountering untouched lands and peoples (Meireles 1960). In keeping with this, photographers who accompanied parts of this project captured on film what seemed to be Indigenous peoples' first moments of contact with modern society, the moment of being handed Western clothing, in contrast to the earlier photographs that showed them habitually wearing clothing. Cinematographer Förthmann, from the SE, was a member of two of these teams. In 1947 he shot a three-hour film of the Xavante's "first contact" (Mendes 2011, 238). Then, in the 1950s, he accompanied the leaders of the central-Brazilian part of the March to the West, the Villas Bôas brothers, when they made their first contact with a group of Kayapó (Mendes 2011, 247). The fragments left of this film show one of the men being offered a shirt by Orlando Villas Bôas and putting it on with discomfort—the shirt was so tight that it constricted the movement of his arms and shoulders (Mendes 2011, 249). The Villas Bôas brothers brought professional photographer Jorge Ferreira on their "second contact" with a Kayapó group and, while cooking techniques and dance sequences are featured in his film, so is the wrapping of a Kayapó women in yards of cloth and putting Western-style bracelets on women's arms (Ferreira 1953). Some of the footage also shows a Brazilian woman who had been kidnapped by the Kayapó as a child transforming from a state of nakedness with a Kayapó haircut into an individual attired in Western fashion by putting on a dress and arranging a scarf to cover her Indigenous hairstyle (Ferreira 1953).

Many other photos shot from the air give the sense of providing a glimpse of native life the instant before first contact took place, as well as showing the power of Western technology to afford this almost magical perspective. A 1945 article in *Life* magazine, for example, features a picture of photojournalist Jean Manzon showing a Xavante village from the air. The military airplane Manzon was shooting from casts a shadow on the lower left over the scene (Costa and Burgi 2012, 52; "Indians Shoot at Plane" 1945, 70). High technology of the era, such as military airplanes from the US, were used to depict an "untouched space" in the heart of Brazil just as earlier modern European photo technology was used to show the state's acculturation of Indigenous peoples.

After 1948, these images fit with and were used to promote the project to create the Xingu National Park, Brazil's first multiethnic, large-scale reservation (Menezes 1999). This area was first packaged as a kind of time capsule of precontact Brazil still present at the heart the modern nation (Menezes 1999; Garfield 2001). The architects of the park, the Villas Bôas brothers, encouraged film and photography within the Xingu by academics, those connected to the SE of the SPI as well those independent of the Brazilian government, and by the popular press. Förthmann of the SE, for example, on the Villas Bôases' invitation, made two thousand photographic plates and three films about Upper Xinguan groups' rituals when he accompanied the Bôas brothers and American cinematographer James Marshall in 1955 (Mendes 2011, 237, 249).

The March also corresponded to the rise in photojournalism in Brazil. The Xingu was a popular destination for photojournalists as the presence of landing strips created by Roncador-Xingu Expedition teams allowed for easy access by air to this otherwise remote location. The Villas Bôas brothers also saw the advantage of publicity with respect to swaying the public to encourage politicians to support the legal creation of the Xingu Park (Menezes 1999). The images shot by photojournalists appeared in the weekly magazine *O Cruzeiro* as well as internationally in magazines such as *Life* and *National Geographic*.

While earlier news stories celebrated the figure and biography of Rondon and left photographers themselves either anonymous or in the background, photojournalism brought the photographer to the fore. Coverage of the Indigenous peoples encountered, such as those from the Xingu, were understood to express the individual artistic style of the photographer. Henri Ballot produced photos described as "hard and disconcerting;" José Medeiros, as "empathetic;" Jean Mason, as "epic" (Costa and Burgi 2012, 42).

The experiences of the photographers were also now part of the story. It was important that their photos were linked to their personal encounters, and articles took pains to note that the photos were not pulled from the archives of the SPI (Costa and Burgi 2012). Part of the story was that the photographers risked their lives in their contact with the unknown. In one 1954 news story, photographer Jorge Ferreira and expedition leader Claudio Villas Bôas were even falsely reported to have been killed by the Kalapalo. This story spawned yet one more about "the tragedy that never was" (Cerqueira 2002). The heroism and daring of the photographer was a theme in this era, on par with the heroism of expedition leaders. Photojournalism in general was tied to the reporting the action in World War II, and some of the photographers who were important in Brazil, such as Jean Manzon, had been journalists in Europe during the war (Moura 2009).

The Kawaiwete Encounters with Photography

Kawaiwete families had different encounters with photography depending on the area in which they lived. Those around Pedro Dantas post could have experienced SPI photographers in the early 1920s. One undated, unattributed photo of Rondon at this post shows Kawaiwete men approaching him after they had swum across the river to meet him (Rondon 1953, 52). Later, in 1927, Max Schmidt's research involved taking photos of people at this post (Bossert and Villar 2013). In the 1940s, Kawaiwete people did not undergo the same degree of photographic documentation by the SE as groups such as the Bororo or peoples of the Upper Xingu had. They did, however, live in the vicinity of both. Kawaiwete individuals visited Bororo villages for extensive periods, some even living for years with the Bororo during the time frame that Förthmann was filming there. Several Kawaiwete people also circulated at the post Simão Lopes set up principally for the Bakairi people, where Förthmann shot a 1948 documentary called *Os Bakairi* (later retitled *Simões Lopes*) (Mendes 2011, 253).

After 1952, when Kawaiwete began to relocate to the Xingu, they became very familiar with photographers who filmed there, principally in the Upper Xingu where several Kawaiwete families worked under the Villas Bôas brothers for periods, until the families moved more permanently to the Lower Xingu. As members of teams led by the Villas Bôas brothers to contact isolated peoples and encourage them to relocate to the Xingu Park, many men and women had even more intimate contact with photographers. So while Kawaiwete have not been the subject matter of extensive government photographic documentation themselves, a significant number of individuals were exposed to the general climate of the media documentation of Indigenous peoples in different periods and in various places.

Tymakang's Mythic Account

Tymakang, when I interviewed him in 1992, was an elderly man, born some time approximately in the teens or twenties of the twentieth century. He was monolingual, but his son, who translated his account for me, had become one of the village's schoolteachers. Tymakang had lived in the Teles Pires River area before relocating to the Xingu, a location where SPI teams had sent exploratory teams in 1910 and 1915 and where posts were first set up in 1922 since it was valuable for rubber exploitation and had been under pressure from colonists (Diacon 2004). Tymakang's family tended to distance themselves from posts in this area, and, at some point after 1952, they relocated with others, walking for months to the Xingu Park.

Well known as a masterful narrator, Tymakang recounted the following story about the arrival of whites (i.e., non-Indigenous peoples). Told in the genre of an "ancestor's story" (*eyja porongyta*) or myth, it is not exactly a Kawaiwete version of the history of their contact with any particular SPI team.[7] Rather, his account ties the historical arrival of whites to an earlier mythic time. Others who were listening to his account said they had never heard this particular well-known story from the ancestors linked to the arrival of whites in the way that he did in his narrative. All were appreciative of his artistry in telling the account in this way.

Tymakang recounted that whites had lived with Kawaiwete in the distant past but left them because of gossip and mistreatment to live in the sky above. While living there, they decided to chop down the celestial tree that holds up the sky itself until they were stopped by some of the celestial gods, called *Mait*, who propped the tree back up and saved those who would have been crushed below on earth. In an aside to me about the whites' attempt to chop down the celestial tree, Tymakang commented that the whites had filmed this event up in the sky. He said, "I saw this in that thing that your people always make. In that, it was shown. The thing you call 'cinema.' It showed on the film how they cut the tree, how they went at it again and again." Tymakang's son interrupted to say that he thought his father was referring to an SPI film shown at the opening of the northern Xingu Park post of Diauraum, sometime in the 1950s. The film, *De Santa Cruz*, had been made early in the twentieth century by SPI filmmaker Luiz Thomaz Reis.[8] For Tymakang these details did not matter; the point was that photography was part of the more general habitus of whites, a characteristic they display in many contexts as they work against Kawaiwete interests. Here this includes also being agents of deforestation.

Continuing on with his story, Tymakang said that whites were then called back to earth by a disgruntled Kawaiwete shaman who spoke their language and who set out Kawaiwete delicacies to tempt them back, such as salt, powdered pepper, peanuts, beans, baked potatoes, and corn flour. This shaman also called to them on a jaguar bone flute in the way shamans currently call out to spirits. The whites finally gave in to these temptations and came back to earth in the following way:

> It is said that all of a sudden your people appeared. *Hoop To oo.* I don't know where they came down [from the sky]. . . . They said they came down in a field, yes certainly in a field. . . . It was in the season when fields are burned. . . . They came in the middle of the people. They came through the door of a house like that door. [He pointed to his own house standing in front of him.]
>
> "Whites are coming for us!"
>
> A son, a daughter, they took them. Then they took a woman, the man had gone to hunt. They came together with paper, your plaything. Then maybe they noted down things. Writing "house," writing "hammock," "cord," "arrow." *Tyrk* [a sound that represented taking a picture, he explained]. . . . *Tyrk. Tyrk. Tyrk.* [More pictures.] Then they finished [writing] and left knives for them. They left knives for them on both sides of the mother's hammock, hanging by cords. They left the knives, cords, and hammocks. They took the woman far away, to their people.

The fact that these whites noted things down on paper, took pictures, and left knives suggests the activities of some unspecified SPI workers. In this story, photography is part of the transformative introduction of goods and sinister reorganization of people brought about by pacification. Tymakang also explained that, when the Portuguese explorer Cabral first came to Brazil in 1500, he too had a photographer. It is significant that photography was, for Tymakang, a standard feature of the "first contact" event structure.

Sabino's Autobiographical Account

Sabino, born sometime in the 1920s, described how photography was part of government expeditions at a later point. Unlike Tymakang, Sabino had grown up at an SPI post in the Teles Pires River area after his parents and much of his extended family had been killed by one of the epidemics that spread through indigenous groups from post personnel. Later, as a young man, he himself had worked under the SPI, contacting groups of more-remote Kawaiwete in an area to the east of the Teles Pires River, along the Peixes River. By the mid-1950s, he too had moved to the Xingu Park, where he worked both on construction projects in the park and as a part of other "contact" missions with the Villas Bôas brothers. He was therefore an insider of sorts, someone who knew the SPI very well.

He described the central place of photography in the 1967 failed expedition to attract the Arara (of Pará), under the direction of Claudio Villas Bôas, in the following way:

> We went up river and arrived at one of their ports. Right here an abandoned house was sitting. The people filming, filmed us and filmed us. Like this, like this. They took a lot of photos of me. . . .
>
> Then we left again. We were carrying things on our shoulders, a lot of pans. . . . They were for them, but it did not work out. [We did not find them.] . . .
>
> We got to a field. We passed it a bit and got to a house. There were two houses just the same.
>
> "There are maybe burials inside," we said.
>
> "Someone perhaps died. They buried someone." . . .
>
> Then, those who were taking photos said, "Let's take one of you again." I had the hair of the dead people at my feet for the photo. Then I was [pictured] with cloth. Juruna [another member of the team] asked for the cloth to take a picture [too]. I think the cloth was a hammock, but it was all ripped. It fell to pieces in my hands.
>
> Then they took pictures of us. *Tyrk, tyrk.*

He commented that taking pictures with the hair of the dead and touching the hammock of the dead was frightening. His account recalls the bravado of post-WWII photojournalism. In contact expeditions, remains of the dead are a newsworthy subject matter much as in wartime photography.

Conclusion

I understand Tymakang's and Sabino's accounts not as offering radically distinct cultural perspectives on the twentieth-century pacification missions to the interior—for example, that they were understood to be caused by a shaman, in the case of Tymang's story. Neither are they simply examples of culturally distinct appreciations of photography—for example, that photos can capture a vital aspect of the person (see Wright 2013, among others). (The manipulation of photographic images is thought by some Kawaiwete, in fact, to be a way of exerting control over the person pictured in a way that does contrast with "Western" ideas.) Instead, my argument is that, despite the existence of different appreciations of history and photographs, these Kawaiwete men's accounts of photography offer perspectives that seem to be remarkably consistent with the aims of the government teams. In the early twentieth century, peoples at the margins of Brazil's territory were in the process of being broken down, refashioned, and integrated into the national society. Rondon-era photos of Indigenous people in Western clothing and Tymakang's narrative about how, after being photographed, women were taken away to live with whites both feature this process. The detailed documentation of native life the SPI encouraged, especially after the creation of the SE, also resonates with Tymakang's description of how photography and writing down native words went hand in hand, even in the time of myth. Mid-century photos, in contrast, portrayed Indigenous people as not yet part of the modern world though encapsulated by it. Here, the encounter with danger is portrayed in a controlled, almost theatrical way. Sabino's story about being photographed amid dead Arara recalls the bravado of this style of photojournalism.

Despite the differences in the ways the Brazilian state encouraged the photography of Indigenous peoples over the course of the twentieth century, this photography was at least tangentially part of different projects concerned with nation building, moments when images of Indigenous peoples were used to construct a modern Brazil. The two stories of Kawaiwete encounters with photography discussed here show a consciousness of aspects of this history. An exploration of the use of this media by and in collaboration with government teams, especially as it is registered from the perspective of those photographed, gives a greater appreciation for how national belonging is currently being reshaped by Indigenous Brazilians through their increasing appropriation of this media.

Acknowledgments

An earlier version of this paper was presented at the InDigital: Latin America Conference, held March 2015 at Vanderbilt University. I would like to thank the participants of this conference for their comments, especially Richard Pace, who also provided editorial comments. The field research on which this essay was based was carried out between 1991 and 1993, funded by grants from the Fulbright Institute of International Education, the Wenner-Gren Foundation, and a University of Chicago Travel Grant. I am grateful to Aturi Kayabi and Mairata Kayabi for their work translating Tymakang's and Sabino's narratives. Finally, I wish to thank Tymakang and Sabino for sharing their accounts with me. Research on photojournalism in Brazil was carried out in 2015 with the aid of a Career Advancement Grant from

University of New Mexico and done in the Biblioteca e Centro de Documentação of the Museo de Arte São Paulo. Many thanks to all of the staff members at the archive for their help, but especially to Romeu Loreto.

Notes

1. A number of Kayapó people lived in the park as well for several decades. Kayapó villages relocated to the Xingu Park from 1956 until the 1990s, when they moved to their own Indigenous area (Hemming 2003, 150).
2. Anthropologists and other sorts of researchers have brought some older photos back to Kawaiwete people. For example, in 2015 I brought copies of Father Dornstauder's photos from the 1950s. In the 1990s, when the accounts I focus on here were recorded, I was, however, not aware of the presence of any photos from the Indian Protection Service (SPI) teams which interacted with Kawaiwete or which employed Kawaiwete men to "contact" other Indigenous peoples. In fact, Sabino, the man I quote in this chapter, complained that he never received any copies of the photos taken of him from the SPI photographers.
3. Rondon took charge of the Comissão de Linhas Telegráphicas do Araguaia in 1891, the Comissão de Linhas Telegráphicas no Estado do Matto Grosso from 1900 to 1906, and led the Comissão de Linhas Telegráphicas Estratégicas de Matto-Grosso ao Amazonas in 1916 (Tacca 2002, 2; 2012). He was also the head of SPI from 1910 to 1915.
4. As Walter Benjamin (1968, 221) has pointed out, the remarkable aspect of the photo is that it is able to meet the beholder in his or her own particular situation.
5. One other category of photographer which native peoples encountered was the independent traveler, such as the journalist Mario Baldi. The Austrian born (later Brazilian national) Baldi visited the Bororo in 1934 and left an extensive archive of more nuanced photos, images which serve to underline Fernando de Tacca's argument that the SPI films of the Bororo involved a construction of an "uncontacted" appearance. Baldi's photos show peoples dressed in a mixture of native and Western clothing interacting with Salesian priests in quotidian and ritual activities (Augustat 2013, 98–103).
6. While the orientation of the SE changed briefly with a new director in 1946 to the documentation of the economic activities of posts, it quickly returned in 1947 to ethnological documentation (Mendes 2011, 240).
7. This "first arrival of whites" could have taken place in 1922 when the SPI sent teams to the Verde River to establish a post to attract Kawaiwete. Or it could have taken place in 1910, when a Kawaiwete man killed a labor contractor for a rubber company operating in their territories. The governor of the state of Mato Grosso then hired twenty-six men to attack Kawaiwete villages and kidnap children. Rondon tried to intervene and sent an SPI team to contact this group of Kawaiwete (Diacon 2004).
8. This was a film that was also shown in 1918 during a talk by Theodore Roosevelt sponsored by the National Geographic Society in New York (Tacca 2002, 200).

References

Augustat, C., ed. 2013. *Beyond Brazil: Johann Natterer and the Ethnographic Collections from the Austrian Expedition to Brazil (1817–1835)*. Vienna: Museum für Völkerkunde. Published in conjunction with an exhibition of the same title at the Museum für Völkerkunde, Vienna—Kunsthistorisches Museum.

Benjamin, W. 1968. *Illuminations*. New York: Schocken Books.

Bossert, F., and D. Villar. 2013. *Hijos de la selva / Sons of the Forest: The Ethnographic Photography of Max Schmidt*. Edited by Viggo Mortenson. Santa Monica, CA: Perceval Press.

Boyer, D. 2006. "Turner's Anthropology of Media and Its Legacies." *Critique of Anthropology* 26 (1): 47–60.

Buckley, L. 2010. "Cine-Film, Film-Strips and the Devolution of Colonial Photography in the Gambia." Special issue edited by S. Okwunodu and J. Peffer, *History of Photography*. 34 (2): 147–57.

———. 2014. "Photography and Photo-Elicitation after Colonialism." *Cultural Anthropology* 29 (4): 720–43.

Cerqueira, C. 2002. "O grande reporter do Xingu: Jorge Ferreira." *Estadão*. *www.estadao.com. br/ext/especial/villasboas/jorge.htm*, accessed January 1, 2018.

Costa, H., and S, Burgi. 2012. "A grande reportagem." In *As origens do fotojornalismo no Brasil*, edited by H. Costa and S. Burgi, 41–77. São Paulo: Instituto Moreira Sales.

Diacon, T. 2004. *Stringing Together a Nation*. Durham, NC: Duke University Press.

Ferreira, J. 1953. "Primeiros contatos com os Txucarramãe: Expedição irmão Villas Bôas," video, 14:15. *www.youtube.com/watch?v=626XZlhj324*, posted by NVILLA Nov. 19, 2011.

Garfield, S. 2001. *Indigenous Struggle at the Heart of Brazil*. Durham, NC: Duke University Press.

Ginsberg, F. 2002. "Cultural Activism and Minority Claims." In *Media Worlds: Anthropology on New Terrain*, edited by F. Ginsburg, L. Abu-Lughod, and B. Larkin, 39–112. Berkeley: University of California Press.

Guzman, T. 2013. *Native and National in Brazil: Indigeneity after Independence*. Chapel Hill: University of North Carolina.

Hemming, J. 2003. *Die If You Must: Brazilian Indians in the Twentieth Century*. Oxford: Macmillan.

"Indians Shoot at Plane." 1945. *Life*. (March 19): 70–72. *books. google.com/books?id=K1MEAAAAMBAJ&lpg=PA70&pg=PA70#v=onepage&q&f=false*.

Lima, A. C. de S. 1995. *Um grande cerco de paz: Poder tutelar, indianidade e formação do estado no Brasil*. Petrópolis, Brazil: Vozes.

Maciel, L. 1997. *A nação por um fio*. São Paulo: Editora da PUC-Sp.

Mattos, A. 2011. "Ribeiro e o Serviço de Proteção aos Índios." In *Memória do SPI: Textos, imagens e documentos sobre o Serviço de Proteção aos Índios (1910–1967)*, edited by C. Freire, 213–21. Rio de Janeiro: Museu do Índio.

Meireles, S. 1960. *Brasil Central*. Rio de Janeiro: Ministério da Guerra, Biblioteca do Exército Editora.

Mendes, M. de S. 2011. "Heinz Förthmann: Fotografia e cinema no SPI—1942/1959." In *Memória do SPI: Textos, imagens e documentos sobre o Serviço de Proteção aos Índios (1910–1967)*, edited by C. Freire, 233–54. Rio de Janeiro: Museu do Índio.

Menezes, M. 1999. *Parque indigena do Xingu: Construção de um território estatal*. São Paulo: IMESP-UNICAMP.

Moura, R. 2009. "José Medeiros e o fotojornalismo na revista *O Cruzeiro*." Paper presented at Intercom—Sociedade Brasileira de Estudos Interdisciplinares da Comunicação / XIV Congresso de Ciências da Comunicação na Região Sudeste, Rio de Janeiro, May 7–9, 2009. *www.intercom.org.br/papers/regionais/sudeste2009/resumos/R14-1104-1.pdf*.

Rondon, C. M. da S. 1946. *Índios do Brasil: Do centro ao noreste e sul de Mato-Grosso*, Tomo I. Rio de Janeiro: Ministério da Agricultura, Conselho Nacional de Proteção aos Índios.

———. 1953. *Índios do Brasil: Cabeceiras do Xingu/rio Araguaia e Oiapoque*, Tomo II. Rio de Janeiro: Ministério da Agricultura, Conselho Nacional de Proteção aos Índios.

———. 1956. *Índios do Brasil: Norte do rio Amazonas*, Tomo III. Rio de Janeiro: Ministério da Agricultura, Conselho Nacional de Proteção aos Índios.

Ryan, J. 997. *Picturing Empire: Photography and the Visualization of the British Empire*. Chicago: University of Chicago Press.

Sá, D., M. Sá, and N. Lima. 2008. "Telégrafos e inventário do território no Brasil: As atividades científicas da Comissão Rondon (1907–1915)." *História, ciências, saúde-manguinhos* (online) 15 (3): 779–810. *dx.doi.org/10.1590/S0104–59702008000300011*.

Schmidt, M. 1942. "Resultados da minha expedição bienal a Mato-Grosso." *Boletim do Museu Nacional* 14-16: 241–85.

Tacca, F. 2002. "Rituais e festas Bororo: A construção da imagem do índio como 'selvagem' na Comissão Rondon." *Revista de antropologia* 45 (1): 187–219. *www.scielo.br/scielo.php?script=sci_arttext&pid=S0034–77012002000100006*.

———. 2011. "O índio na fotografia brasileira: Incursões sobre a imagem e o meio." *Imagens* 18 (1): 191–223.

———. 2012. "Luiz Thomaz Reis: Das selvas à metropole." *Jornal da UNICAP* 534 (August 6–12). *www.unicamp.br/unicamp/ju/534/luiz-thomaz-reis-das-selvas-metropole*.

Turner, T. 1991. "Representing, Resisting, Rethinking: Historical Transformations of Kayapó Culture and Anthropological Consciousness." In *Colonial Situations*, edited by G. Stocking, 285–313. Madison: University of Madison Press.

Wright, C. 2013. *The Echo of Things: The Lives of Photographs in the Solomon Islands*. Durham, NC.: Duke University Press.

Young, M. 1998. *Malinowski's Kiriwina. Fieldwork Photography 1915–1918*. Chicago: University of Chicago Press.

Film

The Kayapó: Out of the Forest. 1989. Directed by Michael Beckham. Disappearing World (Granada Television). Baseline. 1991, videocassette. Chicago: Films Incorporated.

PART FOUR

Television

10

As Seen on TV?

Visions of Civilization in Emerging Kichwa Media Markets

By Jamie E. Shenton

[Actresses] make me want to be like them, to be exactly like them. They dress well. They have a good family. Their fathers and mothers live together. I would like to have their bodies. . . . They are truly beautiful. . . . I would like to be like them. If one day I have money, if I complete my dreams, then I will be like them.

Sarafina

Sixteen-year-old Sarafina was a resident of the small, primarily Kichwa community of Sacha Loma, in Napo Province, Ecuador, located on the western edge of the Amazon. Her bedroom walls were plastered from floor to ceiling with magazine images of tall, thin, light-skinned women selling high-end clothes, dramatic make-up, and whiteness—in all, a carefree lifestyle very different from Sarafina's. The termites consumed the pulpy models as avidly as she did.

A straight-A student and reigning local pageant queen, Sarafina wanted nothing more than "to do something with my life." As I interviewed her in her room, she talked about her dreams in a hushed tone—attend university, fall in love, have a family, and provide her future children with "every opportunity." These seemed distant possibilities given the challenges she had already faced as a young woman: the loss of her mother and then Sarafina's relocation to Sacha Loma to be with extended family. "I want my children to be happy because I haven't been very happy," she sighed. She gazed at the female role models on her walls: "They are spectacular," she said dreamily. When I asked what she wanted in life she responded simply, "a good home, to be happy." In Sarafina's view, happy homes came easily to the fashion models whose smiles never dulled, even as they warped in the humidity, and whose bodies never aged or lost their beauty, even as they faded in the sunshine streaming through the cracks in her shrine-like wall.

In many ways, young women's bodies and behaviors in Sacha Loma reflect a desire to enter into the "global village" (Askew and Wilk 2002, 15; McLuhan 1994); to wear modernity's "uniform" (Hall 1992, 302–3); to pluck their eyebrows, highlight their hair, and contour their eyes in heavy black liner; to buy computers, cameras, and televisions; to eat candy, potato chips, and fried chicken; and even to dream and aspire in particular ways, as Sarafina did. Possibly more than any other vector of globalized influence, the mass media has been accused of irreparably homogenizing the world's communities, as internet and cable signals reach the most far-flung places. Even so, Sacha Lomans' buying into these globalized ideals in an acculturative sense is not the subject matter at hand.

It may be true that, as part of the "global village," young people everywhere are increasingly sharing visions of what worldly bodies and behaviors should look like, especially as oft-advertised consumerist, romance-filled, middle-class lifestyles lived by beautiful, happy people overwhelm representations of formerly viable lifestyles, like farming, with which community elders like Sarafina's grandmother would be familiar. It is also true that while there may be a lot pulling young Sacha Loman women toward Western ways of being and behaving, this attraction is not totalizing. Young people hold Kichwa culture in high esteem and maintain a sometimes critical, if almost always interested, stance toward mainstream television and music. While one student blasts Katy Perry on his stereo, a friend next door raises the volume on singer Bayron Caicedo, a local sensation who celebrates the Amazon's beauty in the up-tempo, drums-and-keyboard musical style characteristic of the area. While the Sacha Loma–born English teacher pages through *Yanbal*, a cosmetic sales magazine, her students piece together seeds and feathers to make traditional costumes for a dance exposition. How mainstream bodies and behaviors are interpreted in practice, then, involves the social contexts, cultural values, and structural barriers that global villagers experience as part of kin networks and distinct communities with roots as cosmologically deep as an internet signal is broad.

Focusing on Indigenous Kichwa women, young and old, this chapter probes community readings of mass-mediatized, white, "civilized" bodies and behaviors, like those on Sarafina's makeshift wallpaper, as they are viewed alongside essentialized representations of traditional Indigenous culture in small-scale music videos and hit regional songs.[1] Processes of civilization emerge as a reference point for Sacha Lomans in both local and global forms of media. Analyzing women's own words, I argue that Sacha Lomans imagine their place somewhere along a direct if fraught line toward civilization, as evidenced by their contradictory analyses of Indigenous counterparts in music videos and on postcards. Their interpretations of non-Indigenous (often white) women in the mainstream media, counterintuitively, are constructed in relation to valued local ways of being and behaving, while these women's civilization, which is unquestionable, remains uncompromised.

Scholars of Indigenous media have identified the ways in which Indigenous peoples appropriate media technology to their own cultural ends, but have done so primarily with a focus on media production (Ginsburg 1991, 2000; Raheja 2007; Salazar and Córdova 2008; Turner 1991, 1992, 1995; Wortham 2013). This research has challenged the seemingly neat "Faustian dilemma" (Ginsburg 1991, 96) between Indigenous culture and foreign technologies of production, demonstrating that technologies are transformed by Indigenous producers into renovated yet familiar tools of cultural representation and reproduction (Ginsburg 1991, 93; Raheja 2007, 1160–61, and 1163 on "visual sovereignty"; Himpele 2007, 200, on "indigenization of popular media"; Salazar and Córdova 2008, 40, 55, on "cultural logic of Indigenous media"; Wortham 2013, 12, citing consultant Juan José García on *video indígena* as vehicle of "*comunalidad*"). Moreover, cultural understandings and practices shape how the activity of Indigenous film production is carried out—framing while filming and editing afterward (Turner 1992, 8–11)—and even embodied as in the operation of equipment (Turner 1992, 8; Wortham 2013, 13). Last, and most importantly for my purposes, researchers of Indigenous media production overwhelmingly agree on one point: Indigenous film is used as a vehicle to solidify, reposition, or bridge social relations, either intracultural (Salazar and Córdova 2008, 55), intercultural (Turner 1992, 12–13), or both (Ginsburg 1991, 97 and 104). Even as a tool to mediate major changes to communities and to forge new relationships with outsiders, Indigenous film, as cultural "practice and process" (Wortham 2013, 12), reaffirms longstanding communal ideals and commitments.

While an abundance of attention has been paid to Indigenous peoples as media producers, the same cannot be said of research on Indigenous peoples as media consumers, though there are important exceptions (Becker 2004; High 2010; Meadows 2009). Indigenous audience reception studies are generally less optimistic than those related to production, with some observing the emergence of risky behaviors, like disordered eating, among Indigenous youth (Becker 2004); others note the tension between traditional expressions of gendered agency and newer forms of gendered bodies and behavior advertised in mainstream television and film (High 2010). Still, shifts occur in dialogue with local forms of meaning making (Becker 2004, 543; High 2010, 765–66).

Far-reaching changes are occurring for the Napo Kichwa in the small community of Sacha Loma. The Napo Kichwa are lowland Indigenous peoples in the Ecuadorian Amazon who have made their living hunting, fishing, cash cropping, and subsistence cultivating. While these livelihoods continue, Sacha Loma is a place in transition. The eighteen-household village is home to an ecotourism lodge, a public primary-through-secondary school, and, at the time of this study, a private high school concentrating on ecotourism, sustainable development, and Indigenous empowerment. Farming is declining as the chief occupation of community members; the majority of its youth are in school full time; and there are mounting numbers of computers with internet, cellular phones, television sets, and mp3 players.

One of the biggest transformations in the community has been the presence of images of bodies and behaviors from outsiders that throw Sacha Loman Kichwa bodies and behavior into high relief.[2] The state-sponsored schools and the eco-hotel, especially the wealthy, white tourists who stay there, promote images of civilized bodies and behaviors. According to Sacha Lomans, they have light skin, wear neat clothing and shoes, speak well, and are wealthy. Fifteen-year-old Víctor notes what distinguishes him from the tourists who visit his community: "They are white, more civilized, more developed, and more advanced economically." Similar images of civilized ways of being and behaving are echoed in the television programs and DVDs that youngsters watch and the magazines they read, many of which feature white, wealthy, attractive leads and/or models.

When asked directly for a definition, Sacha Lomans describe processes of civilization in teleological fashion, with Kichwa people being somewhere in the middle. As fifty-four-year-old Medicio elaborates, to civilize means, "a man living in the woods, who doesn't know you, doesn't know anything. . . . You [the civilizer] teach him what is food, how to put on clothes, and how to speak the civilizer's language. . . . To make friends. To change what they are made of." This end-goal definition of civilization almost always impinges upon anyone considered Indigenous, whether living next door or featured in a music video. Sacha Lomans tell me from experience that Indigenous people are held to dominant society's standards by Kichwa and non-Kichwa alike and are often criticized when not being or behaving in ways that would move them toward the civilized pole, like dressing in clean, neat clothing or trying to secure a white-collar job. At the same time, in certain contexts, like performances for tourists, both Kichwa and non-Kichwa praise traditional representations of Kichwa culture for their authenticity and revitalizing potential, even while still considering them slightly uncivilized.

Things change when Sacha Lomans characterize white bodies and behaviors in the context of magazines and popular *telenovelas* (dramatic serials) featuring famous, usually white, women. What is striking about Sacha Loman views of civilization in terms of mediatized, foreign protagonists is that, though they recognize these women to be utterly civilized, residents apply longstanding local values, specifically a commitment to kin, to how they interpret the actresses and models to be in the world. Whiter women get the best of both worlds: a place in civilized modernity and, as I will explain later, assumed adherence to the highly valued Kichwa cultural principles of collective agency and kinship.

Put plainly, Sacha Lomans' evaluation of Indigenous people is much harsher than their evaluation of white people.[3]

New influences from foreign media compete with existing models of bodies and behaviors in Sacha Loma that continue to resonate among community members who consider them to be foundational Kichwa ways of being and behaving, namely embodied, kin-centered production. Kichwa women ascribe social value to producing persons and supportive social relationships. Ideal women are expected to "do" and to do for others. For older women, this is most often expressed in producing crops, food, and children through manual labor on the farm and in the garden; they grow, harvest, process, and circulate their products among kin. Individually produced items immediately enter the economy of social relations as they are exchanged and consumed, thereby building and fortifying social relationships. A woman who chews manioc all day to make *chicha* (manioc home brew) for her family, for instance, not only nourishes her husband and children—a process Michael Uzendoski (2005, 135) describes as "the fermentation of life"—but also reproduces herself within her family and community as a strong Kichwa woman, wife, and mother. These themes of productive sociality are read into white, mainstream women that Kichwa view on television and/or in magazines who Kichwa presume to be "always already" (Foucault 1980, 141) civilized and, in some ways, "always already" providers for their loved ones in a way idealized by Kichwa. They are interpreted to be good looking, economically productive, family women, in other words, the social values that Kichwa have customarily assigned to strong women in the community.

Media Consumption in Sacha Loma

Media consumption is a recent, if growing phenomenon in Sacha Loma. Of those interviewed, 92 percent report having a television in their home (see Table 10.1). The two respondents who report not having a television at home claim they have access to television outside of their home. Eighty-eight percent own a DVD player, 50 percent have magazines in the house, and 33 percent own a computer. Very few (8 percent) report internet access in their own home. Two wireless internet towers in the community capture a signal from satellite, one for the eco-hotel and one for the public school. Unreliable signals persist, however, and there are fewer personal computers than family televisions (see Eddy, Hennessey, and Thompson-Brenner [2007] for a version of the survey on which that of this study is based). While television and DVDs rank as the media most consumed by Sacha Lomans, with magazines, computers, and internet further behind, substantial numbers of community members have access to the scarcer media outside of the home. Notably, half of those interviewed report using computers and internet outside of the home.

Table 10.1. Media type, ownership, and/or access among the Kichwa in Sacha Loma, Ecuador

Media type, ownership and/or access	Percentage positive response
Do you have a TV in your house?	92%
Do you have a DVD player in your house?	88%
Do you have magazines in your house?	50%
Do you have a computer in your house?	33%
Do you have internet access in your house?	8%
Outside of your house, do you have access to TV?	67%
Outside of your house, do you have access to DVDs?	63%
Outside of your house, do you have access to magazines?	54%
Outside of your house, do you have access to a computer?	50%
Outside of your house, do you have access to the internet?	46%

Note: N=24, male and female ages 15–64

But what counts as consumption? I asked Sacha Lomans about the quantity of media they consume on a regular basis (see Table 10.2). Nearly one-third consume some hours of television daily. Over two-thirds report watching either "some hours per week" or "some hours per month," with the majority finding time to watch television on a weekly basis. Very few (4 percent) report watching no television at all. Nearly one-third report viewing DVDs daily, while many respondents (38 percent) watch DVDs on a weekly basis. Many Sacha Lomans interviewed find time to consume magazines and internet on a monthly basis (46 percent and 33 percent, respectively), though large portions—almost a third in the case of magazines and over half in the case of internet—do not engage with these media forms at all. These numbers are consistent with the data regarding ownership and access to media detailed above. Most families have television, and television ranks as the media form consumed most by Sacha Lomans; DVDs, magazines, and internet follow in order of their accessibility. The fact that 46 percent of respondents have access to internet outside their homes and 58 percent report not using internet at all is not an inconsistency because usage and access are not the same thing.

Succinctly, when asked about the popularity of television in Sacha Loma, Dorado, a guide at the local eco-hotel, put it: "The whole world has one." This is gradually becoming the case for other outlets of media consumption.

Table 10.2. Usage of television and other media

Usage of:	Never	Some hours/ month	Some hours/ week	Some hours/ day
Television	4%	29%	38%	29%
DVDs	17%	17%	38%	29%
Magazines	29%	46%	17%	8%
Internet	58%	33%	8%	0%
Trips to city	8%	58%	33%	0%

"The rhythm of our culture": Small-Scale Music Videos

> [Actors, actresses, singers] dress well. Not like *de la cultura* (that of our culture). There are some that sing well, but there are others who don't capture the rhythm of our culture.
>
> *Maximiliana, age twenty*

During my time in Sacha Loma, a group of Waorani tour guides visited the community to partake in a guiding accreditation program.[4] The Waorani guides performed a customary dance for an audience of white tourists at the eco-hotel, in which they made guttural noises and brandished spears. One guide stood out as he wore a T-shirt emblazoned with "Send more missionaries to Ecuador. The last ones were delicious." Next to this text were images of a mosquito and, oddly, the country of Mexico (not Ecuador). The double entendre was clear to Kichwa onlookers: mosquitoes feast on tourists, but so does the savage Waorani T-shirt wearer. While they seemed to look down on these Waorani performers, many of the Sacha Loman bystanders had performed similar dances for tourists in the past in which their "closeness" to nature and "distance" from civilization were foregrounded. Yet Sacha Lomans would say that their performances were in the name of cultural revitalization, which most find deeply important (see Wroblewski 2014), and not an expression of their inherent lack of civilization, as they appeared to assume about the Waorani dancers.

To be "civilized" is a distinction that Kichwa in Sacha Loma make along a continuum. At the furthest extreme of the continuum are the Waorani—whom Kichwa call *auca* (a pejorative term that means "savage" in Kichwa)—who inhabited the territory of Sacha Loma decades ago. Not used to wearing clothes, say Sacha Lomans, Waorani have in the past been stereotyped by Kichwa in this community as much less civilized than Kichwa, though Kichwa acknowledge that this has changed in recent years as Waorani attend school. Sacha Lomans consider themselves to be well on their way to civilization, which they view as something to accomplish to benefit the whole. That is, according to Kichwa, those who behave in an uncivilized way reflect poorly on everyone else; those who behave properly "uplift" all Kichwa.[5] On one hand, then, Kichwa expect their youth to become civilized in body and behavior, in speech and dress, to learn Spanish, and to be educated and employed. On the other hand, they want their children and grandchildren to value their heritage, remember former ways of life, and treasure the forest and farming.

The consumption of music videos that display many of these cultural values is equally if not more prevalent than cable television. While bootlegged copies of mainstream artists like James Blunt, Britney Spears, and Katy Perry are purchased, Napo Kichwa soundtracks and homegrown Ecuadorian artists are also common choices. Many music video DVDs feature Kichwa artists singing Kichwa songs with a backdrop of local scenery (Floyd 2008, 38; also see Straubhaar 2003 on cultural proximity, and Pace and Hinote 2013, 10–11 on heeding). These expressions of Indigenous identity in the videos are important because, unlike cable television programs that frequently portray rural people as backward and ignorant and elevate the "Spanish-speaking White urban context, Quichua media provides a reinforcement of local ways of life" (Floyd 2008, 37). As Floyd puts it when discussing media consumption by Kichwa-speaking peoples in the Ecuadorian highlands, "Instead of watching media that stems from precepts of racial and cultural inferiority of Indigenous people, viewers have access to culturally affirming media that casts Indigenous people in a positive and prominent role" (2008, 38).

Such reinforcement of local ways of life was prominent in the music videos I watched with youngsters. One day, as I talked with seventeen-year-old Dolores, a music video blared in the background. A friend of hers had come to pass some time away from school and plopped down in front of the television, laughing hysterically at what he interpreted to be "savage" Waorani tormenting oilmen as the singer crooned about the Amazon. "It's Bayron Caicedo," Dolores pointed out to me. Bayron Caicedo rang a bell. A few weeks prior, fifty-two-year-old Micaela had approached me with a huge smile: "Bayron Caicedo is coming," she exclaimed, "I am going to dance all night and not go to sleep!" In fact, the entire community uprooted for the evening to travel to the nearby parochial head for the Caicedo concert. For them, seeing the star so close to home was unforgettable. Caicedo, an Ecuadorian artist, appears to capture the rhythm of regional life.

Caicedo and his music tap into values of friendship and family that many in Sacha Loma esteem. With songs like "Mi bella Amazonia" (My beautiful Amazon) and "Por mi Ecuador saco la cara" (I'll stick up for my Ecuador), he appeals to a burgeoning base of patriotic fans across the country. The music video of "Mi bella Amazonia" is a classic representation of his brand of artistry. The video commences with Caicedo rushing to catch a small plane to visit the interior of the rain forest, or what he calls "Ecuador's lungs and the world's." Scenes jump back and forth between him singing, playing a fiddle, and socializing with local Indigenous peoples bedecked in feathers, spears, and body paint, and the activities of a team of surveyors charting the land. The video ends with the surveyors surrounded by Indigenous spearmen, their plans defueled by the savvy guardians of the forest. For videos like this, Caicedo is known for his appreciation of the diversity—of people, culture, and geography—that Ecuador has to offer.

Music videos (and just plain Napo Kichwa music), which play whenever possible during the day and until the electricity gets cut off at night, are literally the soundtrack to Sacha Loma lives. Even more than Caicedo's videos, regional music videos contain images—of people, places, dance moves, and so on—directly identifiable by and relatable to Sacha Loman viewers. They are made by Kichwa, for Kichwa, in Kichwa. These music videos' upbeat constructions of indigeneity—even when overtly essentializing—generate positive feelings toward Indigenous language and culture among Sacha Lomans and anyone else who finds the music appealing. Perhaps most importantly, music and music videos serve as both representations of and vehicles for sociality, or congregation and exchange with others, which is a central preoccupation of Sacha Loman lives.

A propensity for congenial sociality has been identified as a strong orientation in much of native Amazonia (Overing and Passes 2000). Forty-four-year-old Anselmo puts congeniality in his own words: "You know that the Kichwa culture is different? If there is a *minka* (communal work group), the pair goes. For work, I mean, the couple goes. The woman brings food, her little batch of *chicha*, something. They share. But in Hispanic culture, it's not this way." The primary foundational logic of socially driven production operating on a daily basis in Sacha Lomans' engagements with the world and with each other involves practices of person-making grounded in exchanges of substance and products of human labor, like food, brew, and breast milk, that literally constitute bodies.[6] Indeed, the production of sociality is an end in itself. Sacha Lomans are conscious of the essentialness of relationships of exchange among them; it is a source of pride. Music is central in this regard. In addition to themes of sociality as the content of many songs, which often simply exhort listeners in Kichwa to dance with one another over and over, this music, as a background at parties and gatherings, lubricates Sacha Lomans' dancing with one another, sharing food and brew, gossiping, joking, and catching up.

Referring to the production of Indigenous media, Juan Francisco Salazar and Amalia Córdova (2008, 55) explain, "We must bear in mind that Indigenous media constitute a system of social relations and networking aimed at reaffirming communal social solidarities." Likewise, Erica Wortham's (2013, 12) collaborator Juan José García, a Zapotec media professional, remarked: "*Video indígena* is loaded with symbols, codes; it is loaded with what we up in the sierra call '*comunalidad*.' What are its elements? Principally, collectivity, language, facial features, intimacy. That is to say, in *video indígena* the intimacy of a family is there in such a way that it is barely noticeable." What these observations share is a focus on Indigenous media production as a locus of collective agency. Thus, we would expect that, just as Indigenous media production has a role in cultural reproduction of social solidarity, so might consumption of media with Indigenous content and imagery, which it does. Most interestingly, the same themes of social solidarity are being read into Sacha Lomans' interpretations of foreign media and mainstream representations of already-civilized bodies and behaviors.

Does Cultural Rhythm Hold Up to Telenovela Tempo? Contexts of and Motivations for Watching

"My kids can watch cartoons all day. But from four to six the television is mine for *mis novelas* (my dramatic serials)," twenty-six-year-old Nicola emphasized as she cleared a spot for me on her front porch. She swept away the dried mud from the floor and unstacked a plastic chair from the others in the corner for me to sit on. Nicola had asked me if I would come teach her how to make banana bread. "You are here on time! I am not ready. I look like a witch," she said as she stood in front of the mirror hanging on the wall of her bedroom, which was right off the living room. She slicked back her hair into a tangled heap, clipped stray bangs on top of her head, and put on pink lipstick, black eyeliner, and black mascara. She showed me her nails. They were painted white with black stripes and dots for embellishment: "I bought this at the market upriver. It's cheap and flakes off when I do the dishes."

Nicola, the local Yanbal cosmetics saleswoman, and her husband, Rico, the manager at the local eco-hotel, have the most luxurious home in the community. Nicola and Rico clearly stick out in the community, and most other Sacha Lomans hope to expand their homes as this couple has. There are separate bedrooms for them and their two children, a screened-in porch that doubles as the living room, a small storefront, a kitchen, and, most lavishly, an indoor bathroom. The couple subscribed monthly to beam in DirectTV through a satellite dish that sat conspicuously in the middle of their front yard. This meant the family had access to hundreds of channels, including TL Novelas, Cartoon Network, and a variety of news and film channels. Nicola convinced Rico to screen in their porch due to the constant nuisance of young neighbors hopping the rails to indulge in free entertainment. Then one day, the worst happened. "I am behind in my *novelas*," Nicola grumbled during an evening visit to my house. "Our generator is broken, so I can only watch them in the evenings or when it is sunny enough for me to switch on the solar panel."

Nicola's statement demonstrates her dedication to following the lives of the characters she welcomes into her home on a daily basis. Skipping an episode means missing a crucial piece of the plots around which she structures her afternoons. For some families in Sacha Loma, television is a social event, a reason for family members to gather together and relate emotionally (see Pace 2009; Reis 1998). For instance, Nicola's six-year-old son Olivio enjoys staying up until ten o'clock on Friday nights watching telenovelas with her. One day, Nicola recounted to me the plot of an episode of *Huracán* in which a storm caused much rain, flooding, wind, and all-around destruction. An older woman in a threatened house knelt down and began to pray. As she prayed, she cried tears of blood. Olivio was disturbed, but he did not say anything to his parents. After a moment, Olivio ran into his bedroom and got his younger sister. They both emerged and asked their mother, "Why does Jesus cause so much death and destruction?" Nicola giggled and shook her head, "They're crazy." Feliz, who was also visiting me at the time, commented, "Yeah, the people in my house like to watch horror films, the kind where demented dolls eat human flesh."

Television stars and their characters are an important inspiration for meaning making for Kichwa viewers. As in the case of Nicola, tele-viewers establish relationships with stars and the characters they play. For others, like Olivio and Feliz, they elicit deep emotions like fear and anxiety. Overall, Sacha Lomans reported that images stimulated mixed feelings like hope, longing, love, disappointment, envy, and, for some community elders, confusion, dizziness, and headaches.

There are many scholars who have taken a closer look at the telenovela genre, which recycles themes and content (e.g., the volumes edited by Robert Allen 1995 and Ilan Stavans 2010). Common to most are beautiful, pedigreed women as central and empowered figures, whether moral or immoral. Rural characters are frequently portrayed as engaged in buffoonery, and typically there are no Indigenous leads.[7] Even with their plot twists, threats, and vengeance, telenovelas tend to end on a note of hope or renewal. These themes appear throughout other serial dramas mentioned by Sacha Lomans as potential entertainment: *Mañana es para siempre, Huracán de amor, Dos hogares, Aurora, Marimar, Mariana de la noche, El privilegio de amar, Más sabe el diablo*, and, from the United States, *The OC*.

Telenovelas are not the only thing on television in Sacha Loma. When asked about their favorite programming, in addition to the telenovelas listed above, Sacha Lomans mentioned war, fighting, and action flicks with Jackie Chan, Rambo, Chuck Norris, Jet Li, Jean-Claude Van Damme, and Dwayne "The Rock" Johnson; World Wrestling Entertainment; children's programs like *Harry Potter, Ice Age, Lilo and Stitch, The Lion King, Tinkerbell, Tom and Jerry, The Haunted Mansion, Over the Hedge*, and *Dora the Explorer*; religious-themed films; music television (MTV); and documentary features on the Discovery Channel.

Meanings Attached to Mass-Mediatized Bodies and Behaviors

I showed Kichwa women participants magazine images of Latina actresses like Jennifer Lopez, Euro-American actresses like Angelina Jolie, and Ecuadorian socialites and debutantes in local periodicals with the "society pages" featuring both "regular" women alongside prominent telenovela stars and news personalities like Carolina Jaume. I also presented them postcards of Indigenous women, mostly Waorani and Tsachila, I found in a souvenir shop in Quito, Ecuador's capital city. I asked for their first impressions of the images, and then followed up with a series of pointed questions.

What is most interesting about Kichwa interpretations of mass-mediatized women is the assumption that actresses on television and in magazines must be, for the most, good looking, economically productive, and family-oriented—in other words, the social values Kichwa have always attributed to strong women. Implicit, of course, was actresses' civilization, which is not the case for Indigenous people who are presumed uncivilized until proven otherwise. Kichwa women may readily interrogate Western bodily ways of being even while framing them in more familiar terms: what do these bodies do, and what do they do for others? At the same time, traditional representations of Indigenous women on postcards were held to contemporary educational and professional standards—that is, they were interpreted as uncivilized because they failed to conform to requisites characteristic to globalized modernity.

I am not the first to draw connections between mainstream body images and subliminal invitations to civilization in Latin America (see Roth-Gordon 2013, 298). In Ecuador, foreign ideals of beauty advertised in the media, in tandem with racist ideologies of *blancamiento* (whitening), have generated what Erynn Masi de Casanova terms "'the whiter the better' ideal of beauty" (2004, 291). Imported shows have themes consistent with national race rhetoric, which foregrounds "whiteness and its characteristics: light skin; delicate features; straight/wavy, light-colored hair; and light eyes" (291). These are features that have real implications for young women's livelihoods (298) and thus their ability to provide for their kin (see also Miles 2000).

First Impressions: Good-Looking Family Women

I asked Kichwa to give me their first impressions regarding the women in mainstream magazines and souvenir postcards. I recorded their responses to the question, "Do you have any thoughts about these pictures?" Their reactions, separated by age, are shown in Table 10.3.

Table 10.3. First impressions after viewing images

	Latina actresses	Euro-American actresses	Ecuadorian socialites	Indigenous women postcards
Elder women (28–64)	well-dressed, high heels, models, stylish clothes and makeup, pretty, nice, happy, enjoying life, healthy body, skinny to the point of dying, queens, grandmothers	wives and husbands, mothers and children, family, pretty, working, enjoying, playing, models for clothing, skinny, weddings	beauty pageant participants, singers, like to be on stage, family, happy, boyfriends, queens, singers, participate with guitars and traditional dress	not like "us," traditionally dressed, making brew, pretty, aucas (savage), dangerous, kill people within and outside their group, Shuar, Waorani, in the past, they were aucas
Young women (15–27)	pretty, tall, well-dressed, beautiful, skinny, spectacular, good bodies, good people, attractive, people want their clothes, inspire infidelity, normal, good makeup, fat, selling something	pretty, prepared, successful, work in politics, famous, singers, actors, have good families, have good homes, actresses, models, have to be apart from their husbands for travel, family is separated, beautiful weddings, divorce, infidelity, fleeting happiness, work in hotels, have money, well-dressed, happy family, sick, united home, happy, selfless relationships, good bodies, good children, good boyfriends, good lovers, good friends, different from "us," show off clothes, famous	lots of money, good jobs, happy boyfriends, famous people showing off, actors, singers, talented, beautiful, well-dressed, some are skinny and barely dressed, some are fat and covered up, artists, dancers, happy people who have achieved their dreams, models, dedicated businesspeople, young people who want to advance by doing promotions, pretty, different from "us," presenters at parties and social functions	have customs, "a shame" (said laughing); attractive to outsiders; Waorani; showing off culture and tradition; Waorani are like Kichwa but misbehave; happy; as God made him; enjoying his culture; picture of a culture; natural; innocent; clothes from the woods; face paint, not perfectly painted but happy anyway; Waorani with traditional dress and feather crowns; how they look is no matter, only their personality; nakedness could be offensive to outsiders; don't want to lose their culture, which is why they dress and act as they do; different from "us"

Note: Each descriptor reported only once even if used multiple times

From their initial impressions, there seems to be an association of particular looks with particular social positions and relationships: that is, beautiful women have supportive social networks, as Sarafina assumed too. For example, Kichwa women described Latina actresses like Selena Gomez and Eva Mendez using "pretty," "well-dressed," "spectacular," and "good bodies."[8] They presumed Latina actresses were also "enjoying life" and "good people." Similarly, Euro-American actresses like Angelina Jolie were also "pretty," "skinny," and "rich," but to an even greater extent were perceived to have happy and healthy family lives. Common descriptors were "wives and husbands," "mothers and children," "have good families," "have good homes," "united homes," "selfless relationships," "good children," "good boyfriends," "good lovers," and "good friends." Twenty-three-year-old María commented, "These are people who strive to make good couples and good relationships. They have given up something in order to have a united home."[9] Ecuadorian socialites and local performers also received plenty of remarks praising their beauty. They had "good families" and "happy boyfriends." Thus, according to Sacha Loman Kichwa women in this study, all of the magazine women were arguably whiter and more civilized than my Kichwa collaborators. These women also appeared to, on the whole, have ample and happy social relations, which correlated with their good bodies and appearances.

Economically Productive Sources of Aspirational Longing

After probing for general impressions, I asked Kichwa women yes/no questions about the sets of images, among them: "Have they been successful in life?"; "Are they educated?" (i.e., attended school); and "Would you like to be like them?" (see Table 10.4). Latina actresses, Euro-American actresses, and Ecuadorian socialites were deemed successful unanimously or nearly so. Young women commonly associated success in terms of employment with the Euro-American actresses and Ecuadorian socialites. The Euro-American actresses were described as "prepared," "successful," and "working in politics." The Ecuadorian socialites were characterized as "happy people who have achieved their dreams," "dedicated businesspeople," and "young people who want to advance by doing promotions." These are conclusions that Kichwa women drew primarily based on looks, suggesting that particular bodies gain access to economic and social capital more easily than others, assumptions reinforced by the lavish lifestyles of some actresses as part of their shows' plot.

Table 10.4. Responses to magazine image prompts

Question prompt for picture	Older positive response [n= 10]	Younger positive response [n=13]	Combined positive response [n=23]
Latina actresses: Have they been successful in life?	100%	94%	96%
Latina actresses: Are they educated?	89%	94%	92%
Latina actresses: Would you like to be like them?	56%	35%	42%
Euro-American actresses: Have they been successful in life?	100%	100%	100%
Euro-American actresses: Are they educated?	100%	94%	96%
Euro-American actresses: Would you like to be like them?	89%	52%	65%
Ecuadorian socialites: Have they been successful in life?	100%	94%	96%
Ecuadorian socialites: Are they educated?	100%	100%	100%
Ecuadorian socialites: Would you like to be like them?	90%	38%	58%
Indigenous women: Have they been successful in life?	100%	41%	62%
Indigenous women: Are they educated?	78%	35%	50%
Indigenous women: Would you like to be like them?	44%	12%	23%

A negative response to the question of whether or not someone in an image was educated, which is overwhelmingly perceived by Sacha Lomans as a positive trait, does not necessarily reflect a negative perception of that person. In the case of Latina actresses, Euro-American actresses, and Ecuadorian socialites, those in the images may not be educated because they do not have to be—they are already wealthy, their parents must be wealthy, or they are famous and do not have time for it. Yet, in the case of the Indigenous people in the postcards, not being educated is viewed almost exclusively as negative because it demonstrates that they are not civilizing themselves.

Participants made complex associations with the Indigenous images on the postcards. Indigenous women on the postcards were also believed to be educated fairly consistently by older women (78 percent), while younger women were less likely to think so (35 percent). Interestingly, while older women considered Indigenous women in the postcards to be successful in life, a smaller percentage of younger women (41 percent) judged them successful. Furthermore, the largest marker of success—happy families—did not come up. Kichwa women focused on relationships they assumed the Indigenous people in the postcards had with non-kin others rather than their family life. This is notable given the centrality of family in Kichwa women's own lives. Instead, Kichwa women described the Indigenous men and women as "savage," offensively "naked," and "dangerous" in the same breath as "natural," "innocent," and "picture of a culture." On one hand, they "kill people within and outside their own group" and "misbehave"; on the other hand, they are "attractive to outsiders" like tourists because of their traditional look and behavior.[10] On the whole, Indigenous women were considered less beautiful and not as educated, employed, or worth emulating as actresses and socialites. It is possible that negative perceptions associated with these essentialized images had something to do with the fact that uncivilized bodies are more likely to be stereotyped damagingly by outsiders and thus less able to engage in the educational and professional contexts that generate the current forms of social and economic currency that Sacha Lomans find meaningful.

In response to the question, "Would you like to be like them?" elder women responded positively more than younger women in the case of every set of images, including Indigenous women on the postcards: Euro-American actresses (89 percent) and Ecuadorian socialites (90 percent), Latina actresses (56 percent), and Indigenous women (44 percent). Younger women's responses preferred the image sets in the same order—Euro-American actresses (52 percent), Ecuadorian socialites (38 percent), Latina actresses (35 percent), and Indigenous women (12 percent)—but with a much smaller percentage of positive responses for each set.

Elder women almost always associated being like any one of the people in the mainstream images as a good thing, because, as they justified it to me, it likely meant they would have more money or better jobs to support their family. When I asked them to elaborate, those who had a reason almost always said something similar to what fifty-two-year-old Micaela said: "Of course," she snapped, "they have studied, they move their families forward, and they can provide their kids with food and education!" Reading questions of education and professionalism, or lack thereof, into the images, elder Kichwa women believed the same held true for the women in the postcards. Even Indigenous people, they recognized, are likely nowadays to be educated and have decent jobs. As Micaela reasons regarding a Waorani postcard, "Long ago they would have had no work. Now, more than us [Kichwa] they are professionals and have advanced degrees. The government supports them a lot so that they don't kill people anymore: *para que se enseñen con nosotros* (so that they get used to us, that is, are socialized)." This is a backhanded compliment, of course. Micaela does not think very highly of the Waorani, nor does it seem that she thinks very highly of herself as Kichwa, because she concedes to being less educated in some ways than her Waorani foes. If, to this end, a young person chooses not to get an education or to find a job, then the youngster is conformant to uncivilized, selfish behaviors.

In contrast, younger women, when asked directly, often professed to have the *"yo me acepto tal como soy* (I accept myself as I am)" mentality, similar to the discourse of self-respect popular among contemporary Western youth. In more casual conversation, however, they revealed somewhat different feelings. Twenty-three-year-old María described the sentiments of young women in the community as, "I want to have Shakira's body. I want to copy everything. I want to be like the models I see on television. I want to dress like them." This is at least partly because, as I have suggested, their nice appearances mean that stars and their characters have access to professional success and comfortable family life, as Sarafina communicated at the outset of this chapter. In short, these women, they and their grandmothers assumed, are capable of providing for others.

Civilized women on television are not only read in terms of their adherence to conventional beauty standards but also are interpreted through the lens of filial commitment. Longstanding Kichwa cultural dynamics like kin-centeredness frame renderings of mainstream bodies and behaviors such that women who Sacha Lomans know only as attractive according to dominant racial and cultural preferences become providers. Indigenous women are interpreted in terms of these competing discourses as well. At times they are praised for upholding their cultural values, and questions of civilization seem less important. Other times, appearing traditional is a hindrance to civilization, and they are assumed by looks alone not to be as qualified for education or employment.

Conclusion: "Custom-izing" Conventional Western Bodies and Behaviors?

Kichwa understandings of civilized bodies, in practice, are not charted along a direct line from rural/Indigenous to cosmopolitan/white. Essentialist and traditional representations of Indigenous peoples, like those of music videos and postcards, are interpreted as uncivilized in terms of both cultural practices and stereotypes (e.g., they spear outsiders) and the requisites of contemporary society (e.g., these people are not civilized because they have not pursued higher education). Mass media, in contrast, have their own consistent representations of proper womanhood, which include, predominantly, whiteness, conventional attractiveness, and wealth. While Kichwa women, like Sarafina, grasp, criticize, and/or buy into these intended readings of mainstream bodies and behaviors, their understandings are also influenced by the foundational principle of kin-centeredness that their mothers and grandmothers have long found important. That is, Kichwa women are accommodating new types of bodies and behaviors into their images of productive women, or women who "do" for others.

Actresses in telenovelas and magazines, then, are construed as unquestionably civilized. Their bodies and behaviors are not only understood according to standards of Western beauty (e.g., "they are truly beautiful," as Sarafina put it), but also to Sacha Loman Kichwa cultural standards. Themes of productive sociality are read into white, mainstream women when they are interpreted to be good looking, economically productive, family women. These women's bodies and behaviors are literally "custom-ized" when viewed in terms of kin-centeredness (e.g., white actresses provide for their families). This helps, not hurts, their image in Sacha Loman Kichwas' eyes.

At the same time, we must wonder about risks. Given that foreign images and ideals (civilized whiteness) can be fit into local cultural frameworks (kin-centeredness), the effect of these images and ideals on Sacha Loman women may be amplified. Sixteen-year-old Sarafina lived, studied, and dreamt amidst floor-to-ceiling magazine images that depicted ways of being and behaving very distant from her everyday reality. Women in her telenovelas inhabit mansions while she occupies a modest home in the middle of the rain forest. Women on the shows have high-powered jobs while she struggles to get her high school diploma in a society that disparages her indigeneity. Indeed, one day Sarafina confided in me: "Sometimes I feel badly about my body because I see the images [on television or in magazines], and I want to be like them. But the monkey who dresses in silk is still a monkey." Poor self-esteem and internalized racism are but two of many potential downsides to Sacha Loman women's consumption of "soft-lit," mass mediatized images of beauty and success.

Visions of civilization embodied by white women are an ambivalent and new set of pressures that young Kichwa women negotiate, for now, with reference to family and not the self. For Sacha Lomans, at least for the moment, globalized images of individualized bodies and behaviors like those of telenovela leads must contend with highly valued preferences for collective agency. And they do—as often as regularly scheduled programming.

Acknowledgments

I am grateful to Beth A. Conklin for her guidance and insight over the course of this research. Many thanks to Edward F. Fischer, Laura M. Carpenter, Dominique Béhague, Richard Pace, and Jeff Shenton for their comments on earlier versions of this piece. This research was made possible by funding from the National Science Foundation, Vanderbilt's Robert Penn Warren Center for the Humanities, Vanderbilt's Center for Latin American Studies (CLAS), and Vanderbilt's College of Arts and Science. This material is based upon work supported by the National Science Foundation under Grant Number 1123673. Any opinions, findings, and conclusions or recommendations expressed in this material are those of the author(s) and do not necessarily reflect the views of the National Science Foundation.

Notes

1. I use the words "civilized," and its variations in order to adopt Sacha Loman Kichwas' own descriptors even as I acknowledge the terms stem from a deep and troubling historical experience of ethno-racial discrimination (e.g., Martínez Novo and de la Torre 2010). On one hand, Sacha Lomans' self-characterization in terms of becoming civilized is indicative of their having internalized discriminatory perceptions in everyday comparisons and associations with ethnic others in school, at work, and increasingly on television. On the other hand, when Sacha Lomans speak of the past in terms of their culture's being uncivilized, this is not necessarily with shame. Sometimes it is framed unproblematically, at times proudly, as a process of becoming.
2. People in this community self-identify as "Kichwas" and rarely use the term *runa* (person in Kichwa), which other scholars have deployed when referencing the lowland Amazonian Kichwa peoples in Ecuador with whom they collaborate. Here I will use the term "Kichwa(s)" or "Sacha Lomans," while acknowledging that the cultural dynamics of this community are particular, due to its being a "place in transition" and should not be extended without empirically based reasons to other Kichwa-speaking Indigenous peoples in the Napo or in the Ecuadorian Andes, or to Indigenous peoples in the wider Amazon.
3. Similar observations regarding the dynamics of whiteness and Indigeneity have been made by scholars studying beauty pageants in both lowland and highland Indigenous South American contexts. Exploring pageants in both lowland and highland Ecuador, Mark Rogers (1998) notes that the essentialization of Indigenous identity (what he calls "folklorization") serves to both reproduce existing power structures (when done in white pageants) and resist cultural domination (when done in Indigenous pageants). Andrew Canessa (2012, 249–51) notes that white bodies performing indigeneity in pageants are the ultimate in sexual desirability for local men in Bolivia because they combine elements of forbidden fantasy and assumed accessibility.
4. Though I do not have the space to elaborate the depth of Kichwa-Waorani relations, Waorani are another Indigenous group in the Ecuadorian Amazon that Kichwa consider historically violent and only very recently "civilized"; elder Kichwa claim to have become personally "acquainted" with Waorani spears decades ago and have not forgotten their encounters.

5. As fifty-two-year-old Nemar stated, "Better is the young person who wants to get ahead, to overcome, not only for the young person but also for the rest."
6. For more on lowland South American conviviality and substance exchange, see Conklin and Morgan 1996; Garcés Dávila 2006; Guzmán Gallegos 1997; McCallum 2001; Seeger, da Matta, and Viveiros de Castro 1979; Uzendoski 2004; Walker 2013.
7. Laura Beard (2010, 128) describes "Indigenous-looking" characters in a telenovela she analyzes as maintaining stereotypical roles like domestic employees.
8. One elder woman, however, characterized these women as "skinny to the point of dying."
9. Yet Euro-American actresses did receive some negative comments with respect to their family life. Some young Sacha Loman women assumed that their demanding jobs would mean that they would be separated from their families and possibly risk "infidelity," "divorce," or "fleeting happiness"; in other words, these women are still conceptualized in terms of family, including, more rarely, what they are *not* doing for kin.
10. It should be noted that the aversion of Sacha Loman Kichwa women to those women represented in the postcards probably has something to do with their deep-seated opinions, prejudices, and fears of Waorani as, in their words, "different from us," "a shame," and "savage." Older women remember the Waorani as, in their words, uncivilized hooligans who decades ago, when occupying the same rain forest territory, chased them from their homes in the middle of the night. Even so, given some similarities in custom shared between Kichwa women and those women in the postcards—such as the Shuar women making brew, a beverage staple in Kichwa households—it would not be unreasonable for there to be some comments regarding family associations.

References

Allen, R. (ed). 1995. *To Be Continued . . . : Soap Operas around the World*. New York: Routledge.

Askew, K., and R. Wilk (eds). 2002. *The Anthropology of Media: A Reader*. Malden, MA: Blackwell.

Beard, L. 2010. "Whose Life in the Mirror? Examining Three Mexican Telenovelas as Cultural and Commercial Products." In *Telenovelas*, edited by I. Stavans, 116–31. Ilan Stavans Library of Latino Civilization. Santa-Barbara, CA: Greenwood.

Becker, A. 2004. "Television, Disordered Eating, and Young Women in Fiji: Negotiating Body Image and Identity during Rapid Social Change." *Culture, Medicine and Psychiatry* 28 (4): 533–59.

Canessa, A. 2012. *Intimate Indigeneities: Race, Sex, and History in the Small Spaces of Andean Life*. Durham, NC: Duke University Press.

Conklin, B., and L. Morgan. 1996. "Babies, Bodies, and the Production of Personhood in North America and a Native Amazonian Society." *Ethos* 24 (4): 657–94.

Eddy, K., M. Hennessey, and H. Thompson-Brenner. 2007. "Eating Pathology in East African Women." *Journal of Nervous and Mental Disease* 195 (3): 196–202.

Floyd, S. 2008. "The Pirate Media Economy and the Emergence of Quichua Language Media Spaces in Ecuador." *Anthropology of Work Review* 29 (2): 34–41.

Foucault, M. 1980. *Power/Knowledge: Selected Interviews and Other Writings, 1972–1977.* Pantheon Books.

Garcés Dávila, A. 2006. *Relaciones de género en la Amazonia ecuatoriana: Estudios de caso en comunidades indígenas Achuar, Shuar y Kichua.* Quito, Ecuador: ABYA-YALA.

Guzmán-Gallegos, M. 1997. *Para que la yuca beba nuestra sangre: Trabajo, género y parentesco en una comunidad Quichua de la Amazonia ecuatoriana.* Quito, Ecuador: ABYA-YALA.

Ginsburg, F. 1991. "Indigenous Media: Faustian Contract or Global Village." *Cultural Anthropology* 6 (1): 92–112.

———. 2000. "Resources of Hope: Learning from the Local in a Transnational Era." In *Indigenous Cultures in an Interconnected World,* edited by C. Smith and G. Ward, 27–48. Vancouver: University of British Columbia Press.

Hall, S. 1992. "The Question of Cultural Identity." In *Modernity and Its Futures,* edited by S. Hall, D. Held, and T. McGrew, 273–326. Cambridge, MA.: Polity Press.

High, C. 2010. "Warriors, Hunters, and Bruce Lee: Gendered Agency and the Transformation of Amazonian Masculinity." *American Ethnologist* 37 (4): 753–70.

Himpele, J. 2007. *Circuits of Culture: Media, Politics, and Indigenous Identity in the Andes.* Minneapolis: University of Minnesota Press.

Martínez Novo, C., and C. de la Torre. 2010. "Racial Discrimination and Citizenship in Ecuador's Educational System." *Latin American and Caribbean Ethnic Studies* 5 (1): 1–26.

Masi de Casanova, E. 2004. "'No Ugly Women': Concepts of Race and Beauty among Adolescent Women in Ecuador." *Gender and Society* 18 (3): 287–308.

McCallum, C. 2001. *Gender and Sociality in Amazonia: How Real People Are Made.* New York: Berg.

McLuhan, M. 1994. *Understanding Media: The Extensions of Man.* Cambridge, MA: MIT Press.

Meadows, M. 2009. "Walking the Talk: Reflections on Indigenous Media Audience Research Methods." *Participations* 6 (1): 118–36.

Miles, A. 2000. "Poor Adolescent Girls and Social Transformations in Cuenca, Ecuador." *Ethos* 28 (1): 54–74.

Overing, J., and A. Passes, eds. 2000. *The Anthropology of Love and Anger: The Aesthetics of Conviviality in Native Amazonia.* New York, NY: Routledge.

Pace, R. 2009. "Television's Interpellation: Heeding, Missing, Ignoring, and Resisting the Call for Pan-National Identity in the Brazilian Amazon." *American Anthropologist* 111 (4): 407–19.

Pace, R., and B. Hinote. 2013. *Amazon Town TV: An Audience Ethnography in Gurupá, Brazil.* Joe R. and Teresa Lozano Long Series in Latin American and Latino Art and Culture. Austin: University of Texas Press.

Raheja, M. 2007. "Reading Nanook's Smile: Visual Sovereignty, Indigenous Revisions of Ethnography, and *Atanarjuat* (The Fast Runner)." *American Quarterly* 59 (4): 1159–85.

Reis, R. 1998. "The Impact of Television Viewing in the Brazilian Amazon." *Human Organization* 57 (3): 253–57.

Rogers, M. 1998. "Spectacular Bodies: Folklorization and the Politics of Identity in Ecuadorian Beauty Pageants." *Journal of Latin American Anthropology* 3 (2): 54–85.

Roth-Gordon, J. 2013. "Racial Malleability and the Sensory Regime of Politically Conscious Brazilian Hip Hop." *Journal of Latin American and Caribbean Anthropology* 18 (2): 294–313.

Salazar, J., and A. Córdova. 2008. "Imperfect Media and the Poetics of Indigenous Video in Latin America." In *Global Indigenous Media: Cultures, Poetics, and Politics*, edited by P. Wilson and M. Stewart, 39–57. Durham, NC: Duke University Press.

Seeger, A., R. da Matta, and E. Viveiros de Castro. 1979. "A construção da pessoa nas sociedades Indígenas brasileiras." *Boletim do museu nacional*, Série antropologia, 32: 2–19.

Stavans, I., ed. 2010. *Telenovelas*. The Ilan Stavans Library of Latino Civilization. Santa-Barbara, CA: Greenwood.

Straubhaar, J. 2003. "Choosing National TV: Cultural Capital, Language, and Cultural Proximity in Brazil." In *The Impact of International Television: A Paradigm Shift*, edited by M. Flasmar, 77–110. Mahwah, NJ: Lawrence Erlbaum Associates.

Turner, T. 1991. "The Social Dynamics of Video Media in an Indigenous Society: The Cultural Meaning and the Personal Politics of Video–Making in Kayapó Communities." *Visual Anthropology Review* 7 (2): 68–76.

———. 1992. "Defiant Images: The Kayapó Appropriation of Video." *Anthropology Today* 8 (6): 5–16.

———. 1995. "Representation, Collaboration and Mediation in Contemporary Ethnographic and Indigenous Media." *Visual Anthropology Review* 11 (2): 102–6.

Uzendoski, M. 2004. "Manioc Beer and Meat: Value, Reproduction and Cosmic Substance among the Napo Runa of the Ecuadorian Amazon." *Journal of the Royal Anthropological Institute* 10 (4): 883–902.

———. 2005. *The Napo Runa of Amazonian Ecuador*. Chicago: University of Illinois Press.

Walker, H. 2013. *Under a Watchful Eye: Self, Power, and Intimacy in Amazonia*. Berkeley: University of California Press.

Wortham, E. 2013. *Indigenous Media in Mexico: Culture, Community, and the State*. Durham, NC: Duke University Press.

Wroblewski, M. 2014. Public Indigeneity, Language Revitalization, and Intercultural Planning in a Native Amazonian Beauty Pageant. *American Anthropologist* 116 (1): 65–80.

11

Reproducing Colonial Fantasies

The Indigenous Other in Brazilian Telenovelas

By Antonio La Pastina

"Representation becomes narration."

Charles Ramirez-Berg (2002)

In 1996 and 1997, I conducted fieldwork in a small community in rural north-eastern Brazil to understand the ways in which telenovelas entered the lives of people at the periphery of the urban world often represented in those texts (La Pastina 1999). A third of the way through *O rei do gado* (The cattle king), one of the telenovelas I was following with the locals, a child was introduced. In the days before the child's arrival, several youngsters in town were very excited about the impending appearance of this child in the telenovela. They were excited because they were going to see a child on a telenovela, an uncommon occurrence, and they hoped to see how kids lived elsewhere. But the arrival of this child was a major let down to some of my "informants." "Mas é um Índio (But it is an Indian boy)," said Joana, almost crying. Joana was the daughter of a family with whom I often watched telenovelas. Her younger sister echoed her unhappiness. The problem for these two young girls was that in their understanding, "Indigenous people" are not interesting. As I would find in many of the interviews I conducted with adults, Indigenous people are thought to be no-good troublemakers, dirty and primitive. The two young girls, and many other youth in town, had hoped for a boy or girl that would present to them the lives that they imagined urban kids lived; instead, this Indigenous boy remitted them to the life of hunting, fishing, and running shoeless and dirty in the open fields. That was not a reassuring image that allowed them to see themselves in a better (i.e., urban) future, but rather one that brought them closer to the "primitive" lives they wanted to distance themselves from.

Another narrative that shaped my understanding about nonmainstream populations in Brazil and how they relate to the nation and its ideological project predates the previous one by almost two decades. It is a scene in a movie, not a telenovela. In the movie *Bye Bye Brazil* (1980), by Caca Diegues, an Indigenous elder is in a canoe with white "Brazilians" and he refers to the president of Brazil as the chief of their nation, as if the nation he and his people lived in was not a part of Brazil. The sound track by Chico Buarque made that even clearer when he sang: "Eu vi um Brasil na TV (I saw a Brazil on TV)." This Brazil seen on TV was a Brazil that was inhabited by others and produced representations that were foreign to many: poor rural people, people of African descent or Indigenous people, groups often absent from the screen.

These two images guide my concern about the ways in which Others, and particularly Indigenous Others, are represented within mainstream Brazilian media and how these representations or their absences symbolically annihilate these groups and their culture. For Morris-Suzuki (2005) "our knowledge of the past is of course made up of representations, which include 'narratives' in the conventional sense of the word, as well as non-narrative images such as photographs. But it is not just representation. It is knowledge which shapes feelings and actions, and which is itself shaped by the experience of acting in the world" (234). This "knowledge of history," she continues," we have absorbed consciously or unconsciously though a host of media determines who we feel sympathy for, which contemporary events stir us joy, compassion or anger, and how we respond to these events" (235).

Indigenous people in Brazil constitute 0.4 percent of the country's population ("Indígenas: Gráficos e tabelas"), with approximately 240 distinct ethnic groups forming this peripheral population. Nevertheless, Indigenous people occupy a historical and symbolic presence central to that country's imagining of itself. This chapter looks at one way in which representations of Indigenous people are manipulated within the media genre of telenovelas. Analyzing these produced images, this essay argues they increase the marginalization of these ethnic groups while reproducing patriarchal and colonial ideologies about the role and place of Indigenous people in the Brazilian society. The representational power that images of Indigenous people have in Brazil, how they function as stereotypes, and the symbolic annihilation (Gerbner 1972; Tuchman 1981) that they perform are at the core of this essay. According to Means and Yochin (2008) "as it pertains specifically to race, symbolic annihilation means that those racial groups who are not presented as fully developed in media, be it through absence, trivialization, or condemnation, may see their social status diminished" (4).

Telenovelas, a standard Brazilian cultural product and key to the success of the local media industry, are primetime serial fiction that have dominated the evening entertainment in most Brazilian households since the 1950s. These shows last six months to a year, depending on audience ratings, and are aired from Monday to Saturday from late afternoon to late evening. The evening line-up will vary from decade to decade and from station to station, but the dominant network since the late 1960s, TV Globo, has a grid that begins at five p.m. with a soap opera in the mold of US soaps that has evolved under the same premise and title since the 1980s. The six o'clock telenovela normally relies on literary adaptations, a light dose of religiosity, and inspirational messages, normally targeting the elderly and youngsters with their romantic plots. The seven o'clock tends to be a comedy, with caricaturesque representations, closer to a sitcom in its light tone. But the main fare on primetime is the show that airs after the newscast, normally around nine p.m. This will grab the largest audience ratings, include the most well-known actors, and have the highest production values.

Periodically, Globo may broadcast late-night miniseries that range from a few days to a couple of months long and tackle highly complex narratives, with well-known casts and production teams. Telenovelas can also incorporate exotic locations, pro-social messages, or political content, depending on the writer penning the plot. Telenovelas have evolved over the decades to become clearly mass-market auteur narratives. Over the last sixty-five years, since the inception of television in Brazil in 1950, telenovelas have evolved to become a central force in the articulation of the Brazilian identity (Hamburger 2005; La Pastina 2004). Their repetitive nature, the recurrence of stock characters, and the reliance on urban upper-middle-class environments and values have all served to ensconce acceptable ways of life and lifestyles, while also presenting often disruptive narratives intended to raise awareness of nonmainstream issues. In the last decade, the representations of Brazilians of African descent (more than 50 percent of the Brazilian population) have been radically changed from the way they were presented in most of the genre's history. Arguments about the rise of the lower-middle class due to economic transformations as well as the move of the upper-middle-class audiences to cable, satellite television, and streaming options has forced networks to retarget their products to reach a broader audience. Indigenous people, unlike other minority groups, have not benefited from these changes in the economic, social, and mediatic environments.

In his book *Racial Revolutions*, Warren (2001) enlightened the reader on the situation of Indigenous groups in the northeast of Brazil. Many have held onto their cultural heritage in secrecy. Most will claim to be black rather than Indigenous, because the chances of finding a job increase and the chances of discrimination decrease. In Brazil, a country with clearly documented racial discrimination in job opportunities for people of black ancestry (Telles 2006), to be Indigenous means that you move even further down in the racial hierarchy.

In this chapter, I take this context as a point of departure to investigate how

Brazilian Indigenous people have been represented in telenovelas. Those highly popular TV shows are a key source of shared ideas about the nation in Brazil. Even today, in 2016, with an increasing penetration of paid television, a TV Globo telenovela will have ratings hovering between 30 and 40 percent of all television sets. And some of the telenovelas I will be discussing, broadcast in decades past, had much higher ratings.

The objective is first to document how these texts have constructed representations of an oppressed segment of the Brazilian population, whose history, culture, and identity are part of the foundational narratives of Brazil's national identity. There are a range of texts, from artworks (e.g., Tarsila do Amaral's painting *Abaporu*), to Indianist novels (e.g., José de Alencar's *Iracema*), to orchestral works (e.g., Heitor Villa-Lobos' *Floresta do Amazonas*), to avant-garde fiction (e.g., Mario de Andrade's *Macunaíma*) that have revolved around Indigenous characters and themes, sometimes relying on traditional lore but rarely incorporating the voices of Brazilian Indigenous people into those texts. According to Guzman (2010, 37) "the Amazon and its inhabitants appear repeatedly in national cultural productions as a patriotic trope to represent the whole or imagined essence of the country."

Over the last decade an increasingly complex portrayal of African descendants has emerged in telenovelas in Brazil with fully formed urban middle-class families or leading roles played by black Brazilian actors. This is not a panacea and the leading roles and majority of plots remain focused on the white, urban upper-middle class. But it is a change that indicates a different way of thinking about Brazilians of African-descent within media production centers. The situation of Indigenous characters, however, remains quite unchanged. Stam (1997), investigating the representation of Black Brazilians on film, discusses Indigenous representations briefly, arguing that, unlike other Latin American countries, Brazil rarely had Indigenous filmmakers and produced a very limited number of films with Indian directors, themes, and performers. "The Indian thematic, meanwhile, is important during the silent period (a time when Black themes are absent), but then largely disappears during the 1930s, 1940s, 1950s and 1960s. . . . Indian themes emerge again in the 1970s through the 1990s" (20). In describing the range of representations of Indigenous people in Brazilian movies, he lists the following stereotypes: the noble savage, the primitive to be modernized, the comic Indian, the modernist cannibal, the allegorical rebel, the victim Indian, and the self-representing, camcorder-wielding Indian (21). Of those, the primitive to be modernized and the comic Indian are the most commonly found stereotypical representations in the telenovelas discussed in this chapter.

Analyzing the information available on those telenovelas produced by the various networks that existed in Brazil since 1950, I found several patterns of representation.

1. Few of these shows incorporated recurring Indigenous characters. In the next section I will review the key telenovelas with Indigenous characters, but suffice it to say that fewer than twenty telenovelas had any Indigenous plots of recurring characters.
2. These characters were often used to make a point about some of the leading characters or narrative arcs. Very few telenovelas had Indigenous people as leading characters of theme, with *Aritana* (TV Tupi, 1978–1979, 8 p.m.) and *Alma gêmea* (Twin soul, TV Globo, 2005–2006, 6 p.m.) as rare exceptions.
3. Characters are often the result of interracial relationships, and, with one exception, the father was always white and the mother Indian. In my analysis, which relied on archival material such as synopses of telenovelas, newspaper articles, and research on the history of the genre, I found only one exception to this rule, and, at the end of that telenovela, it is the coming together of a white man and an Indian woman that breaks the curse central to the narrative.
4. With very few exceptions, non-Indian actors in make-up portrayed most of the Indigenous people in telenovelas.
5. Indigenous people spoke in broken Portuguese, were often infantilized, and were portrayed as part of a generic Indian society with no clear ethnic, cultural, or linguistic traditions.

Telenovelas and Miniseries

In the early years of the telenovela, when they were often presented live, there were a few representations, but very little documentation exists of those texts. These telenovelas were based on imported scripts and often set in foreign or fictitious locations. *A rainha louca* (The crazy queen, TV Globo, 1967) is one such example, set in Mexico and with a Mexican Indian character played by a white actor in the leading evil role. In *O mestiço* (The 'half-breed,' TV Tupi, 1966) a white actor plays Renato, the son of a white man and an Indian woman. He is discriminated against because of his mixed ancestry. *Minas de prata* (The silver mines, TV Excelsior, 1966–1967), set in the eighteenth century El Salvador, had the Indian-identified actor J. Lopes Índio playing an Indian in the story. This was his only telenovela appearance although he has had a forty-year career in cinema and commercials. TV Culture produced *A muralha* (The wall), based on a novel by Dinah Silveria de Queiroz in 1961. TV Excelsior produced it again in 1968. And in 2000, TV Globo produced *A muralha* as a miniseries with forty-nine episodes as part of the celebration of the five hundredth anniversary of the arrival of the Portuguese in Brazil. In this narrative, set in early colonial São Paulo, Indigenous people are seen as the victims of conquest, destruction, catechization, and slavery. There is very little free will and independence. In the TV Globo miniseries, there was only one Indian actor, Bumba, while white actors played all of the other Indian characters. According to Almeida (2012) only three key characters were understandable to the viewers, while most of the others spoke in an incomprehensible manner.

Almeida (2012) also found that this miniseries did not allow for Indigenous resistance to be explored, only presenting the exploitation of the natives by the colonizers. She cites historical research that documents how the colonization did not happen so smoothly and that there was a well-organized resistance; she concludes that the Indian appears as a passive actor on television. As in many other telenovelas that we will discuss, *A muralha* presented a homogenized view of Indigenous people. Almeida presents a possible explanation to justify this phenomenon, arguing that the story is set in a period during which the colonizers were trying to impose a homogeneous culture, forcing the Indigenous communities to lose their ethnic characteristics (Almeida 2012). In *A muralha* the white elite talked about the Indian women in pejorative tones. The leading patriarch, Don Bráz, refers to them as *bugras*, a pejorative term to mean wild, non-Christian, primitive, and dissolute, "walking alone on the streets and lying down with anyone in the fields" (134). According to Queiroz (1989), *A muralha* ignored the reality of the colonial São Paulo where the elite were not just white people, but also those descended from the early settlers and their offspring with captive Indian women.

In the 1970s three telenovelas with Indigenous characters or themes stand out. Of those, two were remade in the 2000s: *Os irmãos Coragem* (The brothers Coragem, TV Globo 1970 and 2005) and *Bicho do mato* (Wild beast, TV Globo 1972 and TV Record, 2006–2007). *Aritana* (TV Tupi, 1978–1979, 8 pm), probably the most complex representation of Indigenous people, their culture, and their stories, did not have the same fate. In *Os irmãos Coragem*, Potira is an adopted Indian (played in the 2005 version by Dira Paes, an actor descendant of Indigenous people) who is the object of desire of one of the brothers. She is played without context or a sense of culture. During the telenovela she meets Indaiá, her Indian mother. But as the plot develops, little cultural context is provided for these characters. Her indigeneity serves to exoticize her but not to provide a cultural background to her actions and values. *Bicho do mato* is the story of a young man raised in a small town near the fictitious Guaporá Indigenous people, who has to fight to protect his and the Guaporás' lands from diamond prospectors. This telenovela had the potential to address serious issues, but as a comedy it focused on the cultural shock and miscommunications between the small town young man and his Indian friend, Iru, and the urban life they confronted in the big city. Indigenous people are presented as comedic foil. They are disempowered and little of their culture is presented.

Even with representational problems, *Aritana* was a politically sophisticated narrative on Indigenous people and their struggles in contemporary Brazil. No other telenovela to date has engaged with Indigenous themes with such complexity and political consciousness. *Aritana* relied on extensive footage of Xingu Indigenous Park's everyday life as a backdrop to establish the identity of the main character, Aritana, as an Indian. The Yawalapiti and the Kamayurá, two groups living in the Xingu area, helped in the production with the support of the National Indian Foundation (FUNAI) and the Villas-Boas brothers, important activists and Indigenists instrumental in the creation of the Xingu Indigenous Park in 1978.

Aritana is the son of a white man and an Indian woman. He has an "evil" white uncle who wants to take the lands that belonged to Aritana's father and sell it, in the process expelling the Indigenous people living in their ancestral land. Aritana, with his fragmented Portuguese, intense emotions, naïve understanding of the outside urban modern world, and his good heart, has to fight to protect his tribe and his way of life. Handsome and sexy, with most of his body often exposed, he was the embodiment of the noble savage, but also the image of the Indian who needs to be modernized described by Stam (1997) in his work on Brazilian films. Aritana falls in love with a blond, blue-eyed veterinarian. The couple, played by Carlos Alberto Riccelli and Bruna Lombardi, became a recurrent presence on the covers of magazines during the broadcast of the show, often wearing minimal clothes and exotic, pseudo-Indian ornaments.

Carvalho and Neves (2014) provide a context for the broadcasting of Aritana. They argue that in 1978, in the midst of the Brazilian dictatorship and the modernizing and expansionist project of the military regime, many roads were opened to connect the industrial South to Brasilia, the recently built capital in the center of the country, and to the Amazon in the Northern frontier, often cutting through Indigenous lands. News stories on the clearing of the forests for the opening of the Trans Amazon Highway and the Indigenous conflicts that ensued brought greater awareness of the region and the Indigenous groups living in the area. Ivani Ribeiro wrote the political telenovela *Aritana* in a moment of increased awareness of the struggles of the Indigenous people and challenges their existence posed to the ongoing modernization project. *Aritana* embodied the struggle of the Indigenous people and their nascent movement against industrialists who saw the region as a source of riches and the Indian's existence as a hindrance to Brazil's progress. The telenovela did not directly criticize the military government, attempting, I imagine, to minimize the risks of censorship, but indirectly made it clear that the Indian groups were fighting a battle for survival. Toward the end of the program it attained greater commercial popularity without minimizing Indigenous issues and the differences between the Indigenous and mainstream societies. The telenovela's theme song

was entitled "Kraho," the name of an Indigenous group, and recorded by Mar-
lui Miranda in the Kraho language. Miranda has had a long trajectory as a
promoter of Indigenous music. This choice was another innovative and subver-
sive attempt by Ivani Ribeiro, TV Tupi, and the production team to promote
Indigenous culture.

Many viewers saw this telenovela as propaganda for Indigenous rights and
were critical of Ribeiro and the network. Toward the end of the telenovela, TV
Tupi defended the author's intentions by broadcasting *O caso* Aritana, *uma
novela a parte* (The case of *Aritana*: A unique telenovela) in early December.
This documentary was an opportunity for members of the cast and advocates
to speak about Indigenous rights in Brazil, a rare event at that point in time.
TV Tupi was closed less than two years after the broadcasting of this telenovela
by the military regime that did not renew its licenses.

Aritana was progressive and innovative. It is hard to ignore the international
context in which this telenovela emerged. It was broadcast at the cusp of the
massive strikes that began in São Paulo in 1979 and that would help to undermine the military regime, while the international civil rights movements was
still strong and TV shows like *Roots* in the United States were circulating internationally. Ribeiro's insertion of *Aritana* within this context reinforces the discussions of telenovelas' centrality in social and political debates in Brazil.

During the 1980s and 1990s no significant representations of Indigenous
people emerged in telenovelas. *O rei do gado* (The cattle king, TV Globo,
1996–1997), mentioned earlier in this essay, included an Indian character—a
child, the son of a white man and an Indian woman. The child was taken by
the father to be "adopted" by him and his white wife, who was unaware her
husband was the real father. The boy was wild, unruly, and stubborn, rarely
speaking, and, when doing so, he used the stereotypical broken Portuguese
associated with Indigenous people in telenovelas. He was a difficult child un-
willing to change. The scenes in the village were often of traditional rituals in
the Xingu region, presented respectfully and beautifully filmed. But the images
of the Indian mother (a white actress in make-up), however, showed a bitter
and vengeful woman. These were minor characters that served to lengthen the
duration of the melodrama by extending and exploring these narrative threads,
a common practice when a telenovela is attaining high audience ratings, as was
the case with *O rei do gado*.

With the celebrations of the five hundredth anniversary of the arrival of the
Portuguese in 2000, several telenovelas were produced to mark the occasion.
One could argue that this interest and increase in visibility was more prejudicial
than beneficial to Indigenous people and their cause. As noted in the opening
of this essay, representation becomes narration, and the images that circulated
in the six telenovelas and three miniseries broadcast in this decade (two already

discussed, *A muralha* and *Bicho do mato*, which were remakes of telenovelas from earlier decades) helped to solidify the stereotypes already circulating in the Brazilian mediascape. An important characteristic of these telenovelas is that two were comedies aired at the seven p.m. time slot normally reserved for this genre and the other four were broadcast at six p.m., a time normally dedicated to romantic, religiously inclined telenovelas, sometimes adapted from literary texts. The three miniseries were broadcast in the eleven p.m. time slot.

Uga-uga (TV Globo, 2000–2001) was a comedy that relied on the overused trope of intercultural challenges confronted by a white man raised by Indigenous people who has to adapt to urban life. A wealthy family of explorers from southern Brazil was traveling in the Amazon where the father hoped to discover an uncontacted tribe. He left toys for the savages to find and hopefully become interested in meeting. One night they were savagely attacked by the Indigenous people. The scene unfolds in slow motion while the *Bachianas Brasileiras No. 5* plays, an intensely dramatic piece of music composed by Heitor Villa-Lobos, a revered Brazilian composer. They were all killed except for the young son who was raised by the Indigenous people. Twenty years later, after an intense search funded by his grandfather, which dishonest relatives tried to thwart, Tatuapú, as the boy was then called, returned as the grandson of a very wealthy family. But before he was rescued he was captured, caged, and exhibited as a carnival attraction, a real-life, bare-chested, loincloth-wearing Tarzan. He came back as the naïve Indian to be modernized, of gorgeous body and pure heart, and, in this case, long blond hair. He spoke a made-up language, developed by the authors to avoid connecting the character with any real tribe. The white actors representing the Indigenous people were outfitted in a parody of tribal clothing, creating a generic tribal affiliation.

The ideas of hygiene and morals among the members of the tribe were portrayed as questionable, and the *pajé* (shaman) was a trickster. Before the arrival of the real grandson, the family hired and trained an actor to play the lost grandson as a violent and wild Indian. But the real grandson, raised by the Indigenous people, was good and caring. The paradox in the show is that it ridicules Brazilians' stereotypes of Indigenous people while reinforcing them, and sending the message that the only true good Indian is really white. Protesting the representations of Indigenous people in *Uga-uga*, the Indigenous Commission of Bahia sent a letter to the human rights commission of the Brazilian Congress. In it they wrote "*Uga-Uga* presents an image of Indigenous people in our nation . . . of people without sentiment and capacity; we are presented as animals in a circus attraction, used to call the attention of the viewers" (Gonçalves 2000, my translation).

Of all of the problematic telenovelas representing Indigenous characters in Brazil, the comedy *A lua me disse* (The moon told me, TV Globo, 2000, 7 p.m.)

probably caused the greatest outcry among Indigenous groups and their advocates. Índia, the character played by the Indigenous-identified actress Bumba, was verbally abused repeatedly in the show. She was the maid in the house of one of the leading characters. Played as a naïve and instinctual woman, the character is sex-crazy, running after men, screaming: "When Índia wants man she gets naked in hut, Índia likes to see man naked, Índia wants!" Índia spoke in broken Portuguese following the stereotypical third-person structure used in Hollywood movies. In interviews she said she grew up in the city of Belém and did not speak any Indigenous language. When speaking in an Indigenous language in the telenovela she said she just made it up. Índia was often called *Nhanbiquara* by her abusers, consequently using her possible ethnic affiliation as a pejorative term (Vaz 2005).

The Nhanbiquara people and Indigenous organizations formally complained, arguing that the character of Índia denigrated the Nhanbiquara culture specifically and Indigenous women more broadly. On July 29, 2005, the Ministério Público Federal (Brazilian government agency for law enforcement), responding to complaints by Indigenous groups, recommended that TV Globo stop broadcasting scenes that placed the character of Índia in awkward and degrading scenes. TV Globo, the network producing the show, never formally responded to these complaints, but at the end of the telenovela Índia found a very big diamond in the mine and, as a rich woman, had her former oppressors working for her. The lack of a proper name for the character, or a community and sense of belonging, perpetuates the character's, and consequently the broader Indian population's, stereotypical representations as alienated, disconnected, instinctual, and primitive.

The telenovelas *Alma gêmea* (Twin soul, TV Globo, 2005–2006, 6 p.m.) and *Araguaia* (TV Globo, 2010–2011, 6 p.m.) had Indigenous characters and mystic subthemes. In *Alma gêmea*, Serena, the daughter of a white miner and an Indian woman, has visions that she cannot explain. The viewer soon discovers she is the reincarnation of a white woman who had died earlier in the telenovela. Serena was raised in an Indigenous community with Indigenous values. After her village was destroyed and her father killed by a group of invading miners, Serena departed to find her dream. Separated by traditional melodramatic formulas, she finally met and married her true love, the man whose wife had died twenty years earlier and been reincarnated in Serena. The telenovela was heavily enmeshed in spiritual beliefs about reincarnation. Once Serena left her community, her Indigenous life and culture were less present in the narrative, and Serena embodied most of the values and manners of the departed woman, a former ballerina, including dancing like her. Her speech, however, remained broken and fragmentary, becoming a source of discrimination and reproach by members of the true love's family.

Araguaia, on the other hand, relied on the mystical power of Indigenous people who cursed the male line of a white family in the mid-1800s. This is the only story where a white woman and an Indian man fall in love and have a son. This son and all of his descendants were cursed by the Indian woman who was abandoned by the Indian man in love with the white woman. The curse is that all men of that lineage will die on the banks of the Araguaia River prematurely. The last descendant of the Indian tribe that placed the curse on the family must excise the curse by killing the man with whom she has fallen in love. But their love finally breaks the curse, restoring the patriarchal order as the white man possesses the Indian woman.

A invenção do Brasil (The invention of Brazil, TV Globo, 2000, 11 p.m.) was a micro-series of four episodes, part of Globo's celebration of the five hundred years of "discovery." It was later edited into a movie. The director Guel Araes produced a comedy in a style he termed neotropicalist. It narrated the story of Caramuru, a Portuguese man stranded in Brazil at the beginning of the colonization who escaped being cooked by Indigenous people by shooting his pistol up in the air. Because of this magical power he was then made king by the Indigenous people and, while living with the tribe, had romances with two Indian women.

Patterns and Discontinuities: Bodies

Of all the telenovelas discussed in this essay, only *Araguaia* presents a case of a white woman and an Indigenous man having a relationship and a child. Most of the other Indigenous characters in telenovelas with significant relevance in the narratives were the result of an interracial relationship between a white man and an Indigenous woman. This pattern of white males of European descent reproducing with Indian women perpetuates the pattern of Indigenous female exploitation that is the foundation of the colonization of Brazil. Gambini (2000), in his analysis of the formation of the Brazilian identity, discusses at length the relationship between the early colonizers, the Jesuits, and the Indian women. He describes how it was not uncommon for these early colonizers, who had left their wives in Portugal, to have twenty or more Indian women enslaved and used as concubines. The Jesuits, upon their arrival in 1549, were shocked by polygamy and cannibalism and tried to eradicate both from the new colony. They vilified the Indian women and begged the Portuguese Crown to send women—prostitutes, orphans—to help reduce the threat posed by Indian women's available bodies. As we saw, these telenovela narratives reproduce and normalize white European patriarchal rights and authority over the female Indian body, asserting their virility and superiority over the Indigenous women and emasculating the Indigenous male.

The Indigenous body is often presented as sexualized and desirable. It is interesting that *Aritana*, a telenovela in the late 1970s, already presented a highly objectified male body, a trend that would become part of many telenovelas, particularly at the seven p.m. time slot in the 2000s, as was the case with *Uga-uga* and *Bicho do mato*. The exposed body is a recurrent motif of Indigenous representations. The noble savage has the body of a warrior. The Indian maiden has a perfect body. Another characteristic of most of the Indian bodies on telenovelas is that they are the bodies of white actors wearing make-up. Carvalho and Neves (2015), in analyzing the portrayal of Indigenous people on telenovelas, argued that there is a whitening of the Indigenous body, because the "bodies that are accepted to interpret those roles are those of white individuals with European features" (91).

With very few exceptions, Indigenous actors have never worked in speaking roles in telenovelas. Bumba, one of the few Indian-identified telenovela actors, performed in *A lua me disse* and *A muralha*. Dira Paes, who traces her ancestry to Indigenous people as well as white and black Portuguese, acted in the role of Potira in *Irmãos Coragem*. Suyane Moreira is the granddaughter of Indigenous people and has played an Indian woman in *Araguaia* and the miniseries *Amazônia, de galvéz a Chico Mendes* (TV Globo, 2007). These two younger actresses, unlike Bumba, have successfully played many roles not constrained by their ethnic heritage. I could not locate any other Indigenous-identified actors with speaking roles in telenovelas.

Voices

Neves and Carvalho (2015) documented the pattern of broken Portuguese often spoken by Indigenous characters on telenovelas. In their article they focused on three telenovelas, *Uga-uga*, *Alma gêmea*, and *A lua me disse*, and found a consistent pattern of incorrect grammatical and structural use of the Portuguese language, with Indigenous characters often adopting an infantilized and naïve way of speaking and communicating. It seems that the Indigenous people in these telenovelas also followed a Hollywood formula of speaking in the third person. Neves and Carvalho's observations can be expanded to most of the telenovelas discussed in this essay. When Indian characters were extras, they often had no voice or were made to speak in made-up languages or in ways that were not understandable by the audience. I could not document the use of any specific Indigenous language spoken with subtitles used to provide translation into Portuguese. Consequently, it is fair to say that Brazilian telenovela writers and producers have not made an effort to represent the linguistic diversity of the Indigenous population in Brazil.

The few characters described in the previous sections that had recurring roles with sustained participation spoke in broken Portuguese. Often these characters' lack of Portuguese proficiency was equated with a limited understanding of the cultural complexities of the non-Indian world. Ultimately, this limited language proficiency and the infantilized form they spoke transformed even serious discussions into comic moments for audiences who interpreted these interactions in the broader context of representations of Indigenous people in Brazilian and Hollywood media.

Identities

Hundreds, if not thousands, of locations through Brazil are named after Indigenous words. The diet and cuisine of Brazilians is heavily indebted to Indigenous tastes, products, and technologies. The mystical creatures and legends of the Indigenous people populate the folklore and myths that pervaded the childhoods of most people growing up in Brazil. These are just a few of the ways in which Indigenous culture and knowledge pervades the everyday of Brazilians. But watching the telenovelas discussed in this essay, no viewer would be able to appreciate the complexity of Indigenous cultures or the indebtedness of Brazilian identity to its Indigenous roots. Indigenous people on telenovelas are deprived of their cultural practices, values, and ways of being, and instead are produced as a mishmash of Hollywood movies' imagery and colonial iconography.

A few telenovelas tried to carefully represent Indigenous practices and environments, but often as a background to the scenes involving the main characters. In *Aritana* as in *O Rei do gado*, careful portrayal of the exterior of the Xingu houses and their environs were presented, and *O Rei do gado* also presented long sequences of traditional dances. But the actual Indigenous characters with speaking roles are often deprived of a sense of identity and culture and a process of assimilation seems to be the goal. Characters in *Uga-uga* or *A lua me disse* are parodic trivializations of Indigenous cultures, desensitizing viewers to the lives of real Brazilian Indigenous people who remain at the margin of society.

Conclusion

In this chapter, I presented an overview of the ways in which Brazilian television, throughout its history, has produced Indigenous Others within telenovelas, a highly popular prime-time entertainment genre. I argue that their absence and trivialization have worked to produce a form of symbolic annihilation of a group oppressed and living at the margins of Brazilian society.

Over more than sixty years of telenovela production in Brazil, very few of these narratives included Indigenous characters. Of those that did, Indigenous people were often presented as inarticulate, comedic, oversexed, gullible, and violent, but also of good heart, naïve, docile, submissive, and passive. These portrayals add up to a characterization that leaves little for viewers to identify with or relate to, and even less for Indigenous people to be proud of.

Indian women are seduced, or taken, by the white men, and they reproduce children who grow up straddling two worlds. Their children never truly fit in either world, which is a not-so-subtle critique of miscegenation in a country where the majority of the population is of mixed ancestry. The Indian men are emasculated, living at the margins, often functioning as the noble savage or the buffoon. But mostly, Indigenous people are absent, and when they are presented, they are portrayed by white actors in exaggerated make-up and costumes, with caricatured gestures and speech.

Unfortunately, the portrayals that have existed over these six decades do not show any progression toward more inclusive or positive representations; they are frozen in a particular time and mindset. Indigenous people in Brazil remain at the margins of society and mostly absent from the main source of entertainment in that nation. This silencing and symbolic and de facto annihilation of the first inhabitants of Brazil continues.

References

Almeida, V. 2012. "*A muralha* e a representação indígena na televisão, na literatura e nas ciências socias." *Proa: Revista de antropologia e arte* 1 (4): 194–209.

Gonçalves, Patricia. 2000. "Índios apelam a direitos humanos contra novela." Câmara dos deputados (website) November 14, *www2.camara.leg.br/camaranoticias/noticias/2506. html*.

Carvalho, V., and I. Neves. 2014. "O indígena na telenovela brasileira: Discursos e redes de memória." Paper presented at the 37th Brazilian Congress of Communication Science, Foz do Iguaçu, Brazil, September 2–5, 2014.

———. 2015. "O corpo indígena nas telenovelas brasileiras: Memória, nudez e embraquecimento." *Redisco* 8 (2): 88–94.

Gambini, R. 2000. *Espelho índio: A formação da alma brasileira.* Sao Paulo: Axis Mundi/ Terceiro Nome.

Gerbner, G. 1972. "Violence in Television Drama: Trends and Symbolic Functions." In *Television and Social Behavior, Vol. 1: Content and Control,* edited by G. Comstock and E. Rubinstein, 28–187. Washington, DC: US Government Printing Office.

Guzman, T. 2010. "Our Indigenous People in Our American: Anti-Imperialism Imperialism and the Construction of Brazilian Modernity." *Latin American Research Review* 45 (3): 35–62.

Hamburger, E. 2005. *O Brasil antenado: A sociedade da novela.* Sao Paulo: Jorge Zahar editora.

"Indígenas: Gráficos e tabelas." n.d. Instituto Brasileiro de Geografia e Estatística (website), *indigenas.ibge.gov.br/graficos-e-tabelas-2.html*. Accessed on May 5, 2016.

La Pastina, A. 2004. "Selling Political Integrity: Telenovelas, Intertextuality and Local Elections in Brazil." *Journal of Broadcasting and Electronic Media* 48: 302–25.

———. 1999. "The Telenovela Way of Knowledge: An Ethnographic Reception Study among Rural Viewers in Brazil." PhD diss., University of Texas at Austin.

Means, R., and E. Yochin. 2008. "The Symbolic Annihilation of Race: A Review of the 'Blackness' Literature." *African American Research Perspectives* 12: 1–10.

Morris-Suzuki, T. 2005. *The Past within Us: Media, Memory, History.* New York: Verso.

Neves, I., and V. Carvalho. 2015. "A 'fala errada' dos Indígenas nas telenovelas brasileiras: Entre o saber e o poder." *Linguagens midiáticas* 9 (3): 69–85.

Queiroz, M. 1989. "Identidade cultural, identidade nacional no Brasil." *Revista tempo social* 1 (1): 29–46.

Ramirez-Berg, C. 2002. *Latino Images in Film: Stereotypes, Subversion, Resistance.* Austin: University of Texas Press.

Stam, R. 1997. *Tropical Multiculturalism: A Comparative History of Race in Brazilian Cinema and Culture.* Durham, NC: Duke University Press.

Telles, E. 2006. *Race in Another America: The Significance of Skin Color in Brazil.* Princeton, NJ: Princeton University Press.

Tuchman, G. 1981. "The Symbolic Annihilation of Women by the Mass Media." In *The Manufacture of News: Deviance, Social Problems and the Mass Media*, edited by S. Cohen and J. Young, 169–85. Beverly Hills, CA: Sage.

Vaz, F. 2005. "O estrago que a índia da Rede Globo faz." Fenajufe (website), August 23, *www.fenajufe.org.br/index.php/imprensa/artigos/62-o-estrago-que-a-india-da-rede-globo-faz.*

Warren, J. 2001. *Racial Revolutions: Antiracism and Indian Resurgence in Brazil.* Durham, NC: Duke University Press.

12

Kayapó TV

An Audience Ethnography in Turedjam Village, Brazil

By Richard Pace, Glenn H. Shepard Jr.,
Eduardo Rafael Galvão, and Conrad P. Kottak

Ever since they appeared in the documentary film *Kayapó: Out of the Forest* (1989) toting cameras like war clubs and deploying video images in an international mobilization against a proposed dam on the Xingu River, the Kayapó or Mebêngôkre people of Brazil have been indelibly associated with the field of Indigenous media studies. The scholarly literature on Kayapó media has explored concepts of agency, representation, and political struggle with an almost exclusive focus on Kayapó uses of film and video (Turner 1991, 1992; Conklin and Graham 1995; Conklin 1997; Silva-Muhammad 2015). Entirely absent from the literature on Kayapó media engagement are studies of other technologies such as the internet, radio, cell phones, DVDs, and commercial television. Brazilian commercial television, in particular, is crucial to understanding Kayapó media strategies and ongoing processes of sociocultural change for several reasons. First, television is a fairly new medium for most Kayapó, but one with which they now engage frequently, if not daily, creating an opportunity for significant cultural impact. Second, unlike Indigenous video, and, more recently the internet, none of television's content is designed for Indigenous audiences in general, much less the Kayapó specifically. Thus Kayapó engagements with television may reveal different pathways and modes of agency and influence when compared with other media, particularly the self-produced videos about which so much is written.

In this chapter we will describe and analyze Kayapó televiewing and reflect on how their engagement with television and other electronic media fits into broader Kayapó strategies of self-representation and self-determination. Fieldwork was conducted in the village of Turedjam, located in the northwestern section of the Kayapó Indigenous Lands in the state of Pará, Brazil, located about thirty kilometers from the small town of Ourilândia do Norte. Our research is part of a larger multisite project called the Evolution of Media

Influence in Brazil, funded by the National Science Foundation. The project compares media engagement in Turedjam with four other non-Indigenous rural communities in different regions throughout Brazil.[1] Research was co-ordinated across all five sites with parallel methodologies of audience ethnography and a standardized interview schedule. Together, these methods were designed to explore viewers' or users' engagement with various forms of electronic media in daily life and assess the influence of such engagement on processes of sociocultural change. In this chapter we report principally on our findings concerning televiewing in Turedjam, complemented by observations on the Kayapó's use of other media technologies and preliminary comparison to other research sites.

Anthropology, Television Studies, and Indigenous Peoples

For over forty years anthropologists and other researchers using anthropological concepts and methods have studied audience engagement with television in different cultural contexts (Lie 2003; Ginsburg 2005; Osorio 2005, 2001; Peterson 2003). These studies reveal a multitude of ways that television has been incorporated into people's daily lives without resulting in a concomitant acculturation to dominant Western cultural norms (Peterson 2003, 11; Shohat and Stam 2014). Instead, media messages appear to become indigenized or transformed through a complex process of hybridization (Abu-Lughod 2005; Canclini 1997; La Pastina 1999; Lull 1990; Machado-Borges 2003; Mankekar 1999; Reis 2000; Straubhaar 2007; Tufte 2000; Wilk 2002). Still, the overall number of such studies is relatively small given TV's global reach and its massive potential for stimulating sociocultural change (Lie 2003, 151–52). Particularly in anthropology, this blind spot toward television reflects both anxiety about and resistance to modern technology and its presumed power to homogenize and erode the cultural distinctiveness and authenticity that anthropologists celebrate (Kottak [1990] 2009, 12).

Rarer still are studies of television engagement by Indigenous peoples. Most studies about television among Indigenous people focus on the production and distribution of television programming (McCallum and Waller 2013). What is sorely missing from these studies is research on actual engagement with and reception of media technologies (Lie 2003, 157). Of particular importance are audience ethnographies that collect data on media engagement situated in daily life, including details about the wider web of social interactions and the broader socio-historic framework (see La Pastina 1999, 80; 2005, 142; Peterson 2003, 8–9; Pace and Hinote 2013, 8; Descartes and Kottak 2009, 5). Overall, audience ethnography provides a better understanding of the complex roles media play in sociocultural transformations (Peterson 2003, 8–9; Tufte 2000, 3; La Pastina 2005, 142).

We carried out audience ethnography and administered a standardized interview schedule in each house in Turedjam village to understand this Kayapó community's engagement with television over the five years since it arrived there. The period encompasses the founding of the new village and the arrival of electric power and television. As other studies in Brazil have shown, the initial phasing-in of television in a media-naïve community can be a period of potentially rapid change (Pace and Hinote 2013, Kottak [1990] 2009). In Turedjam, we looked for alterations in behavior and inquired into people's views and opinions about media and what it means to engage it. We focus on five primary areas (see Williams 1986, 9–10; Peterson 2003, 127–40):

1. the technological constraints to media engagement, including questions of ownership and access;
2. the signification or meaning of the medium both as a material object and a communication modality;
3. the purpose and goals of engagement (e.g., entertainment, education, distraction, prestige);
4. habits of spectatorship, including viewing etiquette, kinds of gaze, social interactions, engagement in parallel tasks while watching; and
5. displacement of other social activities to allow viewing.

Intertwined with each of these elements is the fundamental question of whether television is measurably affecting thought and world view. In other words, how do people engage media messages by heeding, missing, ignoring, reworking, or resisting them within their own cultural context? And what changes are created by such engagement? (See Pace 2009.) The literature on media studies demonstrates an array of perspectives for addressing such impacts, ranging from analyses of the power of media messages in shaping thought and behavior (so called "media effects" research), to approaches that prioritize individuals' agency in mediating or resisting messages ("active audiences" research; see Kitzinger 2004, 24, Corner 2000, 383). This literature is typically polemical, even parochial, and scholars tend to dismiss the work of those who do not conform to their own views. In this sense, the study of televiewing and its cultural impacts is as contentious as it is complex. We suggest such problems be addressed through long-term ethnographic fieldwork focusing on media engagement (see Pace and Hinote 2013). According to this standard, our field work among the Kayapó is still preliminary and will require more research over a longer time-span to draw more substantial conclusions. However, the results obtained so far permit an overview of the Kayapó's current engagement with television and its general degree of influence (or not) on ongoing processes of cultural change.

Authors Pace and Shepard, as well as our research assistant Eduardo Rafael Galvão, collected data on media engagement and sociocultural change in Turedjam village over a five year period (2011–2015), although the principal ethnographic study occurred in 2013. Data collecting methods include participant-observation and structured observations in Turedjam; a standardized interview schedule administered at each household in Turedjam; formal and informal interviews with Kayapó consultants in Turedjam, the city of Belém, and during a trip with three Kayapó cinematographers to the US (see Chapter 2 this volume); and analysis of communications with a few Turedjam community members and other Kayapó on Facebook.

Study Site

The village of Turedjam is a community of approximately three hundred people, located thirty kilometers by dirt road from the Brazilian town of Nova Ourilândia do Norte, population 30,100 (IBGE 2014. A bridge built in 2013 over the Riozinho (Little river), a small tributary stream of the Rio Branco that separates demarcated Kayapó lands from adjacent cattle ranches, makes Turedjam reachable in just thirty to forty-five minutes by ordinary car from Ourilândia. This proximity enabled the municipal government, interested in good relations with (and votes from) the community, to extend electric power lines to the village. Since 2011, all homes receive around-the-clock electricity from the municipal power grid. This proximity has also made the village a target for illegal gold-mining operations, which the Brazilian Federal Police recently broke up in a series of high-profile arrests and confiscations in July of 2016 ("Polícia Federal desarticula" 2016).

The village has a large satellite dish providing five stations of Brazilian commercial television. Privately owned satellite dishes outside a few homes provide additional channels for viewing. The village is at the very fringes of local cell phone coverage, such that cell phones work sporadically at a few "sweet spots" around the central plaza. A few households own "rural antennas" mounted on poles seven to ten meters high that provide access to the cell phone network. Many, though not all, individuals have cell phones they use through prepaid access plans. The cell signal is too weak to allow 3G access, so internet services are available only in town.

A throwback to earlier days of telecommunications, the village also owns a two-way radio that is used to communicate with more remote Kayapó villages and government agencies such as FUNAI (Fundação Nacional do Índio, or the National Indian Foundation), the federal Indian agency. FM and AM radio signals reach the village from nearby towns, although reception is weak due to obstructions from the hilly terrain. Despite these limitations, Turedjam is nonetheless among the better-connected villages in this part of the Kayapó territory.

Turedjam was founded in 2010 in an episode of violent village fissioning resulting from demographic growth and political and economic tensions, which is a common part of Kayapó political dynamics (see Turner 1965; Bamberger 1979; Fisher 1991; Verswijver 1992; Chernela and Zanotti 2014). Turedjam is an offshoot of the older village of Kikretum, which in turn descended through several fissioning episodes from the ancestral village of Gorotire. In 2013, the village consisted of thirty-eight houses arranged in the traditional circular pattern, with the ceremonial "warriors' house" at the center. Houses were built from a combination of materials, including palm thatch, *Brasilit* roof tiles, and plastic tarps over mud-and-daub or wooden structures, mostly with dirt floors, though a few had concrete floors. The houses lack running water, but since 2012 the village has been provided with running water pumped from a well into a large water tank that distributes potable water to several communal taps. Bathing and laundry were done in the nearby Riozinho stream, though the latest news is that gold mining activities have contaminated the stream so much that it is no longer safe for bathing.

Electric street lamps are arranged around the circular central plaza, conforming to traditional village architecture, and two street lamps are arranged on opposite sides of the warriors' house in much the same arrangement as the wooden masts used in certain rituals. The village has a brick and concrete health post and a small wooden school house with concrete flooring located just outside the residential circle. The health post is staffed by Brazilian health workers who reside in the village on an established schedule, assisted by a local Kayapó nurse-aid. School teachers commute daily from Ourilândia on motorcycle, assisted by one Kayapó teacher and several local teaching-aids who reside in the village. In 2012, Pentecostal missionaries from the Assembly of God congregation built a concrete brick church, which approximately 30 percent of villagers regularly attend.

The Kayapó subsist on agriculture (with manioc and sweet potatoes as their main staples), hunting, fishing, and gathering. A few individuals receive government salaries as health workers, teachers, or teacher-aids; some work for local NGOs; and one is a part-time mason. Most families make additional money selling beadwork and forest products such as açaí (*Euterpe oleracea*) fruits. Many households receive a monthly government welfare payment through the *Bolsa Família* (family grant) program designed to alleviate poverty. The funds are used mostly to buy staple commercial foods such as rice, beans, coffee, and canned food. Thus, household incomes are low, placing the villagers in the bottom decile of the Brazilian economic stratum. Yet their constitutional rights to a vast traditional territory where they are free to fish, hunt, farm, and collect forest resources insulates them from the degree of poverty experienced by poor Brazilians with similar cash income levels.

Turedjam is politically autonomous from other Kayapó villages. Still, the population maintains an extensive network of kinship and exchange relationships with other villages structured through matri-uxorical residence and traditional social formations including ceremonial moieties, age sets, ritual associations, and men's clubs (Verswijver 1983; Lea 1992; Fisher 2003). Internally, the village is organized by extended family household units structured according to age sets and political and ceremonial associations (Turner 1995, 102). Each association or set supports its leader or leaders as a collective unit in both secular (political, economic) and ceremonial contexts. The leader or leaders, however, have limited power in enforcing decisions (Verswijver 1983, 18–20).

History of Media Access

Older villagers we spoke with remembered their first encounters with electronic media devices dating back to the 1970s and 1980s. At that time many lived in Gorotire village, which Turner (1991) describes as possessing a communal shortwave communication radio. Presumably, some must have seen the early videos produced there by the Kayapó Video Project. Vanessa Lea (2012, 26) describes the impact of television and videos in Gorotire as far back as 1976. Access to commercial radio and especially television was limited, however, and mostly encountered only during time spent in Brazilian towns and cities —which for most individuals amounted to a few days or at most weeks per year. Reading materials, ranging from newspapers and magazines to Kayapó-language Bibles, were presumably available, but most people of this older generation were not literate at all, much less in Portuguese.

When the new village of Turedjam was first founded in 2010, a few households brought small gasoline generators which they used to power television sets and DVD players and charge batteries for cell phones and FM/AM radios. They could receive commercial radio broadcasts from the nearby town of Ourilândia on battery-powered radios, but reception was poor. The arrival of electricity direct from the power grid eliminated the need for batteries and generators, but TV and radio reception remained weak. In 2011 the community obtained a satellite dish, and individual families began purchasing television sets. This marked the first time that the majority of villagers had access to Brazilian commercial television in their homes on a regular basis.

Cell phones, purchased in nearby towns with prepaid calling plans, also became more common, although their use in the village requires an external antenna for service. Many cell phones in Brazil come with the Facebook application pre-installed, however the limited range of cell phone reception renders 3G internet access impossible. Only 8 percent of survey respondents reported ever having used the internet, and just two individuals said they use it weekly (during visits to town), mainly for Facebook, YouTube, and email.

By 2013, eleven families had purchased their own satellite dishes, giving them access to about thirty TV stations. By far the most popular network is Globo, Brazil's dominant free-access commercial station. Other networks, in order of popularity, are: SBT, TV Camara, Record, Esporte, and Bandeirantes. Around 2011, people began purchasing DVD players to watch Brazilian, foreign, and especially Kayapó video productions on their television sets. Kayapó-made films on DVDs produced in distant villages such as Gorotire circulate in informal networks among villages. In 2012, a group of Kayapó youth, including two young men from Turedjam, received training through a Goeldi Museum project (see Shepard and Pace 2012). Thereafter, a growing number of videos, recorded and eventually edited in Turedjam by Kayapó filmmakers, began circulating. Recently, a more diverse set of works have begun to circulate on USB drives and camera or cell phone memory cards. These include MP3 music files, video shorts, and digital slide shows. They range from commercial media and internet downloads to home-grown Kayapó productions.

Media Inventories, Technological Constraints, Ownership, and Access

To understand how media technologies are being consumed, by whom, and under what conditions and constraints, we conducted a media inventory in all homes in Turedjam. We found that twenty-six of the thirty-eight homes had a television set, eleven had a satellite dish, twenty-one had a DVD player, twenty-three owned DVDs, twenty-one had one or more simple cell phones, one had a smart phone, six had a sound system, six had a laptop computer (although not all of them were working), three had a transistor radio, and two had MP3 players. The inventory data, together with our observations and interviews, made it clear that television is the main and most frequently used media technology in the village. TV sets are used both to watch commercial television programming and to play DVDs and music CDs. All twenty-six TVs in Turedjam are color sets, and most are flat-screen models. Because electricity is free to villagers and available twenty-four hours a day, viewing can occur at any time of the day or night. The only constraints to viewing are occasional power outages, household rules on watching at certain times, and malfunctions of devices due to power surges, exposure to the elements, or poor product quality contributing to a short life span.

Television sets are owned individually or collectively by family members. Since access to cash income was fairly limited in Turedjam at the time of the study, families pooled their money to amass sufficient funds to buy TV sets, selling beadwork and various forest products, requesting money from salaried relatives, and occasionally receiving supplemental money or gifts from politicians, visitors, government, and NGO representatives. Most families had purchased or received their first-ever television set after moving to Turedjam. The recentness of television ownership is clearly reflected in the televiewing survey results (see Table 12.1) in that among the sample (which were all adults eighteen years or older) 71 percent of respondents reported six years or fewer of television watching, corresponding closely with establishment of the new village of Turedjam. In comparison to the non-Indigenous study sites in our comparative sample across Brazil, Turedjam rates as the least impacted in terms of years of exposure to the medium (also see Pace and Hinote 2013; Kottak [1990] 2009).

Table 12.1. Years of televiewing in Turedjam (respondents' estimation)

	Percentage
1 year or less	29
1–6 years	42
6 or more years	29

All TV sets in Turedjam are kept in a family's residence, although on special occasions they may be carried temporarily to the warriors' house or other locations for communal viewing (see below). People living in homes without televisions still have ready access to daily viewing by visiting nearby houses of neighbors, kin, age-set fellows, or friends. Their egalitarian social organization means that no Kayapó is denied access to TV, if they seek it out.

Signification: Material Object and Communication Modality

Within Kayapó homes, television sets are typically placed on a makeshift wooden table along a wall in the main house area; most homes have only one room, though a few have a separate sleeping area. Rarely are there any decorations or things of prestige or value associated with the display of the sets, unlike non-Indigenous Brazilian rural populations where the television is often a centerpiece surrounded in an almost shrine-like arrangement by valued objects such as family portraits, trophies, religious icons, souvenirs, or religious calendars. The Kayapó seem to give no special importance to the television set as a material object. In addition, television screens are seldom visible from outside the house, unlike the case for non-Indigenous rural Amazonian homes, where the television is often positioned prominently so it can be seen from outside the house through an open window or door (see Pace and Hinote 2013, 96). Only on special occasions, such as a World Cup soccer match or the arrival of a recently edited DVD of a ceremony in Turedjam or elsewhere, is communal viewing arranged by setting up a large TV at the warriors' house or under an improvised awning.

The placement of the set, the lack of decoration, and other observations made during research suggest that Turedjam villagers are not quite certain about television's importance as a material object. There is an ongoing contemplation of the place of the sets in the world of valuables (as well as for cell phones, DVD players, digital cameras, and computers) and whether they should become part of the universe of *nekret* (ceremonial wealth). In Kayapó culture, the concept of nekret refers to relationships between people, objects, and social prestige (Gordon 2006; Lea 2012). The term has been translated variably by different researchers as "heritage" (both tangible and intangible; Menget 1999), ceremonial wealth or "goods of value" (Turner 1993), and "prerogative" (Lea 1986), in the sense that nekret implies a privilege of exclusive or semi-exclusive use of ritual objects by certain people or groups.

Traditionally, valued possessions such as weapons, ornaments, names, and songs that were captured from enemies during warfare were classified as nekret (Lea 1986). Today, the concept also appears to apply to manufactured goods and other Western trappings that confer power and social prestige, notably firearms, computers, video cameras (Shepard and Pace 2012) and even pop music (Shepard 2013); all things that have been obtained or in some sense "captured" and appropriated from the world of the *kuben,* (i.e., non-Indigenous Brazilians or "whites").

Some people in Turedjam consciously consider electronic devices such as cell phones, DVD players, video cameras, and computers to be part of the universe of nekret. Cell phones especially, which circulate at a breathtaking pace from one hand to the next along kinship or age set lines, appear to have entered the symbolic realm of nekret as transferrable prestige objects. Not all people agree, however, reserving the term nekret for a more specific category of traditional prestige objects and knowledge.

Current funerary practices certainly reinforce the association, conscious or not, between Western goods and the traditional category of nekret. Traditional nekret objects such as body ornaments, headdresses, and weapons are piled on top of graves in Turedjam alongside valued manufactured objects such as television sets, satellite dishes, bicycles, sports trophies, and mattresses. Nekret are deposited on grave sites, since, during life, they can only be transferred between individuals in special ceremonies, usually from adults to adolescents (see Fisher 2003). When such objects from the deceased are kept by family members without the appropriate rituals of transfer, they attract the soul or 'image' (*karon*, curiously, the same word used to refer to television and other visual images) of the dead, which can lead to soul loss, illness, and death (Bamberger 1974, 368; Fisher 2003, 125, 131).

Just as local opinions on the status of television sets as material objects vary, so do significations of television as a communication modality. Those who see value in the medium comment about its positive influence through the expanded information base it provides about the world of the kuben. Many of those interviewed cited the importance of obtaining information about Brazilian land, forest, and development policies, and international environmental initiatives that directly affect Kayapó land rights. Others noted the benefits of being aware of current prices for commodities like fuel and food through advertising so they do not get taken advantage of by merchants. One man noted how both advertisements and television soap operas (where conspicuous product placement is used to reach consumers) help the Kayapó learn about the comparable features, qualities, and available "models" (he emphasized the Portuguese word, *modelo*) of different manufactured goods like cell phones, watches, and gas ovens, for example, so they do not automatically buy cheaper, inferior brands.

Others noted the value of televiewing in improving Portuguese fluency to allow for better interaction with Brazilians. Several mentioned that it was good for the youth to watch television and learn Portuguese in order to better prepare them for dealing with Brazilian society in the future. Others noted the sheer pleasure and entertainment value of watching television. Several people mentioned that they enjoyed seeing beautiful imagery, particularly unfamiliar natural landscapes, and exotic animals. Men in particular like watching televised soccer matches. A few people said they took pleasure in laughing at the silliness of white Brazilian society as depicted in the evening soaps or *telenovelas* (see below).

To ascertain the overall value of television as a communication modality, we asked survey respondents whether they had an overall positive, negative, or neutral opinion of TV. Only a few expressed a negative opinion, and over a third had a positive opinion, but a surprising 52 percent were neutral in their opinion about television. By contrast, respondents in non-Indigenous communities elsewhere in Brazil had an overwhelming 61 percent positive perception of television, and only 22 percent had a neutral opinion. These results indicate a high level of ambivalence toward television in Turedjam (see Table 12.2). When we asked more specific questions about what they found good in television, 25 percent of respondents mentioned the use of the TV screen as a monitor for showing Kayapó film productions through DVD players or other devices, making this the second most common response, after "news and information" (Table 12.3). The high value the Kayapó attribute to television as a medium for viewing their own native productions turns McLuhan's dictum that "the medium is the message" on its head.

Table 12.2. Overall opinions about television in Turedjam

	Percentage
Television is very positive or positive	37
Television is neither good nor bad	52
Television is not positive or simply bad	11

Table 12.3. "What is good about television?" in Turedjam

	Percentage
News and information	46
Used to show Kayapó films	25
Just a pleasure to watch	13
Telenovelas	8
Sports	4
Watching films other than Kayapó productions	4

Goals and Ends

Despite the general ambivalence toward television, people in Turedjam appear to watch TV programming with certain goals and ends in mind. According to 46 percent of respondents (Table 12.3), television's primary importance is for obtaining news and information about the wider world. Villagers are most interested in watching, learning about, and monitoring outside events that bear a direct impact on their lands, livelihoods, and society. A good example of this tendency occurred in 2013 during major street protests throughout Brazil against the government of President Dilma Rousseff. The people of Turedjam watched with great attention as nationwide protests came to dominate the news cycle (see Pace, Shepard, and Kottak 2014). Despite an incomplete understanding of the wide range of popular complaints and political motivations underlying the unrest, people in Turedjam realized that the federal government was weakened by the national and international news coverage. Jointly with other Kayapó villages, they perceived an opportunity to express specific grievances against proposed laws and constitutional amendments that would weaken Indigenous land rights, unkept promises about public health services, and the imminent threats of the newly revived Belo Monte Dam project.

During the peak of the unrest, a television was brought to the warriors' house where Kayapó men congregated in full regalia. All-day meetings were convened there while village leaders held intense radio and cell phone communications with other Kayapó villages and FUNAI in order to plan and coordinate protest activities. The entire village seemed to be preparing itself for battle, as men sharpened their arrows and carved their clubs, women painted their husbands' bodies in solid black *Genipa* war paint, and village leaders and elders gave vociferous, angry speeches to motivate the assembled warriors. The initial idea was to block traffic on a nearby stretch of highway to make their demands heard. After several days of tense discussions, the blockade was abandoned in favor of direct talks with government officials in Brasilia. A commission of six chiefs and warriors from Turedjam went to Brasília, where they joined with more Kayapó leaders and many other Indigenous peoples in the widely publicized Indigenous protest movement in September and October 2013.

As we observed these events unfolding, we noted how the people of Turedjam monitored events on the television news with a skeptical eye. On this and other occasions, Turedjam televiewers often criticized or even rejected the information on TV as false or distorted, particularly Globo's *Journal nacional* evening news program, which is the most commonly watched. The people of Turedjam especially distrust news stories involving Indigenous people. The harshest critiques we heard during the field research period focused on the Belo Monte Dam construction project and a series of proposed legal reforms that would undermine Indigenous land rights.[2]

As noted above, an important goal identified by the people of Turedjam in viewing television is to educate themselves, and even more so young people, about the outside world of non-Indigenous Brazilians, or kuben. While parents hope their children will learn the Portuguese language and gain a better understanding of Brazilian customs, culture, laws, and politics, they also caution the young to mistrust the information they receive from TV and to question the actions, motives, and intentions of the often-treacherous kuben. Thus, the overall goal would appear to be to encourage the younger generation to gain skills, knowledge, and a critical capacity for understanding the kuben world while defending Kayapó rights and interests.

Entertainment was also mentioned explicitly as a goal of watching television. Sports programs, mostly soccer, are the main source of entertainment, a preference reflected in the almost daily informal soccer matches young men play on the central plaza. In other cases, viewers appear to find pleasure in viewing a world far removed from their own experiences, whether it be exotic landscapes or animals, or the often silly antics of Brazilians. Yet overall, the entertainment value of television is much lower than that expressed in comparative non-Indigenous, rural Brazilian audiences (see below), easily understandable due to the Kayapó having limited familiarity with the language itself, much less the cultural norms and subtle social cues than most programs assume of their audience.

Habits of Spectatorship

People watching television in Turedjam stand, or else sit on plastic chairs, wooden benches, hammocks, beds, wood planks, or directly on a concrete floor. The more senior in age or prestige, the more likely a person will claim one of the limited number of chairs or benches to sit on. Televiewing shows no apparent segregation by age or gender, particularly within the family unit. Most people watch television with their kin or age set, since televisions are usually housed in individual homes where these groups typically congregate. We did not observe social tensions disrupting joint televiewing between or among families and friends.

Unlike novice televiewers among non-Indigenous Brazilians, the Kayapó do not stare silently and motionlessly at the screen (see Pace 1993; Pace and Hinote 2013, 94–95). Instead, the Turedjam villagers continue to talk among one another in Kayapó, perform domestic tasks, take care of children, and especially (for women and girls) do beadwork while the television is on. Viewers frequently disengage from viewing to do some other activity or leave the locale altogether, possibly returning to view later on.

Such a fractured and semi-attentive viewing pattern stems from the noted cultural disjuncture with program content. The concepts of "cultural capital" and "cultural proximity" allow us to understand these habits of spectatorship. Bourdieu's (1984) notion of cultural capital, as applied to televiewing, includes the viewers' implicit familiarity with narrative structures and strategies; genre rules; and stereotypical images, characters, and motifs found in programming (La Pastina 2004, 306). Viewers' life experiences dictate the degree of shared cultural capital and thus influence their ability to read and interpret a televisual text. Limited Portuguese fluency is a crucial barrier to understanding as well. The idea of cultural proximity (Straubhaar 2007, 203) stipulates that viewers' capacity to decode and interpret texts depends on their ability to recognize visual elements (such as landscape, clothing styles), verbal elements (including the language itself, as well as historical, political, and cultural references), and other distinctive features associated with a particular culture.

For Kayapó televiewers, shared cultural affinities with wider Brazilian society are constrained, thus limiting their full understanding of television genres, advertising such as product placement, intertextual messages such as drama emerging from stereotypes or subversions of race or social class, and more sophisticated humor beyond mere slapstick (which the Kayapó indeed enjoy). The relatively low interest in televiewing in Turedjam, compared with non-Indigenous rural Brazilian populations, certainly owes in a large part to these difficulties. Among Kayapó survey respondents (see Table 12.4), 58 percent state they that they watch no television at all or less than one hour of television per day; among survey respondents in non-Indigenous rural populations, only 13 percent report such a low level of viewing. Thus, the majority of people at Turedjam would be considered nonviewers or light viewers of television (see Gerbner and Gross 1976; Pace and Hinote 2013; Kottak [1990] 2009).

Table 12.4. Daily television viewing in Turedjam (self-reported on survey)

	Percentage
0 hours	29
1 hour or less	29
2 to 4 hours	32
5 or more hours	10

One illuminating example of such local variations in cultural capital was apparent in Kayapó responses to a popular commercial aired on the Globo television network during the 2014 World Cup soccer tournament. In the ad, referred to as "Neymar's Hair," the Brazilian soccer superstar Neymar da Silva Santos Jr. takes his friends on a back-country trek in a Volkswagen vehicle to reveal the secret of his creative and highly variable coiffure: a wild-looking Indigenous medicine man, living in an isolated village. The extreme conditions of the journey (muddy roads, splashing water, savanna grasslands), the arrival in a "primitive" Indigenous village (modeled after those found in the upper Xingu region), the exotic but generic dress of the medicine man (grass skirt, face paint, culturally nonspecific body ornaments), the rustic, throne-like wooden barber's chair, and the grunting noise the man makes all draw on stereotypes that sensationalize, decontextualize, and trivialize Brazil's rich and diverse Indigenous heritage (see Stam 1997; Carvalho and Neves 2015; Neves and Carvalho 2015; also see La Pastina this volume). However, Kayapó viewers in Turedjam, far from taking offense, laughed heartily at the commercial. When we asked why they laughed, several observed that the implausibility of such an important Brazilian celebrity actually visiting an Indigenous village just to get a haircut made the short clip absurdly funny. When we pressed further as to why they did not find the depiction of Indigenous people offensive, they saw no connection between the generic Indian depicted briefly in the clip and their own culture and lifestyle. In other words, the generic, ethnocentric, and demeaning representation of Indigeneity, which speaks so directly to Brazilian prejudice and stereotype, made no connection with Kayapó experience, therefore rendering it irrelevant and hence inoffensive, at least from their point of view (see Monteforte 1992 and Villarreal 2017, 175 for similar observations in Mexico and Bolivia).

For 91 percent of Kayapó survey respondents, television news was either their first or second favorite program. News programs on the Globo network were the most popular, with 45 percent listing this as their favorite program. News is followed by equal interest in sports and variety shows: 17 percent each. Only 11 percent of Kayapó respondents chose the evening soaps, or telenovelas, as their favorite kind of program, increasingly negligibly to only 14 percent if both first and second choice are combined. In the relatively nearby non-Indigenous township of Gurupá, also located in Pará state in the Brazilian Amazon, nearly 50 percent of those surveyed chose telenovelas as their favorite programs, increasing to 81 percent when combining first and second choice (Pace and Hinote 2013, 39). The telenovelas, so beloved elsewhere in Brazil, fail to hold the attention of the people of Turedjam because of the noted barriers in cultural capital and cultural proximity.

Opinions about how enjoyable it is to watch TV vary widely in Turedjam (see Table 12.5). Those who articulate negative views about television note how both broadcast news and telenovela storylines often focus on illegal and immoral behavior. As expressed in spontaneous survey responses, the people of Turedjam are especially disturbed by news and fictional stories about drug trafficking and kidnapping. As noted above, many complain about falsehoods, misinformation, and negligence in covering the political, economic, and environmental issues that most directly impact the Kayapó. Some complained about what they perceive as "false advertising" when local prices for goods and services appear higher than those advertised on television. Finally, many complained about violence as portrayed on the news as well as in films on TV or DVDs, particularly crime and horror films.

Table 12.5. Enjoyment of television viewing in Turedjam

	Percentage
Pleasurable	39
Indifferent	53
Unpleasant	8

Opinions on the actual impact of television programming in the community are mixed. Because of the newness of the technology and the relatively light viewing practices of most people, the vast majority of the people in Turedjam (66 percent of survey respondents) claim that television has made no impact in the community. Among those who do see impacts, only a few observe positive changes stemming from improved knowledge of Portuguese, Brazilian government policies, and the broader outside world. Most of those who do see changes, however, point out negative influences and worry that excessive televiewing might lead to loss of Kayapó language, traditions, and culture. One example noted independently by several respondents is the near universal substitution of the Portuguese terms *pai* (father) and *mãe* (mother) for the traditional Mebêngôkre words for father (*djunsã*, or *nãm* for short) and mother (*irwa*, or *bãm* for short). Some pointed out a growing defiance of parental authority among the youth, attributed to watching these behaviors on television. Others expressed concern over increasing imitation of kuben clothing and hair styles, especially short haircuts for men. To be fair, these changes occur within a wider context of direct contact with Brazilians in town as well as in the village. And yet, although television is only one among many sources of outside influence, the people of Turedjam single out television as the culprit in bringing about these undesired changes.

Displacement of Social Activities

Despite these local apprehensions about possible negative effects of television, our observations showed that television does not generally displace traditional social activities. News shows, telenovelas, and other programs mentioned in the surveys are broadcast mostly in the evening, when people have returned from local subsistence and social activities, or from trips into town. Evenings are a time for socializing and cultural instruction in the household, and, most importantly, for long nocturnal meetings at the warriors' house, where men discuss local or national events, plan for hunting expeditions and festivals, gossip, and tell stories under the stars, sometimes all night. When at home in the evening, families often turn on the television, but they continue to socialize and carry out other domestic tasks. Some ignore the television altogether, and those who do watch will also talk, do chores (especially beadwork), or otherwise continue their evening routine with minimal interference or restriction to their normal social behaviors. People easily and frequently disengage from televiewing to engage in other activities as necessary, whether a meeting at the warriors' house, a community festival, or an informal social visit. Non-Indigenous Brazilian communities, by contrast, undergo a significant disruption of household and public lifestyle during their initial years of exposure to television, most notably interrupting their habitual activities to watch telenovelas (Pace and Hinote 2013).

The only exception we witnessed to this tendency occurred in 2013 during the final episodes of a popular telenovela, *Salve Jorge* (Hail Saint George), which captured the attention of the community like no other program during our research stint. One of the multiple plot lines involved a human trafficking ring that promised unsuspecting poor women from the slums of Rio de Janeiro lucrative jobs in Turkey, only to ensnare them in prostitution. The most popular character among the men and women of Turedjam was an attractive young woman whose nickname, *Morena*, refers to her brown skin color. Through a combination of strategic deception and handiness with a pistol, she managed to escape her captors and avenge herself of their abuse. Many woman of the village would point her out on the screen and call out her name, "Morena!" when she appeared. They commented favorably on her ability to use the handgun. For several nights during the closing episodes, the top chiefs of Turedjam shortened or postponed meetings at the warriors' house to avoid missing the broadcast. The storyline of Morena's confrontation with her oppressors and her skill in using a gun fit with the Kayapó warrior ethos, with the added twist of placing a woman in the aggressive role. The actress who played Morena, Nanda Costa, is not noticeably Afro-Brazilian, but she does have a darker complexion and a stockier build than many popular "white" Brazilian actresses. This closer physical approximation to Kayapó body type may have also sparked added interest in the actress's performance.

Television as a Monitor for DVDs

A major use for television sets by Turedjam villagers is as a monitor for watching DVDs; only two people reported watching DVDs on laptops. When we asked people how many DVDs they had watched during the previous week, answers ranged from none to three or more (Table 12.6). By far the most frequently watched DVDs are Kayapó productions, accounting for 42 percent of respondents' reports, nearly twice the frequency of the second place genre, "action films," at 26 percent (Table 12.7). When asked generally about DVD genre preferences, an overwhelming 69 per cent say Kayapó productions are their favorites (see Table 12.8).

Table 12.6. Number of DVDs watched in previous week in Turedjam

	Percentage
None	18
1	16
2	32
3 or more	31

Table 12.7. Genre of DVDs watched in Turedjam

	Percentage
Kayapó productions	42
Action films	26
Adventure	14
Horror	10
Others	8

Table 12.8. Favorite genre of DVDs in Turedjam

	Percentage
Kayapó productions	69
Action films	17
Horror	8
Cartoons	3
Sports	3

The stated preference for Kayapó productions in survey responses was easily confirmed in our own direct observations of viewing activity in the village. By the same token, "Kaya-pop" (Kayapó-language pop music; see Shepard 2013) is also frequently heard on boom boxes and portable MP3 players around the village. All important village ceremonies are filmed and edited by local videographers in Turedjam who were trained through a prior Indigenous media project (Shepard and Pace 2012). Editing is usually completed within a few days after the ceremony is over, and the productions are distributed on DVD and other digital media throughout the village and the wider Kayapó territory. After a new ceremony is filmed, edited, and copied, people throughout the community play the DVD over and over for days if not weeks. The repetitive viewing of the latest "hit" DVD ends when a new ceremony is performed and filmed, or when the DVD wears out. Our structured observations also confirmed that more people gather to watch Kayapó productions, for longer intervals, than when viewing television. Unlike watching television shows, which is done mostly in the evenings, Kayapó DVD productions are often viewed repeatedly throughout the day.

As with televiewing, there is potential for DVD viewing to displace traditional activities. In Turedjam, however, people express little concern over displacement. People's viewing habits with television already show considerable flexibility. If there some other pressing need or demand for a person's attention, they simply stop viewing and start again later. Because in most cases the DVD has already been watched several times, disengagement is easy.

Conclusion

This research project sought to investigate the role of television in the daily life, reception of outside media messages, and self-representation of the Kayapó community of Turedjam. Our initial analysis suggests that any current influence is limited by the relatively recent history of exposure and the minimal levels of daily viewing. When compared to the non-Indigenous rural communities we have studied in Brazil, Turedjam rates as lightly impacted. Moreover, most people in Turedjam are light viewers by choice, since television is readily accessible to all, any time of the day or night.

Even though most people watch television only an hour or less per day, our media inventories indicate that television, both as device for watching commercial broadcasts as well as a monitor for DVDs, is nonetheless the most significant media technology in the village. Its signification as a material object reflects a somewhat uncertain status. The technology is considered valuable enough that twenty-six of the thirty-eight homes have managed to buy a set, and eleven more have purchased their own satellite dishes. Television sets and other foreign prestige goods resonate at least partially with the traditional category of nekret, or heritable ceremonial wealth; however, opinions on the subject vary. Likewise, television's signification as a communication modality is ambiguous, with more than half of respondents expressing a neutral opinion about the medium, a far less enthusiastic opinion than comparable non-Indigenous rural populations surveyed. Even among those who judged televisions in a positive light, one-fourth did so because of the television's usefulness as a medium for watching Kayapó DVD productions.

A similar ambivalence governs ends and goals for viewing. The people of

Turedjam express an interest in gaining knowledge of the outside world through televiewing, particularly by monitoring political events, learning Portuguese, and understanding Brazilian culture. Yet they also express a clear distrust toward the medium and its messages.

A semi-attentive viewing pattern witnessed in our observations of spectatorship behavior clearly relates to cultural disjunctions and incomplete comprehension of the messages. Hindrances to comprehension include limited Portuguese-language fluency, lack of cultural identification with actors and settings, and difficulties related to cultural capital in the interpretation of narrative devices, plot, class and cultural stereotypes, product placement, intertextual messages, and so on. These difficulties detract from the pleasures of televiewing as indicated by the high levels of indifference to the medium.

Televiewing currently does not appear to result in significant displacement of normal social activities. People easily disengage from viewing and continue their social activities despite the presence of a television set. Even when viewing their preferred Kayapó productions, they easily disengage after the initial rounds of viewing.

Nonetheless, Turedjam villagers themselves have identified specific changes associated with the arrival of widespread in-home TV sets over the last five years. While these changes are clearly related to a wider context of direct contact with Brazilian society, the people of Turedjam identify television as an important source of such changes, notably the use of certain Portuguese language terms in discourse among the young, changes in clothing and hair styles, and challenges to adult authority by the youth. At present, these developments are seen as an inconvenience for older generations, but not as insurmountable obstacles to Kayapó cultural well-being. Especially when we consider the Kayapó's clearly articulated distrust of and resistance to media messages about politics and Indigenous rights, and their general ambivalence toward the medium, television has not had an observable negative impact on processes of self-determination and self-representation in Turedjam.

The future, of course, is impossible to predict. The tendency certainly seems to be increasing exposure to television and other media, particularly the internet; improving Portuguese language skills; and growing cultural proximity with Brazilians in Turedjam and other Kayapó villages. What will be key to future television engagement, we can speculate, is Kayapó resilience. We do not use the term "resilience" to suggest the strict maintenance of pure and unchanging Kayapó cultural forms, but rather to a process of selective appropriation and creative integration of certain aspects of outside technology and culture into the Kayapó cultural repertoire. The Kayapó have demonstrated this kind of resilience over the past half century of interactions with Brazilian society. Indeed, resilience appears to be fundamental to the Kayapó's own notion of culture, which from their point of view has always been an additive process whereby knowledge, weapons, ceremonial objects, songs, and names are captured from enemies, rivals, and cultural others. By continually appropriating, incorporating, and re-signifying the cultural production of their enemies, the Kayapó highlight the strength and perseverance of their own "warrior ethos" (Turner 2009, 1995, 1991). The Kayapó's enduring success in appropriating foreign cultural elements without losing their agency and identity provides them with a resilient framework for engaging with new media technologies and messages without sacrificing their cultural uniqueness or compromising their survival as a people.

Notes

1. National Science Foundation Grant 1226335, The Evolution of Media Influence in Brazil: A Longitudinal and Multi-Sited Study of Electronic and Digital Media, Principal Investigator, Richard Pace, and Co-principal Investigator, Conrad P. Kottak. The study examines the scope and intensity of sociocultural changes associated with viewer/ user engagement with media in daily life over a three decade period in five locations: Turedjam (Pará), Gurupá (Pará), Arembepe (Bahia), Cunha (São Paulo), and Ibirama (Santa Catarina). Specific methodologies examine how people engage media and modify their talk, thought, and behavior as they fashion, alter, or reinforce social identities; create and interact with expanded social networks; participate in new forms of economic, political, and religious activities; record and share their own representations of their worlds; and basically reshape world views in myriad of ways. Seven ethnographers conducted fieldwork in a total of five rural communities and collectively administered a total of 893 interview schedules.
2. The proposed law 227 sought to modify Article 231 of the Brazilian Constitution in order to end Indigenous peoples' rights to exclusive and permanent usufruct of resources on their ancestral territories. The revision would allow the appropriation of land and resources for relevant public interest such as dam-building, mining, and road building (see Ramos 2013).

References

Abu-Lughod, L. 2005. *Dramas of Nationhood: The Politics of Television in Egypt.* Chicago: University of Chicago Press.

Bamberger, J. 1974. "Naming and the Transmission of Status in a Central Brazilian Society." *Ethnology* 13: 363–78.

———. 1979. "Exit and Voice in Central Brazil: The Politics of Flight in Kayapó Society." In *Dialectical Societies: The Ge and Bororo of Central Brazil,* edited by D. Maybury-Lewis, 129–46. Cambridge, MA: Harvard University Press.

Bourdieu, P. 1984. *Distinction: A Social Critique of the Judgment of Taste.* Cambridge, MA: Harvard University Press.

Canclini, N. 1997. "Hybrid Cultures and Communicative Strategies." *Media Development* 44 (1): 22–29.

Carvalho, V., and I. Neves. 2015. "O corpo indígena nas telenovelas brasileiras: Memória, nudez, e embraquecimento" [The indigenous body in the Brazilian telenovelas: Memory, nudity and whitening]. *Redisco* 8 (2): 88–94.

Chernela, J., and L. Zanotti. 2014. "Limits to Knowledge: Indigenous Peoples, NGOs, and the Moral Economy in the Eastern Amazon of Brazil." *Conservation and Society* 12 (3): 306–17.

Conklin, B. 1997. "Body Paint, Feathers, and VCRs: Aesthetics and Authenticity in Amazonian Activism." *American Ethnologist* 24 (4): 711–37.

Conklin, B., and L. Graham. 1995. "The Shifting Middle Ground: Amazonian Indians and Eco-Politics." *American Anthropologist* 97 (4): 695–710.

Corner, J. 2000. "'Influence': The Contested Core of Media Research." In *Mass Media and Society*, edited by J. Curran and M. Gurevitch, 376–97. London: Arnold.

Descartes, L., and C. Kottak. 2009. *Media and Middle Class Moms: Images and Realities of Work and Family.* New York, NY: Routledge.

Fisher, W. 1991. "Dualism and Its Discontents: Social Process and Village Fissioning among the Xikrin Kayapó of Central Brazil." PhD diss., Cornell University.

———. 2003. "Name Rituals and Acts of Feeling among the Kayapó (Mebengokre)." *Royal Anthropological Institute.* 9: 117–35.

Gerbner, G., and L. Gross. 1976. "Living with Television: The Violence Profile." *Journal of Communication.* 26: 173–99.

Ginsburg, F. 2005. "Media Anthropology: An Introduction." In *Media Anthropology*, edited by E. Rothenbuhler and M. Coman, 17–25. Thousand Oaks, CA: Sage.

Gordon, C. 2006. *Economia selvagem: Ritual e mercadoria entre os índios Xikrin Mebêngôkre.* São Paulo: Fundação Editora da UNESP (FEU).

IBGE (Instituto Brasileiro de Geográfia e Estatística). 2014. *Censo demográfico e censo econômico.* Rio de Janeiro: IBGE.

Kitzinger, J. 2004. *Framing Abuse: Media Influence and Public Understanding of Sexual Violence against Children.* London: Pluto.

Kottak, C. (1990) 2009. *Prime-Time Society: An Anthropological Analysis of Television and Culture.* Walnut Creek, CA: Left Coast Press.

La Pastina, A. 1999. "The Telenovela Way of Knowledge: An Ethnographic Reception Study among Rural viewers in Brazil." PhD diss., University of Texas at Austin.

———. 2004. "Seeing Political Integrity: Telenovelas, Intertextuality, and Local Elections in Rural Brazil." *Journal of Broadcasting & Electronic Media* 48 (2): 302–26.

———. 2005. "Audience Ethnographies—Media Engagement: A Model for Studying Audiences." In *Media Anthropology*, edited by E. Rothenbuhler and M. Coman, 139–48. Thousand Oaks, CA: Sage.

Lea, V. 1986. "Nomes e nekrets Kayapó: Uma concepção de riqueza." Doctoral thesis, PPGAS-Museu Nacional-UFRJ.

———. 1992. "Mebengokre (Kayapó) Onomastics: A Facet of Houses as Social Facts in Central Brazil." *Man* 27: 129–53.

———. 2012. *Riquezas intangíveis de pessoas partíveis: Os Mẽbêngôkre (Kayapó) do Brasil central.* São Paulo: EDUSP.an

Lie, R. 2003. *Spaces of Intercultural Communication: An Interdisciplinary Introduction to Communication, Culture and Globalizing/Localizing Identities.* Creskill, NJ: Hampton Press.

Lull, J. 1990. *Inside Family Viewing: Ethnographic Research on Television's Audiences.* London: Routledge.

Machado-Borges, T. 2003. *Only for You! Brazilians and Telenovela Flow.* Stockholm Studies in Social Anthropology 52. Stockholm: Dept. of Social Anthropology, Stockholm University.

McCallum, K., and L. Waller. 2013. "Indigenous Media Practice." *Media International Australia* 149: 67–69.

Mankekar, P. 1999. *Screening Culture, Viewing Politics: An Ethnography of Television, Womanhood, and Nation in Postcolonial India.* Durham, NC: Duke University Press.

Menget, P. 1999. "Entre memória e história." In *A outra margem do ocidente*, edited by A. Novaes, 153–66. São Paulo: Companhia Das Letras.

Monteforte, G., ed. 1992. *Pidiendo vida / Petition to Life.* Mexico City: INI.

Neves, I., and V. Carvalho. 2015. "A 'fala errada' dos Indígenas nas telenovelas brasileiras: Entre o saber e o poder" [Indians' "broken speech" in the Brazilian telenovelas: Between knowledge and power]. *Linguagens Midiáticas* 9 (3): 69–85.

Osorio, F. 2001. "Mass Media Anthropology." PhD diss., University of Chile.

———. 2005. "Proposal for Mass Media Anthropology." In *Media Anthropology*, edited by E. Rothenbuhler and M. Coman, 36–45. Thousand Oaks, CA: Sage.

Pace, R. 1993. "First-Time Televiewing in Amazonia: Television Acculturation in Gurupá, Brazil." *Ethnology* 32 (2): 187–205.

———. 2009. "Television's Interpellation: Heeding, Missing, Ignoring, and Resisting the Call for Pan-National Identity in the Brazilian Amazon." *American Anthropologist* 111 (4): 407–19.

Pace, R., and B. Hinote. 2013. *Amazon Town TV: An Audience Ethnography in Gurupá, Brazil.* Austin: University of Texas Press.

Pace, R., G. Shepard Jr., and C. Kottak. 2014. "Street Protests and Electronic Media in Brazil: Views from Small Towns and Villages." *Anthropology News*, Online (June), *www.anthropology-news.org/index.php/2014/05/20/street-prorests-and-electronic-media-in-brazil.*

Peterson, M. 2003. *Anthropology and Mass Communication: Media and Myth in the New Millennium.* New York: Berghahn Books.

"Polícia Federal desarticula esquema de garimpo em terra indígena no PA." 2016. *Globo comunicação*, globo.com (July 7), *g1.globo.com/pa/para/noticia/2016/07/policia- federal-desarticula-esquema-de-garimpo-em-terra-indigena-no-pa.html.*

Ramos, A. 2013. "O que está em jogo no PLP 227/2012?" *Blog do PPDS* (blog). *Instituto socioambiental* (July 16), *www.socioambiental.org/pt-br/blog/blog-do-ppds/o-que-esta-em-jogo-no-plp-2272012.*

Reis, R. 2000. "'A gente se fala depois da novela': An Ethnography of Television Viewing in the Brazilian Amazon." *Boletim do Museu Paraense Emílio Goeldi – Antropologia* 16 (2): 109–275.

Shepard, G., Jr. 2013. "Kaya-Pop: The Brave New World of Indigenous Music in Brazil." *Anthropology News* (June 14). *www.anthropology-news.org/index.php/2013/06/14/kaya-pop.*

Shepard, G., Jr., and R. Pace. 2012. "Through Kayapó Cameras: A Report from the Field." *Anthropology News* (April). 53 (4): 18–19.

Shohat, E., and R. Stam. 2014. *Unthinking Eurocentrism: Multiculturalism and the Media,* 2nd ed. New York: Routledge.

Silva-Muhammad, C. 2015. "Eliciting Self-Determination: The Kayapo Mobilization through Activism and Global Indigenous Media." Rapoport Center for Human Rights Working Paper Series. Austin: University of Texas at Austin School of Law. *law.utexas.edu/humanrights/projects/eliciting-self-determination.*

Stam, R. 1997. *Tropical Multiculturalism: A Comparative History of Race in Brazilian Cinema and Culture.* Durham, NC: Duke University Press.

Straubhaar, J. 2007. *World Television: From Global to Local.* Los Angles: Sage.

Tufte, T. 2000. *Living with the Rubbish Queen: Telenovelas, Culture and Modernity in Brazil.* Luton, UK: University of Luton Press.

Turner, T. 1965. "Social Structure and Political Organization among the Northern Cayapo." PhD diss., Harvard University.

———. 1990. *The Kayapó Video Project: A Progress Report.* Montreal: Revue de la Commission d'Anthropologie Visuelle (Université de Montréal).

———. 1991. "The Social Dynamics of Video Media in an Indigenous Society: The Cultural Meaning and the Personal Politics of Video-Making in Kayapó Communities." *Visual Anthropology Review* 17 (2): 68–76.

———. 1992. "Defiant Images: The Kayapó Appropriation of Video." *Anthropology Today* 8 (6): 5–16.

———. 1992b. "Os Mebengokre Kayapó: História e mudança social, de comunidades autónomas para a coexistência interétnica." In *Historia dos indios no Brasil,* edited by M. Cunha and F. Salzano, 311–38. Sao Paulo: Fundação de Amparo à Pesquisa do Estado de São Paulo, Companhia das Letras, and Secretaria Municipal de Cultura, Prefeitura do Município de São Paulo.

———. 1995. "An Indigenous People's Struggle for Socially Equitable and Ecologically Sustainable Production: The Kayapó Revolt against Extractivism." *Journal of Latin American Anthropology* 1 (1): 98–121.

———. 2009. "Valuables, Value, and Commodities among the Kayapó of Central Brazil." In *The Occult Life of Things: Native Amazonian Theories of Materiality and Personhood,* edited by F. Santos-Granero, 152–69. London: Routledge.

Verswijver, G. 1983. "Cycles in Kaiapó Naming Practices." *Communication and Cognition* 16: 301–23.

———. 1992. *The Club-Fighters of the Amazon: Warfare among the Kaiapo Indians of Central Brazil.* Gent, Belgium: Rijksuniversiteit te Gent.

Villarreal, G. 2017. *Indigenous Media and Political Imaginaries in Contemporary Bolivia.* Lincoln: University of Nebraska Press.

Wilk, R. 2002. "'It's Destroying a Whole Generation': Television and Moral Discourse in Belize." In *The Anthropology of Media*, edited by K. Askew and R. Wilk, 286–98. Malden, MA: Blackwell.

Williams, T. 1986. "Background and Overview." In *The Impact of Television: A Natural Experiment in Three Communities*, edited by T. William, 1–38. New York: Academic Press.

Worth, S., and J. Adair. 1972. *Through Navajo Eyes: An Exploration in Film Communication and Anthropology*. Bloomington: Indiana University Press.

Film

The Kayapó: Out of the Forest. 1989. Directed by Michael Beckham and Terence Turner. Disappearing World (Granada Television). Baseline. 1991, videocassette. Chicago: Films Incorporated.

Contributors

Amalia Córdova is a filmmaker, curator, and scholar specializing in Indigenous film. She is the Latino Curator for Digital and Emerging Media at the Smithsonian Institution's Center for Folklife and Cultural Heritage. For over a decade she was a Latin American program specialist for the Film + Video Center of the Smithsonian Institution's National Museum of the American Indian in New York City. She has served as assistant director of New York University's Center for Latin American and Caribbean Studies and teaches at NYU's Gallatin School of Individualized Study. She has juried at Indigenous film festivals, has co-directed three documentary shorts, and co-produces *Urban Indians*, a web series. Her publications include essays in *New Documentaries in Latin America* (2014), *Film Festival Yearbook 4: Film Festivals and Activism* (2012), and *Global Indigenous Media* (2008).

Eduardo Rafael Galvão is a project coordinator for the Association for Protected Forests, an NGO dedicated to protecting the Mẽbêngôkre/Kayapó territories, natural resources, and cultural heritage in Brazil. He is part of the Audiovisual and Computer Training Project, which trains and provides the necessary tools for the Kayapó to take advantage of audiovisual technologies with the general objective of strengthening their culture and improving their territorial and environmental management capacities.

Laura R. Graham is a filmmaker and professor of anthropology at the University of Iowa. In 1991 she initiated the first video project among the Xavante of Pimentel Barbosa in Mato Grosso, Brazil. Her scholarship concerns Indigenous language, media, and communication, with a focus on representation in national and international arenas. She is an active human rights advocate. Graham is author of *Performing Dreams: Discourses of Immortality among the Xavante Indians of Central Brazil* (1995), *Performance de sonhos: Discursos de imortalidade Xavante*, with audio CD (2018), and *Performing Indigeneity: Global Histories and Contemporary Experiences* (2014, with Glenn Penny) and numerous articles and book chapters on Xavante and Wayuu peoples. She is also producer and co-director, with David Hernández Palmar (Wayuu) and Caimi Waiassé (Xavante), of the film *Owners of the Water: Conflict and Collaboration over Rivers* (Documentary Educational Resources, 2009).

Faye Ginsburg is founding and ongoing director of the Center for Media, Culture and History at New York University, where she is Kriser Professor of Anthropology and director of the Graduate Certificate Program in Culture and Media.

Her work as a scholar and advocate focuses on cultural activism, from her early, multiple-award-winning book *Contested Lives: The Abortion Debate in an American Community* (1989), to her co-edited volume *Media Worlds: Anthropology on New Terrain* (2002), to her longstanding work (since 1988) on Indigenous media in Australia, the US, Canada, and Aotearoa, New Zealand. She is part of the curatorial team for the Margaret Mead Film Festival, held every fall in NYC with special attention to Indigenous work, and in 2005 co-curated a groundbreaking showcase, First Nations, First Features, at both the Museum of Modern Art and the National Museum of the American Indian, that brought twenty Indigenous directors from around the world to screen and discuss their work.

Guilherme Orlandini Heurich is currently a British Academy Newton International Fellow at the Department of Anthropology, University College London. His research among the Araweté, a small Amerindian society in Eastern Amazonia, focuses on the place of songs and music in the Araweté's relations with Others—such as enemies, spirits, and divinities. He has published "Imagining Memories" (*Current Anthropology*) and "Outras alegrias: Cachaça e cauim na embriaguez mbyá-guarani" (*Mana*), and co-edited the book *Araweté: Um Povo Tupi da Amazônia*, updated 3rd edition (2017).

Conrad P. Kottak is the Julian H. Steward Collegiate Professor Emeritus of Anthropology at the University of Michigan-Ann Arbor. He has conducted ethnographic field work in Brazil (since 1962), Madagascar (since 1966), and the United States. His general interests are in the processes by which local cultures are incorporated—and resist incorporation—into larger systems. This interest links his earlier work on ecology and state formation in Africa and Madagascar to his more recent research on global change, national and international culture, and the mass media. He is the author of *Prime-Time Society: An Anthropological Analysis of Television and Culture* (2009) and, with Lara Descartes, *Media and Middle Class Moms: Images and Realities of Work and Family* (2009). Among his other books are *The Past in the Present: History, Ecology and Cultural Variation in Highland Madagascar* (1980), *Researching American Culture: A Guide for Student Anthropologists* (1982), *Anthropology: The Exploration of Human Diversity* (18th ed., 2019), *Cultural Anthropology* (18th ed. 2019), and *Mirror for Humanity: A Concise Introduction to Cultural Anthropology* (11th ed., 2018). Kottak's articles have appeared in academic journals including *American Anthropologist, Journal of Anthropological Research, American Ethnologist, Ethnology, Human Organization*, and *Luso-Brazilian Review*. He has also written for more-popular journals, including *Transaction/SOCIETY, Natural History, Psychology Today*, and *General Anthropology*.

Antonio La Pastina is an associate professor in the department of communication at Texas A & M University. His research focuses on the longitudinal understanding of how communities engage with mediated forms of communication. Utilizing ethnography, he has conducted research in rural Northeast Brazil, southern Italy, and along the Texas-Mexico border. He has written extensively on telenovelas and representations of otherness in that genre. He has published his research in *Popular Communication*, *Qualitative Inquiry*, *Critical Studies in Media Communication*, *Gazette*, *Journal of Broadcasting and Electronic Media*, *Global Media Journal*, and *International Journal of Cultural Studies*, among other journals.

Mario A. Murillo is professor of communication and Latin American studies at Hofstra University in New York, and is the author of *Colombia and the United States: War, Unrest and Destabilization* (2004), and *Islands of Resistance: Puerto Rico, Vieques and US Policy* (2001). He has written about Latino culture, immigration, Indigenous issues, community media, Latin American affairs, human rights, and US foreign policy for many years. His articles and essays have been published in academic journals, edited collections, newspapers, websites, and popular magazines in the US and abroad. A long-time media activist and award-winning journalist, he has served as program director, director of Public Affairs programming, and a host and producer at WBAI Pacifica Radio, was a feature correspondent for NPR's *Latino USA*, and was a regular guest host on WNYC New York Public Radio.

Suzanne Oakdale is an associate professor in the department of anthropology at the University of New Mexico. She is a socio-cultural anthropologist who specializes in the study of ritual, history, and narrative with a focus on Brazil and the Kawaiwete/Kayabi people. She has written an ethnography, *I Foresee My Life: The Ritual Performance of Autobiography in an Amazonian Community* (2005), edited with Magnus Course *Fluent Selves: Autobiography, Person, History in Lowland South America* (2014), and published articles in the *Journal of the Royal Anthropological Institute*, the *Journal of Anthropological Research*, *American Ethnologist*, *Ethos*, and *Ethnohistory*.

Richard Pace is a professor of anthropology at Middle Tennessee State University. His research interests are in media anthropology with a focus on Brazil, particularly the Amazon. He has published *Amazon Town TV: An Audience Ethnography in Gurupá, Brazil* (2013) with Brian Hinote and *The Struggle for Amazon Town: Gurupá Revisited* (1998), as well as articles in the journals *American Anthropologist*, *Ethnology*, *American Ethnologist*, *Luzo-Brazilian Review*, *Boletim do Museu Goeldi*, *Reviews in Anthropology*, and *Journal of Anthropological Research*.

Ingrid Carolina Ramón Parra is a PhD candidate in anthropology at Purdue University. She recently completed extended fieldwork with Kayapó women in the Central Brazilian Amazon. Her contribution to this edited volume is her first academic publication; she has published poetry in *Mujeres de Maiz* zine and a short story in *The Truth about the Fact*.

Jamie E. Shenton is assistant professor of anthropology at Centre College in Danville, Kentucky. She is a medical anthropologist specializing in issues of gender, body image, and social change among Indigenous Kichwa women in the Napo Province region of the Ecuadorian Amazon. In addition to her work on globalization, intergenerational transformation, and media consumption featured here, her current research interests include productive intersections of contemporary feminist theory and Amazonian ethnography, as well as sexual violence on college campuses and questions of awareness and prevention.

Glenn H. Shepard Jr. is an ethnobotanist, medical anthropologist, and filmmaker who has worked with diverse Indigenous peoples of Latin America, especially in Amazonia. Publications include research articles, commentary and reviews in *Nature, Science, Science Advances, American Anthropologist, Economic Botany, Conservation Biology, PLoS One*, and the *New York Review of Books*. His work in the Peruvian Amazon was featured in recent stories in *National Geographic* and the *New Yorker*. He has participated in the production of several films, including the Emmy Award–winning documentary *Spirits of the Rainforest*, as well as *Zapatista Memories*, which debuted in 2016 at the Margaret Mead Film Festival. He is currently a staff researcher in the Human Sciences Division at the Goeldi Museum in Belém. He blogs at "Notes from the Ethnoground" (*ethnoground.blogspot.com*).

Diego Soares da Silveira is an anthropologist working for the Institute of Social Sciences of the Federal University of Uberlândia, Brazil, as well as a research associate at the Center for Research in Social Sciences (NUPECS-UFU), the Laboratory of Anthropology of Science and Technology (LACT/UNB), and the Center for Anthropology and Citizenship (NACI/UFRGS). His research interests include ethnographic study of traditional environmental knowledge, symmetrical anthropology, actor-network theory, biopolitics, and governmentality. He researches principally in the Brazilian Amazon with Indigenous and ribeirinho populations. His publications include the book *Redes Sociotécnicas na Amazônia: Tradução de Saberes no Campo da Biodiversidade* (2012) and journal articles in *Antares: Letras e Humanidades, Saúde e Sociedade, Enfoques*, and *Antropolítica*, as well as numerous book chapters. He is currently active in the Collaborative Anthropology and Community Empowerment project which seeks the transfer of audiovisual technologies to the Mebêngôkre-Kayapó people of the village A'Ukre.

Erica Cusi Wortham is a cultural anthropologist and interdisciplinary social scientist with special interests in Indigenous media, visual heritage, and community archiving. She is the author of *Indigenous Media in Mexico: Culture, Community and the State* (2013) and has also published in *LIMINAR, Estudios sociales y humanísticos, World Studio Sphere*, and *American Anthropologist*. She is a lecturer in the department of anthropology at George Washington University and is currently engaged in the development of a Special Collection of Indigenous Media at New York University's Bobst Library. This special collection incorporates many of the key elements of the Indigenous Latin American Digital Media Archive (ILADMA) discussed in this volume.

Laura Zanotti is an environmental anthropologist and interdisciplinary social scientist whose research program partners with communities to better understand how local, mostly rural, livelihoods and well-being can be sustained for future generations. Using a feminist political ecology framework, Zanotti maps out spatial inequalities and injustices experienced by resource-dependent communities and highlights local creativity in the context of acute change. She has partnered with the Kayapó of Brazil for over ten years and is currently working on projects around the United States and in Latin America on "media sovereignty" and digital landscapes, environmental justice and valuing nature, and community resilience and healing. She is the author of *Radical Territories in the Brazilian Amazon: The Kayapó's Fight for Just Livelihoods* (2016) and has published in *Science, Anthropological Quarterly,* and *Journal of Political Ecology.* She is an associate professor of anthropology at Purdue University.

Index

Adair, John, 5, 55, 75
archiving, 5, 13, 15, 20, 32, 34–39, 54, 96,
    97–98, 106, 113, 215, 217–18
    accessible archive, 103
    Ara Irititja project (Australia), 37–38
    via internet, 102
    MCHAP Mapuche videos, 67–68
    Mukurtu CMS (Australia), 103
    repatriation, 100, 111
audience ethnography
    body images and TV, 186–88
    Kayapó, 213–14
    Kichwa of Sacha Loma, 179–81
    perceptions of indigeneity and TV,
        189–92

cell phones, 11, 21–22n3, 31, 33, 107,
    111, 218–19, 220
CLACPI (Latin American Coordinators of
    Indigenous Peoples' Film and Video), 7,
    34, 63–64, 84, 88
Cohn, Norm, 41–43
collaborative video, 108, 113, 115–16, 118,
    121, 123n6
    capacity building, 107, 113, 122
Córdova, Amalia, 7, 14, 87
Córdova and Salazar, 4

Deger, Jennifer, 40
Dowell, Kristin, 6, 9
DVDs, 54–55, 100–101, 179–81, 218,
    221–22, 228–30

embedded aesthetics, 4–5, 40, 60, 76,
    88–89, 97, 100
ephemeral materiality and media, 97–99,
    101, 103

Facebook, 14, 57, 69–70, 102, 104,
    122–23n3, 215, 218
    power asymmetries and Indigenous
        media, 9, 43–44
Faustian contracts, 2, 32, 177
flash drives/USB
    recording Arawaté shaman songs,
        148–50
    recording dead vs. live shaman's voice,
        152, 154–56

Galvao, Eduardo, 19
García, Juan José, 5–6, 8, 177, 183–84
Ginsburg, Faye, 3, 4, 6, 9, 11, 13, 60, 76,
    97–98, 177
Graham, Laura, 14

Hernández Palmar, David
    childhood, 78–80
    and CLACPI, 84
    as fashion photographer, 81
    Indigenous cosmopolitan, 77
    MICIV (Venezuela's International
        Indigenous Film Showcase), 84–85
    Owners of the Water, 85
    Xavante interactions, 82–84
Heurich, Guilherme, 16–17
Himpele, Jeff, 8
hybridity, 7, 14, 60, 71, 213

Indigenous media
    as cultural activism, 31–32, 33
    not real work, 99
    range of work, 33–34
    sustainability and role of universities,
        36–37
    talking back, 31

243

Indigenous media studies
    authenticity, 5, 32, 53, 98
    decentering the West, 11
    decolonizing, 6, 8–10, 11–12, 42, 98,
        100, 107
    definitions, 3–11
    founders, 3
    media engagement, 10
    research lacuna, 2
InDigital Latin America Conference, 2–3
    Terence Turner's participation, 3, 13
infrastructure stratification, 43

JAAS. See Silva, Jennifer

Kayapó-Mebengôkre, 1, 3, 8, 12–13, 35,
        40, 56–57, 106, 158–59, 163–64,
        170n1
    Cherokee visit, 55
    Disneyworld visit, 55–56
    film aesthetic, 5–6, 40, 53–55
    film history, 50–52
Kottak, Conrad, 19

Landzelius, 22n3, 42
La Pastina, Antonio, 18–19
Lea, Vanessa, 110, 217, 220

Magallanes Blanco, Claudia, and José
        Ramos Rodríguez, 7–8, 20–21, 22n4
making culture visible, 5, 7, 21
Mapuche media
    bilingual radio and repression, 68–69
    media makers and resistance to
        repression, 70
    Ralco dam and resistance through film,
        62
media effects, 40, 214
Metuktire, Kiabieti
    challenge to indigeneity, 52–53
    friendship with Turner, 49
    interview with Turner, 50–52
    National Geographic video, 57
    US travels, 55–56
Michaels, Eric, 40
Murillo, Mario, 16
music videos, 66–67, 181–83

new media nation, 9

Oakdale, Suzanne, 17–18
ONIC (National Indigenous Organization
    of Colombia) digital platforms, 138

Paillán, Jeannette, 60, 63, 71
parallax view, 11–12
Parra, Ingrid, 15–16
photography
    as cultural domination, 161
    Kawaiwete views on pacification and
        photographs, 168–69
    photojournalism and Brazilian
        Indigenous groups, 163–64
    portraits, 112
    Rondon's photographs of pacification in
        Brazil, 160
    taxonomic photographs in Brazil, 162
postura, 9–10

radio
    Araweté radio, 148
    creation of indigenous identity, 131–32
    exclusion from Colombian national
        identity, 130–31, 134–36
    history of Colombian radio, 132–35
    history of Indigenous Colombian radio,
        137–42
    radio is like a shaman, 153–54
    resistance and inclusion, 129–30,
        142–44
    tejido as foundation of organizing,
        139–40
Radio y Video Tamix (Mexico), 97, 99–103
Raheja, Michelle, 9, 33, 90n1, 106–7
respectful listening documentaries, 39

Salazar, Juan, 4, 7, 10, 12, 21, 60, 68, 71n4
Salazar and Cordova, A., 7, 177, 183
Schiwy, Freya, 6, 9, 57n1
Shenton, Jamie, 18
Shepard, Glenn, Jr., 1–2, 56, 220, 229;
    Shepard, G. and R. Pace 5–6, 54, 110,
        218, 229
Silva, Jennifer (JAAS), 61, 65–67, 71
Soares da Silveira, Diego, 15–16

sovereignty, visual 9, 33, 106–7, 116
 media, 32–33, 36, 44, 107

telenovelas, 178, 184–85, 198–99
 depictions of Brazilian Indigenous
  peoples, 201, 207–8, 209–10
 depictions of race, 179, 197
 representations of language, 208–9
 symbolic annihilation, 198
television
 Isuma TV (Canada), 41, 102–3
 Kayapó displacement of social activities,
  227–28
 Kayapó goals of watching, 222–24
 Kayapó spectatorship habits, 224–27
 NITV (Australia), 38–45
 signification by Kayapó, 219–22
 television studies of Indigenous peoples,
  213–14

Turner, Terence, 6, 8, 35, 49–58, 110, 117,
 121, 217
 Wakampy, 50, 57

Video nas Aldeias, 41, 57n2, 110
Villarreal, G., 5–6, 9–10
Viveiros de Castro, Eduardo, 150, 152–53

women and media engagement, 110, 112,
 117–20, 122
 body images, 176–78
 Mapuche filmmakers, 60–61, 63–64,
  65–67
 restrictions on Kayapó female media
  makers, 119–20
Worth, Sol, 5, 55, 75
Wortham, Erica, 5–9, 10, 14–15, 35, 177

Zanotti, Laura, 15–16

www.ingramcontent.com/pod-product-compliance
Lightning Source LLC
Chambersburg PA
CBHW031126270326
41929CB00011B/1512